# THE NOTION OF PROGRESS
# IN INTERNATIONAL LAW
# DISCOURSE

# THE NOTION OF PROGRESS
# IN INTERNATIONAL LAW
# DISCOURSE

Thomas Skouteris

T·M·C· ASSER PRESS

The Hague

*Front Cover Image*:
Désiré Despradelle, "Beacon of Progress, Comparison of the Beacon of Progress with the Great
Monuments of the World", ink and watercolor on paper, Boston/Paris 1900,
MIT Museum.

ISBN 978-90-6704-299-4

PRINTED IN THE NETHERLANDS

# PREFACE

This book takes issue with the notion of progress in public international law. Terms such as progress or progressive are familiar slogans in international law rhetoric and writing, commonly used to accentuate proposals for improvement or change. They are not the only ones. Claims about progress find their place next to stories of disenchantment, declension, stagnation, which carry their own slogans and narrative forms. In this book I only focus on progress as a manner of speaking about international law. Progress is and has been for over two centuries an indispensable part of the everyday language of international law. It continues to fulfill an essential role in the choice of suitable doctrinal, procedural, or institutional solutions. At the same time, the notion of progress is rarely explored as such in the literature. The book hopes to begin addressing this gap by offering some reflections on its function in international law discourse.

A few preliminary remarks are due here to explain the approach to such a broad topic. My aim is not to devise a scientific method to define progress in international law or a yardstick to measure the 'progressiveness' of reform proposals. The intention is not to embark on a conceptual history of the use of progress either. This is, in other words, neither an ontology nor a genealogy of progress. Instead, this book is concerned with the function of the notion of progress in public international law discourse. It aims to address fellow public international law scholars and practitioners and begin a debate about how our professional community constructs/ is constructed by progress narratives. The objective is therefore circumscribed narrowly: it is to explore 'what is it' that makes a given development *appear* as constituting progress in international law. It is an investigation of how meaning about progress may be produced and a study of the consequences of the production of such meaning. Instead of developing a theory or a method to find the meaning of progress, this book demonstrates how a given event may become synonymous with progress, regardless of whether 'it is' progress or not.

The book does not therefore belong to the genre of theory of science whose task is the development of normative or descriptive theories of progress. By using different techniques, such analyses are concerned with an investigation of the nature of progress.[1] To follow John Losee's classification,[2] theories of progress typically apply themselves to any of three different types of investigation. The first is to identify the distinguishing features of progress and the conditions necessary for science to be 'good', which normally leads to prescriptions about how science evolves. A classic example here is Thomas Kuhn's claim that real scientific revolutions occur only when a major taxonomic system is replaced with a new one.[3] The second is to define the kind of 'goodness' that needs to be attained for science to achieve progress. This 'goodness' could be about developing models that lead to a closer approximation to truth, increasing effectiveness in problem solving, or a myriad other goals. The example here is Larry Laudan's claim that true progress occurs only through increased success in the problem-solving ability of theory and not through claims to better approximation to truth, which he considers to be a false promise.[4] A third type of investigation involves an explanation of why science develops the way it does, i.e. it is about uncovering the underlying mechanisms or conditions that are chiefly responsible for the attainment of scientific progress. Answering such questions could lead to making (normative version of the approach) or avoiding (descriptive version) recommendations about how science should be practiced. The example here is Karl Popper's evolutionary analogy, namely that progress in science may be regarded as a means used by the human species to adapt itself to the environment.[5]

---

[1] See, e.g., J.B. Bury, *The Idea of Progress: An Inquiry into Its Origins and Growth (1920); J. Baillie, The Belief in Progress* (1950); L. Edelstein, *The Idea of Progress in Classical Antiquity* (1967); G. Sorel, *The Illusion of Progress* (1969); W.W. Wagar, ed., *The Idea of Progress Since the Renaissance* (1969); R.A. Nisbet, *Social Change and History: Aspects of the Western History of Development* (1969); D.W. Marcell, *Progress and Pragmatism: James, Dewey, Beard and the American Idea of Progress* (1974); F.J. Teggart, ed., *The Idea of Progress: A Collection of Readings* (1929); R.A. Nisbet, *History of the Idea of Progress* (1980). See generally, J. Losee, *Theories of Scientific Progress: An Introduction* (2004). For the concept of progress in public policy studies, see C.L. Anderson and J.W. Looney, eds., *Making Progress: Essays in Progress and Public Policy* (2002).
[2] Losee (Theories of Scientific Progress), Ibid., at 1-3.
[3] Th. Kuhn, *The Structure of Scientific Revolution*, 2nd edn. (1970).
[4] See, e.g., L. Laudan, *Progress and Its Problems* (1978).
[5] See, in particular, K. Popper, The *Rationality of Scientific Revolutions* (1981); and K. Popper, *The Logic of Scientific Discovery* (1959).

This book steers clear from such investigations. This is a book about international law discourse. It looks closely at concrete examples in international law's everyday practice in order to make the following argument: while progress may be a convenient label to caption a certain event (doctrine, process, institution, action, etc.), it is ultimately a notion empty of meaning unless placed in the context of a narrative – a story about how things were, how things are, and how things need to become. Such narratives, it is argued, give meaning to the idea of progress. But narratives do not 'speak themselves': their plot does not unfold in a world out there for the observer to record – it is not objectively true. Instead, their plot is constructed, based on concrete epistemic, ideological, or other choices and presented by means of assumptions, images, metaphors, and other discursive structures. Instead of recording reality 'as it is', narratives discursively represent and construct our perception of reality. Narratives of progress compete with and exclude alternative accounts. They also constitute the basis for policies and decisions that produce tangible effects on everyday life. In this light, progress narratives, and everyday invocations of the notion of progress in international law, are no longer descriptions of an objective reality but powerful rhetorical strategies of (de)legitimation. The term 'vocabulary of progress' is used throughout to refer to the conglomerate of discursive structures that produce meaning about progress in international law argument.

Although this argument may sound uncontroversial to some, it is at loggerheads with the claim of objectivity (truth, universality, neutrality, and so on) that continues to be ascribed overtly or covertly to many of international law's founding narratives. It is also at loggerheads with much of the mainstream understanding about the potential of our work to represent reality 'as it is', to achieve a 'more correct' representation of reality, or to lead to 'more efficient solutions', without necessarily asking what is left out by such characterizations. While international law debates are becoming increasingly accustomed to critiques that challenge the universality or objectivity of some of its doctrines and techniques, such critiques have not necessarily altered traditional perceptions about the possibility of international law to achieve or contribute to some sort of true progress that 'speaks itself'. And while narrative may be an inevitable rhetorical form for the expression of international law reformist proposals, not enough has been said about the capacity of progress narratives to simultaneously include and exclude, legitimize and delegitimize, or present the world as 'speaking itself'.

Hence this book is not a manifesto 'for' or 'against' progress narratives but a contribution to the understanding of their discursive function. Without doubt, there are several international law events that enjoy the endorsement of a majority or minority of international lawyers as progressive or good, the present author being no exception. This is not incompatible with seeking to understand the mechanisms by which the very same events and their accompanying explanations may also produce a whole range of exclusionary outcomes, either unanticipated or hidden from sight. Commitment to individual goals certainly does not prevent the re-evaluation of foundational narratives of the discipline that claim to represent reality 'as it is' and therefore constrain the horizon of available possibility for action. Commitment to individual goals certainly does not mean loyalty to traditional narratives of progress or traditional forms of telling international legal histories either. In that sense, the examination of the function of the notion of progress is part of a wider legal-political constructionist project of realizing the limits and potentials of legal discourse as well as the beneficiaries of their social outcomes.

Writing this book has been a long process that started over a decade ago in the context of my doctoral study, research fellowships, and teaching in different places. I am deeply indebted to several institutions and persons that provided the intellectual, institutional, and personal support that enabled this journey to come to an end. The Dissertation Program of the T.M.C. Asser Institute in The Hague and the European Law Research Center of Harvard Law School made early years of research possible by providing exceptionally stimulating environments and important financial support. The Faculty of Law of Leiden University kindly granted an eight-month sabbatical leave in 2006 and leeway in my working hours to complete the manuscript thereafter. Many of the reflections that became part of this book were generated in discussions with colleagues in different locations, such as the Asser Dissertation Program; the Graduate Program of Harvard Law School (1997-1999); Dighton weekends and gatherings; Foundation for New Research in International Law and Birkbeck University workshops; and discussions with colleagues at Leiden University and the Leiden Journal of International Law. My appreciation goes to T.M.C. Asser Press and, in particular, Philip van Tongeren and Marjolijn Bastiaans, for their enthusiasm, patience, and professionalism. Finally, I am thankful to Paola Gaeta and Laurence Boisson de Chazournes for the hospitality of the University of Geneva during the last month of the production of the text.

While all remaining shortcomings are my own, different parts of the manuscript have benefited from the thoughtful commentary and caring advice of John Dugard, David Kennedy and Martti Koskeniemi. I am beholden to them for all they have done for me over the years. A profound thank you also goes to Juan Amaya Castro, Martin Björklund, Claudio da Silva Correa, Matt Craven, Eric Durrer, Vangelis Herouveim, Florian Hoffmann, Rikki Holtmaat, Orsalia Lambropoulou, Frédéric Mégret, Sundhya Pahuja, Nikolas Tsagourias, Panos Triantafyllou, Frank Turner, and Michael Vagias for their friendship. They are all present in this book, each in their different way. My last word, one of boundless gratitude, goes to Riikka Koskenmäki and to my parents, Eleftheria and Michalis, for their love.

Earlier versions of Chapters 2 and 4 first appeared as 'The Vocabulary of Progress of Interwar International Law: An Intellectual Portrait of Stelios Seferiades', 16 *European Journal of International Law* (2005) 823-856; and 'The New Tribunalism: Strategies of (De)Legitimzation in the Era of Adjudication', *XVII Finnish Yearbook of International Law* (2006) 307-356.

*Cairo/Geneva, Autumn 2009*                                    Thomas SKOUTERIS

# TABLE OF CONTENTS

# LIST OF ABBREVIATIONS

| | |
|---|---|
| CRPC | Commission for Real Property Claims of Displaced Persons and Refugees in Bosnia and Herzegovina |
| CRT | Claims Resolution Tribunal for Dormant Accounts in Switzerland |
| | |
| ECHR | European Court of Human Rights |
| EFTA | European Free Trade Agreement |
| | |
| GATT 1947 | General Agreement on Tariffs and Trade |
| | |
| HPCC | Housing and Property Claims Commission in Kosovo |
| | |
| ICC | International Criminal Court |
| ICJ Rep | ICJ Reports |
| ICJ | International Court of Justice |
| ICSID | International Center for the Settlement of Investment Disputes |
| ICTY | International Criminal Tribunal for the former Yugoslavia |
| ITLOS | International Tribunal for the Law of the Sea |
| IUSCT | Iran-US Claims Tribunal |
| | |
| NGOs | Non-governmental organizations |
| | |
| OAPEC | Organization of Arab Petroleum Exporting Countries |
| | |
| PCIJ | Permanent Court of International Justice |
| PICT | Project for International Courts and Tribunals |
| | |
| RCADI | Recueil des Cours de l'Académie de Droit International de la Haye |
| | |
| TWAIL | Third World Approaches to International Law |
| | |
| UN | United Nations |
| UNCC | United Nations Compensation Commission |
| UNCLOS | United Nations Convention on the Law of the Sea |

VCLT              Vienna Convention on the Law of Treaties

WTO DSM           World Trade Organization Dispute Settlement Mechanism
WTO               World Trade Organization

# Chapter 1
# INTRODUCTION – THE NOTION OF PROGRESS IN INTERNATIONAL LAW DISCOURSE

## 1.1    Progress and International Law Debates

International law is strewn with accounts of progress. Academic and professional talk teems with stories about events that stand in the collective understanding of international jurists as examples of some sort of improvement or advance. They form much of the knowledge basis of the discipline and standard points of reference in textbooks, class education, and everyday practice. We speak of different institutional, doctrinal, methodological, or other developments as milestones in international law's long evolutionary march, as moments to be cherished or 'never again' repeated. Terms such as progress or progressive and their antonyms (regression, declension, regressive, conservative, and so on) are familiar expressions in our daily speech and writing to emphasize, accentuate, or accompany our claims about how to further professional methods and objectives.

The idea of progress seems ever-present, so perfectly embedded in international law's everyday life that its constant use passes unnoticed. Take for example the Kantian mantra that legal internationalism is an important catalyst of social progress, which animates the discipline's self-conception and lays the groundwork for many of our starting assumptions. Progress in our doctrines and processes, in our understanding of the nature of international relations, in our approximation to truth, in our capacity to respond to international crises, in achieving goals (e.g. maintaining peace, bringing justice, protecting human rights or the environment, and so on) remains the paramount driving force, promise, and aspiration of our projects. Belief in the very possibility of progress by means of internationalism, in the sense of advance constituted in stages each one of which is superior to its predecessor, is central to the identity of the international jurist and the reason why many of us joined the field.

Examples of the use of progress abound. Let it suffice here to recall, by means of a first reference, that the term progress has enjoyed widespread and unabated use for nearly two centuries in specialist international law writing. It has been used with great fervor in the period preceding the Great War[6] but also during the inter-bellum,[7] post-World War II,[8] and post-Cold War[9] periods. Most of us would concede a list of 'generally accepted' events

[6] For a few characteristic examples, see H. Wheaton, *Histoire des progrès du droit des gens en Europe depuis la paix de Westphalie jusqu'au Congrès de Vienne: avec un précis historique du droit des gens européen avant la paix de Westphalie* (1841); P. Pradier-Fodéré, *Traité de droit international public européen et américain suivant les progrès de la science et de la pratique contemporaines* (1885-1906); T.E. Holland, *The Progress Towards a Written Law of War* (1881); C. Calvo, *Le droit international théorique et pratique précédé d'un exposé historique des progrès de la science du droit des gens* (1896); L. Poinsard, *Comment se prépare l'unité sociale du monde: le droit international au XXe siècle, ses progrès et ses tendances* (1907); L. Renault, *Les progrès récents du droit des gens* (1912); International Peace Forum, *The World Court: A Magazine of International Progress Supporting a Union of Democratic Nations* (1916-1919).

[7] E.g., League of Nations Union, *The Progress of the League of Nations* (1923); G.A. Johnston, *International Social Progress: The Work of the International Labor Organization of the League of Nations* (1924); F.B. Boeckel, *Progress of the Centuries toward World Organization* (1927); J.B. Scott, *Le progrès du droit des gens* (1930); H. Wehberg, 'La contribution des conférences de la paix de La Haye au progrès du droit international', 37 *Recueil des Cours* (1931); M. Hudson, *Progress in International Organization* (1932); D. Mitrany, *The Progress of International Government* (1933).

[8] E.g., G. Hutton, *The War as a Factor in Human Progress* (1942); F.K. Bieligk, *Progress to World Peace: A Study of the Development of International Law and the Social and Economic Conditions of Peace* (1945); C.C. Lingard, *Peace with Progress* (1945); N.G. Ranga, *The Colonial and Colored Peoples: A Programme for their Freedom and Progress* (1946); C.G. Fenwick, 'The Progress of International Law during the Past Forty Years', 79 *Recueil des Cours* (1951); D. Eisenhower, *The Atom for Progress and Peace* (1953); C. Rousseau, *Scientific Progress and the Evolution of International Law* (1954); Q. Wright, *Problems of Stability and Progress in International Relations* (1954); I. Claude, *Swords into Plowshares: The Problems and Progress of International Organization* (4th edn. 1988); N.S. Chruschev, *Peace and Progress Must Triumph in Our Time* (1959); J.F. Kennedy, *Alianza para progreso, U.S. Government Printing Office* (1961); A. Ross, *The United Nations: Peace and Progress* (1966); *International Labor Office, The ILO in the Service of Social Progress* (1969); T. Buergenthal, 'The American Convention on Human Rights: An Illusion of Progress', in *Miscellanea: W.J. Ganshof van der Meersch*, Vol. 1 (1972); P. de Lapradelle, 'Progrès ou déclin du droit international', in *Mélanges offerts à Charles Rousseau* (1974); *Progress and Undercurrents in Public International Law: The International Law Association's Committee on Legal Aspects of a New International Economic Order* (1986).

[9] E.g., R. Beddard, *Economic, Social and Cultural Rights: Progress and Achievement* (1992); L. Arbour, 'Progress and Challenges in International Criminal Justice', 21 *Fordham International Law Journal* (1997) 531-540; J. Charney, 'Progress in International Criminal Law?', 93 *American Journal of International Law* (1999) 452; S.D. Murphy, 'Progress and

that symbolize international law's progress. Such is the case, for instance, with 1899 and 1907 and the Hague Peace Conferences, often described as pivotal for the codification of the obligation to peacefully resolve international disputes.[10] Such is also the case with 1920 and the Statute of the Permanent Court of International Justice, regarded as the first and standard-setting global judicial institution, whose spin-off effect was the crystallization and codification of many doctrines, from the sources of international law to principles of international procedural law.[11] One would never omit the Nuremberg and Tokyo Trials, founding moments that dared the paradigm-shift from a state-centered model of responsibility to one that provides for international criminal responsibility for individuals when their actions affect a fundamental interest of *l'ordre public international*.[12] Who could ignore the Breton Woods institutions and GATT 1947, for their con-

---

Jurisprudence of the International Criminal Tribunal for the Former Yugoslavia', 93 *American Journal of International Law* (1999) 57; A. Gillespie, *The Illusion of Progress: Unsustainable Development in International Law and Policy* (2001); C. Wellman, *The Proliferation of Rights: Moral Progress or Empty Rhetoric?* (1999); L. Condorelli, 'Les progrès du droit international humanitaire et la circulaire du secrétaire général des Nations Unies du 6 août 1999', in *The International Legal System in Quest of Equity and Universality* (2001); M. Delmas-Marty, 'Present-day China and the Rule of Law: Progress and Resistance', 2 *Chinese Journal of International Law* (2003) 11; E.C. Luck, 'Reforming the United Nations: Lessons from a History of Progress', in *The Politics of Global Governance: International Organizations in an Interdependent World* (2005); P. Bearman, *The Islamic School of Law: Evolution, Devolution, and Progress* (2005); R. Miller and R. Bratspies, eds., *Progress in International Law* (2008).

[10] The Hague Peace Conferences are typically portrayed as crucial moments for international law's (and international dispute settlement's) transition into the modern era. See Wehberg (Contribution), *supra* note 7; S. Rosenne, ed., 'Editor's Introduction', *The Hague Peace Conferences of 1899 and 1901 and International Arbitration – Reports and Documents* xv-xxi (2001).

[11] John Fischer Williams joins other scholars of the interwar to proclaim the adoption of Art. 38 as "the solid bed of rock of which the fabric of international law must be built". See J.F. Williams, *Aspects of Modern International Law – An Essay* (1939) at 37-38; see also Chapter 3.2, *infra*.

[12] Contemporary accounts of international criminal law and international criminal tribunals typically trace their origins to the International Military Tribunals in Nuremberg and Tokyo, as the first brave (albeit faulty in many respects) steps in the prosecution of individuals for the commission of international crimes. See, e.g., M.C. Bassiouni, 'From Versailles to Rwanda in Seventy-Five Years: The Need to Establish a Permanent International Criminal Court', 10 *Harvard Human Rights Law Journal* (1997) 11; W. Schabas, *The UN International Criminal Tribunals: The Former Yugoslavia, Rwanda and Sierra Leone* (2006) 11.

tribution to the stability of the post-war economic order and for planting the seeds for the liberalization of world trade and today's World Trade Organization?[13] Then there is a long list of international treaties and agreements in the field of human rights and humanitarian law: 1948 and the Universal Declaration of Human Rights, for providing the legal basis for the celebration of the universality of human rights, often regarded as one of humanity's greatest accomplishments;[14] 1949 and the Geneva Conventions, a watershed on humanity's perception of the conduct of warfare;[15] 1950 and the European Convention of Human Rights, introducing the most successful regional human rights system. Same with 1969 and the Vienna Convention on the Law of Treaties, which led to doctrinal harmonization on the most important law-making technique, thus increasing the certainty and predictability of international relations;[16] 1982 and the United Nations Convention on the Law of the Sea, which remedied many of the shortcomings of the pre-existing regime and offered a global and unified framework;[17] 1992 and the Rio Conference on Environment and Development, which rejuvenated awareness on the environment and provided the basis for many subsequent changes;[18] 1995 and the World Trade Organization;[19] 1998 and the

---

[13] Similarly, GATT 1947 is typically described as a founding moment for the development of a global liberalized trading system. See, J. Jackson, *The World Trading System: Law and Policy of International Economic Relations* (1997) 35-43.

[14] See, e.g., H.J. Steiner and P. Alston, *International Human Rights in Context: Law, Politics, Morals* (2008).

[15] F. Kalshoven, *Constraints on the Waging of War* (2001).

[16] I. Sinclair, *The Vienna Convention on the Law of Treaties* (1984).

[17] See, e.g., the editor's introduction about recent developments in the theory and practice in the Law of the Sea since 1982, in R. Barnes, D. Freestone and D.M. Ong, eds., *The Law of the Sea: Progress and Prospects* (2006) 1-27.

[18] The 1992 Rio Conference on Environment and Development is typically described as a landmark event for international environmental law, parallel to the 1972 Stockholm Conference. Although both events are deemed to have had much less impact on international affairs than initially hoped, and although they failed to produce any binding international instruments, they are generally regarded as pivotal moments for the evolution of the field. See P. Birnie and A. Boyle, *International Law and the Environment* (2002).

[19] The WTO and the emergence of the new economic law of the 1990s was proclaimed a 'revolution' in international affairs, replacing the waning UN system with a new, much more capable agent of international governance. See J. Trachtman, 'The International Economic Law Revolution', 17 *Pennsylvania Journal of International Economic Law* (1996) 33.

Rome Statute and the fulfillment of a dream of generations;[20] 2001 and the Articles on State Responsibility, which brought closure to one of international law's most important doctrines. Numerous examples can be found also in accounts of slower processes that have undercut longer periods of international law's development. Such is the case with the codification of international law and the ensuing expansion of its regulatory reach;[21] the limitation of the reserved domain of states, especially with regard to accountability for human rights violations; the codification of the use force and the calamity of its subsequent erosion;[22] the rise of international arbitration.[23] The list is truly endless.

The above observation that progress is intertwined with everyday international law work becomes arresting the moment one realizes that the language of progress is also a language of authority, to legitimize and de-legitimize. Invoking or evoking the notion of progress is a common and perfectly acceptable rhetorical move. But when we speak of something as progressive we don't merely describe reality the way we perceive it. We also assume, postulate, propose a desirable improvement compared to the *status quo ante*. Antonyms of progress (such as regression or regressive) are to be avoided at all cost. Indeed 'making progress' is the tenor of many claims about newness, renewalism and avant-gardism in international law.[24] 'Talking progress' is a common strategy of legitimation and delegitimation. The same certainly holds for accounts of declension or regression.[25] Progress

---

[20] "We have an opportunity to create an institution that can save lives and serve as bulwark against evil"; Address by the UN Secretary General at the Rome Conference on 15 June 1998, as cited in I. Tallgren, 'We Did It? The Vertigo of Law and Everyday Life at the Diplomatic Conference on the Establishment of an International Criminal Court', 12 *Leiden Journal of International Law* (1999) 683, at 683.

[21] For example, K. Oellers-Frahm, 'The Evolving Role of Treaties in International Law', in Miller and Bratspies (Progress), *supra* note 9, at 173-195.

[22] T. Franck, 'Who Killed Article 2(4)?', 64 *American Journal of International Law* (1970) 809.

[23] M.A. Bedikian, Triumph of Progress: 'The Embrace of International Commercial Arbitration', in Miller and Bratspies (Progress), *supra* note 9, at 517-538.

[24] For different strategies of renewalism see D. Kennedy, 'When Renewal Repeats: Thinking Outside the Box', 32 *New York University Journal of International Law and Politics* (2000) 335; N. Berman, 'In the Wake of Empire', 14 *The American University International Law Review* (1999) 1521; O. Spiermann, 'Twentieth Century Internationalism in Law', 18 *European Journal of International Law* (2007) 785.

[25] Narratives may use a similar form of determinism when speaking of regression or decline instead of progress. See for example de Lapradelle (Progrès), *supra* note 8, at 139-

talk is not just hortatory but often becomes the decisive discourse for policy making. From academic education to the way we choose to provide solutions to concrete situations or allocate resources, ideas of progress have palpable political salience in everyday life. Arguments about progress (or regression) mete out resources, power, justice, legitimacy, and set aside competing claims or understandings. One does not need to look far for examples. The Preamble of the UN Charter reads:

> "We the Peoples of the United Nations
> Determined to save succeeding generations from the scourge of war, which twice in our lifetime has brought untold sorrow to mankind, and [...]
> to promote social progress and better standards of life in larger freedom,
> And for these Ends [...]
> to employ international machinery for the promotion of the economic and social advancement of all peoples,
> Have Resolved to Combine our Efforts to Accomplish these Aims [...]."

Accounts of progress in international law come in a dazzling variety. They differ in their narrative form, in the manner they imagine the relationship between progress and international law, in the goal to be achieved, in the beneficiaries of the goal. There may be a strong correlation between the rhythm, the poetic form, the metaphors, the conception of temporality used and the traction of a narrative form in specific locations and times. It would be interesting to catalogue international law's narrative forms and discern relationships between form its salience in different situations. A comprehensive typology of progress accounts is not our main focus. Among many possible typologies, three generic types (or styles) of progress narrative are sketched by means of indication. These three categories are commonly found across the literature and are identified on the basis of how they register the relationship between international law and progress.

*First*, narratives of international law *as* progress, in other words the idea that international law itself has an immanent progressive value for the world, for civilization, for humanity. The underlying rationale here is the Kantian idea that international law (see internationalism, the creation and use of

---

152; or, more recently, E.A. Posner, 'The Decline of the International Court of Justice', in S. Voigt, M. Albert and D. Schmidtchen, eds., *International Conflict Resolution* (2006).

more and better international law and institutions, the rule of law in international affairs, etc.) signifies a desirable move towards a superior state of social development. This has been understood in different situations as a move of internationalism away from power, politics, injustice, war, impunity, absolutism; and a corresponding move towards rules, standards, processes, rule of law, justice, peace, accountability, democracy. Needless to say, the reverse course has been called progressive with equal fervor. Rosenne writes:

"I have given this course the title *The Perplexities of Modern International Law*. [...] The perplexities follow from the conviction that universal peace will become a reality when we have a workable, rational, balanced and accepted general system of international law and competent, impartial and appropriate instruments to enforce it when necessary, that it in times of crises. The World has not yet reached that state. That is what it is trying to find."[26]

*Second*, narratives of progress *within* international law. Here the idea is that international law achieves progressive internal development as a working pure. According to such accounts, international law (as a science, as a discourse, as a tool, as a governance system, as a technique, and so on) becomes better in its methods, efficiency, techniques, or in attaining its goals. In different periods and places 'better' international law has stood for a broad range of goals, such as more/less rules, standards, processes, institutions, empirical analysis, radical critique, formalism, codification, determinacy, and so on. During the interwar period, for instance, some international lawyers considered that in order to make progress international law needs to codify more rules in the form of international treaties and based on sociological-empirical analysis of the needs of the international community.[27] In international criminal law, more recently, scholars have considered that international criminal law has made progress through its elucidation and elaboration in the work of International Criminal Tribunals for the Former Yugoslavia and Rwanda.[28] The adoption of Article 38 of the Statute of the Permanent Court of International Justice was welcomed as a moment of disciplinary progress *within* international law:

---

[26] S. Rosenne, *The Perplexities of Modern International Law* (2004) 2.

[27] A. Álvarez, 'The New International Law', 15 *Transactions of the Grotius Society* (1930) 35-51.

[28] Charney (Progress), *supra* note 9.

"There was no established permanent court of international law; the lawyer advising a client, perhaps the government of his own country in the guise of a client, was often quite uncertain whether the matter in question would ever be referred to a tribunal at all; if it was to be referred to a tribunal, he had no knowledge of how that tribunal was likely to be constituted, and he might not even be sure what were the sources to which that tribunal was likely to appeal of the determination of the legal points at issue. The Institution of the Permanent Court of International Justice has changed all this. We now have it laid down, by the authority of all states which have become parties to the Statute of that Court, what are the sources of international law. [...] Many international lawyers of outstanding eminence and authority might have drafted this article differently had they been called on to do so in 1920, but nevertheless it stands as the text of capital importance, the solid basis of rock on which the fabric of international law has to be built."[29]

*Third*, there are instances where a single disciplinary development is described as embodying both categories (international law *as* progress; progress *within* international law) at the same time. This is the case in recent debates about the proliferation of international judicial institutions where the establishment of international tribunals is seen as having an intrinsic progressive value. This holds both for humanity as a whole (e.g., social progress) and for the techniques and methods of international law, the story goes. The proliferation of tribunals completes the missing piece in international law's institutional architecture while strengthening the fabric of the law.

"An international judicial or arbitral body has in itself some claim to be regarded as a good thing: opposition to the establishment of such a body has to be based on questioning whether it is actually needed rather than on any denial of its virtues. The creation of new tribunals may indeed be regarded as an encouraging sign, as amounting to the 'expression d'adhésion plus grande des acteurs de la vie internationale à la doctrine de la primauté de la règle de droit dans les rapports internationaux [...]'."[30]

---

[29] Williams (Aspects), *supra* note 11.

[30] H. Thirlway, 'The Proliferation of International Judicial Organs: Institutional and Substantive Questions: The International Court of Justice and Other International Courts', in N. Blokker and H. Schermers, eds., *Proliferation of International Organizations* (2001) 251-278 at 255.

These broad categories encompass and spawn a whole range of sub-variations revolving around additional properties such as the pattern with which progress is described to occur, the narrative form used, or the goal that progress needs to serve.

In terms of the pattern in which progress occurs, progress is seen by many to take place in single revolutionary episodes or in gradual processes of incremental change. Along these lines, some see individual bursts of progress in the Treaty of Westphalia of 1648 and the creation of the concept of nation-state sovereignty as we know it today. Others see a leap forward in The Hague Peace Conferences in 1899 and 1907 and the creation of the League of Nations, inaugurating a new era of international organization. The same could be said of the 1949 Geneva Conventions and the way in which they helped re-conceive the *jus in bello*. Some saw a true scientific revolution in the emergence of International Economic Law, as a new paradigm of international governance, replacing the dysfunctional UN system. Alternatively, progress could take place through a slow process of incremental change. This change occurs through accumulation of knowledge, crystallization, induction, reduction, deduction, natural selection of the strongest theory, rise and fall, or numerous other ways. Some see progress evolving in a linear way, others in the form of a spiral, of a river strengthened by tributaries, a revolutionary overthrow of paradigms, natural selection, by means of an 'invisible hand'. Accounts of gradual progress give context and meaning to individual events by interpreting them and relating them to one another into coherent historical or causal relationships. It is very hard to understand why the 1899 and 1907 Hague Peace Conferences are important unless one refers, and among other things, to the significance of the codification of the obligation to resolve disputes peacefully and how this process started with the Jay Treaty of 1794 and culminated in recent events. Likewise, the establishment of the International Criminal Tribunal for the former Yugoslavia (ICTY) or the International Criminal Court (ICC) acquires its meaning as a key development only when placed in the context of an argument about the importance of individual international criminal responsibility for global peace, security or justice. One could also recall here the stories about the de-mystification of the absolute conception of sovereignty into a bundle of rights and obligations; the codification of international law and the ensuing expansion of its regulatory reach; the limitation of the reserved domain of states, especially with regard to human rights

violations; the prohibition of the use force and the establishment of an obligation to peacefully resolve international disputes; the crystallization of
important doctrines, such as sources or state responsibility, into generally
accepted formulations, and many others.

Narratives may also differ in the way in which the story is emplotted in
narrative form. Sometimes international law's evolution is described as a
struggle of overcoming and vindication (e.g., the eradication of global pov-
erty, nationalism, or legal indeterminacy), as a prophecy to be confirmed
(e.g., the democratic peace thesis, according to which democratic states are
reluctant to go to war with one another), as a Manichean struggle that needs
to be won (e.g., the battle between democracy and absolutism), a morally
just cause to be defended by righteous actors (e.g., the legitimacy of humanitarian intervention), and so on. David Scott, for example, suggests that
most early post-colonial critique has been emplotted in the distinctive narrative form of a Romance of vindication.[31] Others speak of the "rise and
fall" of doctrines, ideas, institutions.[32]

In terms of the goal that progress serves, the picture is even more complex. The normative undertaking involved in figuring out the postulated
goals of the progressive sequence of the discipline has led to a variety of
radically different claims. The two main categories are, first, about models
that enhance the discipline's approximation to truth and, second, models
that increase its effectiveness in problem solving. In the first category,
progress involves a better understanding of the nature of the world, of the
science of international law, of the foundational concepts of the discipline
(state, community, truth, justice, fairness, etc). The purpose would be to
reach a superior understanding, i.e., one that is more/less pure, coherent,
realistic, empirical, objective, inter-disciplinary, universal, political, sociological, flexible, etc.[33] In the second category, emphasis is shifted to pro-

---

[31] D. Scott, *Conscripts of Modernity: The Tragedy of Colonial Enlightenment* (2004) 7.

[32] See, e.g., E. Brown Weiss, 'The Rise or the Fall of International Law?', 69 *Fordham Law Review* (2000) 345-372; T. Waelde, 'A Requiem for the "International Economic Order": The Rise and Fall of Paradigms in International Economic Law', in N. Al-Nauimi and R. Meese, eds., *International Legal Issues Arising out of the United Nations Decade of International Law* (1995) 1301-1338; G. Scott, *The Rise and Fall of the League of Nations* (1973).

[33] See, for instance, A.M. Slaughter, *A New World Order* (2004), whose description of the international legal order is presented as a sophisticated correction to previous under-standings of the structure of international relations.

ducing better results, such as more/less correctness, efficiency, prevention, prediction, justice, closure, welfare, equality, liberty, determinacy, health, human rights, peace, etc.[34] Accounts of progress here involve anything from codification of rules to the development of standards; from formalization of our idea of law to de-formalization; from power-oriented systems to rule-oriented systems; from separating law from politics to embracing power within our concept of the law; from solutions by means of processes and political institutions to solutions based on institutionalized judicial dispute settlement; from coexistence to cooperation; from privileging sovereign will to privileging community ends; from an international community of states to a global community of persons; and so on.

The nature of progress has been the subject of extensive enquiry in the social sciences for over two centuries.[35] Yet, no similar investigation has taken place in international law. Despite the central position that progress continues to occupy in international law's language, little or no examination of the ontology or history of progress has been offered to date. By and large, progress is used in its dictionary sense of a passage or transision from one 'inferior' state of affairs to a 'superior' one, while reflections on more theoretical dimensions of the concept are rare. Two significant exceptions to this rule need to be mentioned here. First, there is the important contribution of Newstream and Critical legal scholarship to the study of narrativity, history, and ideology in international law. This body of work has addressed on occasion the idea of progress and has produced findings of great significance for the present analysis, as explained in the next section.[36] The second exception is a recently published compilation of essays, entitled *Progress in International Law*.[37] This is the first book-sized effort that specifically takes issue with the notion of progress in international law and, as such, it deserves our full attention.

In *Progress in International Law* Russ Miller and Rebecca Bratspies aspire to "survey the state of the contemporary legal order".[38] This is a

---

[34] See, for instance, N. Pillay, 'Protection of the Health of Women through International Criminal Law: How Can International Criminal Law Contribute to Efforts to Improve Criminal Justice', 22 *Emory International Law Review* (2008) 15-27.

[35] See note 1, *supra*.

[36] See the analysis in Section 1.2, *infra*.

[37] Miller and Bratspies (Progress), *supra* note 9. For a more extensive review, see T. Skouteris, 'Review Essay: Progress in International Law', 22 *Leiden Journal of International Law* (Vol. 3, 2009) (Forthcoming).

[38] Ibid., at 11.

broad and unusually ambitious scholarly project aimed at "cataloguing this generation's tangled international legal order" and hoping "to map the current tendencies, theories, doctrine, and trends". The most intellectually intriguing aspect of the book is the manner in which editors and contributors posit the relationship between international law and progress. The editors acknowledge in their editorial note that, at the beginning of the new century international law finds itself yet again in a state of "flux" and uncertainty.[39] This condition is brought about by "three epochal developments" which are no other than the end of the Cold War, the rise of the era of global terrorism, and the rapid pace of technological change. These new conditions, according to the editors, have "eroded" the universal nature of foundational assumptions in international law. Setting aside this factual-political context, references by the editors to the writings of Martti Koskenniemi, David Kennedy, and even Jacques Derrida point between the lines to yet another development that shapes the historical conjuncture in which the book is written. Post-modern critique of the grand narratives of the Enlightenment, such as the one of human progress, has persuasively entered the stage of international law argument. In the advent of such critique, the editors find it hard to speak meaningfully about progress without at least reckoning with the complex relationship between history, ideology, truth, and narrativity.

The book appears to have been inspired by a remarkable monograph published in 1932 by Manley O. Hudson.[40] Hudson's book, coincidentally or not, is central to Chapter 3 of the present enquiry as well.[41] The title that Miller and Bratspies have chosen, *Progress in International Law*, is a paraphrase of the title of Hudson's initial publication ("Progress in International Organization"). This choice underscores the intricate relationship between the two projects. In not so many words, the aspiration of the book, like Hudson back in 1932, is not a head-on definition of the notion of progress in the context of international law. Rather, the desire is to record the state of affairs at the beginning of the new century, much as Hudson did in the beginning of the tumultuous decade of the 1930s. It is more about putting on record views by academics and practitioners involved in everyday inter-

---

[39] Ibid., at 9.
[40] Hudson (Progress), *supra* note 7.
[41] See Sections 3.2 and 3.3, *infra*.

national law about 'how things stand' at the moment of writing. Thus the editors hope to create an "artifact", a "snapshot" of our times, for the benefit of present and future generations. The ulterior motive, similar to Hudson, is to accumulate data for an informed assessment of whether international law is able to meet its goals. Consequently, the objective is to answer the question of whether international law has achieved internal disciplinary progress or whether it has contributed to wider social progress at the moment of writing.

How does the book aspire to catalogue international law in its current state, while acknowledging post-modern critique? The editors express their hope that explorations of the intricate relationship between progress and international law will at least "color" their book. Their answer however really comes in the language of editorial pragmatism. They make it clear that the book "does not directly confront the indeterminacy at the heart of the progress narrative".[42] Instead, questions of progress "operate mostly as a backdrop to this book" and this is "in part, a result of conscious editorial choice" – i.e., they did not wish to "narrow the contributors' gaze" on the materials. Although the answer provided is clear, it stands in some tension with the contestation of the editors that the book "was not intended to diminish the fundamental critique that progress narratives are inherently slippery and value laden".[43]

The reason is the following. Choosing not to address critiques of narratives of progress in a book dealing with *Progress in International Law* is not without consequences. Editors and authors pass on a great opportunity to engage the centerpiece of modern social sciences, namely the idea that there 'is' such a thing as progress and, the international lawyer's version of the story, that international law is a crucial agent for its materialization. In addition, in its quest for firm ground that sidesteps the post-modern critique, the book resorts to Hudson's own "modernist-positivist" (as the editors brand it) epistemology as an inspiration for the articulation of its research questions. The most crucial concession is that most of the essays in the volume "generally proceeded from the unspoken assumption that progress could be measured, debated, and agreed upon". Authors and editors alike seem to experience Marshall Berman's modernist anxiety that *All That is*

---

[42] Miller and Bratspies (Progress), *supra* note 9, at 24.
[43] Ibid.

*Solid Melts into Air*:[44] At the century's dawn, "the accepted grounds of international consensus and cooperation seem to be shifting under our feet".[45] Hence the book operates on the assumption that the cataloguing of today's reality for the assessment of progress achieved is a meaningful exercise which retains its own inherent value in recreating some sovereign ground for international law: "Aware that we are succumbing to this particular facet to international law's progress narrative" the book proceeds "with the belief that an accounting of the state of contemporary international law would prove both challenging and enriching".[46]

Let us see how that happens. In the opening essay of the book Jordan Paust draws parallels between the interwar period and today.[47] He concludes that certain developments since the interwar period, such as increased human interdependence, the increased recognition of private and public individual roles, and the growth of international and regional institutions have brought the gradual effectuation of certain human values. These values include human dignity, tolerance, human rights, democratic values and the cooperative use of armed force. For Paust, gradual effectuation of these values provides "both an evidence and promise of progress in international organization".[48] The point here is not to question whether Professor Paust is right or wrong but, rather, to observe the way in which the relationship between law and progress is drawn. For example, the author's notion of progress is not defined as such in the text, whereas attainment of the said values offers evidence and promise of its materialization. The precise relationship between values and forward movement is not explained but taken as self-evident – who can doubt that 'more human dignity' is a 'good thing'? Although the answer would appear self-evident to most, one could legitimately ask what does 'more human dignity' really mean, whether the listed achievements do lead to more human dignity on the global level, what are the costs or exclusions of recent developments, and so on. Now, despite the

---

[44]  M. Berman, *All That is Solid Melts into Air – The Experience of Modernity* (1982).

[45]  Miller and Bratspies (Progress), *supra* note 9, at 25.

[46]  Ibid.

[47]  J. Paust, 'Evidence and Promise of Progress: Increased Interdependence, Rights and Responsibilities, Areas of Interaction, and the Need for More Cooperative Armed Force', in Miller and Bratspies (Progress), *supra* note 9, at 33-50.

[48]  Miller and Bratspies (Progress), *supra* note 9, at 50.

absence of such ruminations, Professor Paust's argument does not alienate the reader. The reason is precisely that the argument operates self-referentially against the background of a liberal-democratic narrative of progress, which is never spelled out but assumed as true throughout the text. This narrative adopts the said values as yardsticks of progressive internationalism over the past hundred years. The liberal-democratic narrative, however, is not questioned. Its various failures, critiques, potential bias, or exclusions are not part of the account. As a consequence, the essay concludes that during the last hundred or so years progress has been achieved.

*Progress in International Law* makes great reading and succeeds in offering a snapshot of today's state of affairs in international law. At the same time, it passes on a great opportunity to enrich its investigation with a much-needed dialogue on progress narratives and their role in international law. Is "succumbing" to the traditional understanding of progress narratives, as Miller and Bratspies put it, a 'good' or a 'bad' thing? Is it part of some progressive or regressive political project? This brings us to the next point.

## 1.2    THE PROBLEM: PROGRESS AS A NOTION THAT 'SPEAKS ITSELF'

Accounts of progress in international law texts, such as the ones listed above, have something in common. Beyond expressing a conviction or aspiration, they also appear to 'speak themselves'. With this phrase I do not refer to the lack of supportive arguments, although that may also be the case. I rather suggest that the expression "social progress and better standards of life in larger freedom" (Preamble UN Charter), the benefits of codification for international law, or the desirability of increased accountability for human rights violations, all allude to a kind of progress that exists on a plane independent from subjective judgment. Unless a narrative of progress convincingly demonstrates that it belongs on such a plane it collapses into pure opinion.

This is a very important point that is often missed. Although we all have different ideas about what true democracy is and how to achieve it, we all think that achieving more democracy means progress because, ultimately, there is an essence in democracy (democratic institutions, democratic processes, in the social outcomes of the institutions, etc.) which transcends all

16                                                                        CHAPTER 1

our individual definitions and truly constitutes a greater good. Similarly, for progress to be true in international law it needs to claim properties that rise above the subjectivity of the author and exist in some objective (immanent, obvious, true, neutral, universal, transcendental, etc.) meta-dimension. "Social progress and better standards of life in larger freedom" exists not because I say so but because it is so, regardless of whether I say so or not. The beneficiary must be a decisive totality (e.g., international community, humankind, civilization, etc.) greater than the author of the claim or the group she represents. This is certainly the case with the UN Charter's preambular commitment to social progress but also with debates about more international law, more democracy, more rule of law, more human rights, more accountability, more international tribunals, and so on.

Take the relatively uncontroversial thesis that the mere accretion of knowledge constitutes progress for science.[49] According to this thesis the accumulation of knowledge about a topic is a 'good thing' in itself. International law can be described as having progressed on account of the fact that, ever since its early years, it continues to amass in-depth knowledge by means of an increasing body of scientific work, legislation, case law, and so on. We now know 'more' about international law and transnational legal relationships than we ever did before. Most people would agree that this is a form of progress that 'speaks itself' in the sense that it is an a-political, uncontroversial statement that transcends subjective opinion and benefits the totality of human society. Indeed most scientific work aspires to modestly participate in some way or another to the accretion of knowledge. But the accretion of knowledge thesis is meaningless without a meta-theory that demonstrates how the accumulation of information, data, evidence, teachings, doctrines, histories, makes 'better' science. Better science could mean anything from better approximation to truth (e.g. more accurate representation of how international relations 'are'), more efficiency in problem solving (e.g., 'more' justice), and so on. This meta-theory needs to explain what is a better representation of reality or more justice. But it will have to do so in a manner that is decisive and transcends subjective judgment. It will have to speak itself.

One will immediately counter-argue that there is nothing wrong with using a notion of progress that 'speaks itself' this way. The absence of the

---

[49] This thesis was central in Miller and Bratspies (Progress), *supra* note 9.

"I" of the narrator could be a mere cultural or aesthetic convention, not necessarily a commitment to objectivity or universality. Third person accounts of how things are could be seen also in positive light, as the projection of a subjective conviction or aspiration on a grand scale. Such rhetorical projections are legitimate and necessary on different grounds, from the humble (making formal theories of general application is the prescribed way of advancing science) to the noble (it is my hope that my ideas will become universally accepted) and the savvy (I use universalist vocabulary strategically in order to sound more convincing). Most of us acknowledge the temptation to use accounts of progress and admit to have done so on occasion. Such accounts seem to be intuitive; they seem to facilitate rhetorical economy; they effectively drive the points across. Besides, there seems to be general agreement among the invisible college of international lawyers that international law *is* in a better state today than it was a hundred years ago, and so is the world at large, even though 'better' is understood differently by each person. Even Roland Barthes has famously written that narrative is a universal form of verbal representation so seemingly natural to human consciousness that to suggest that this is a problem might well appear pedantic.[50] So, what exactly is the problem?

Let me explain. For a narrative of progress to be persuasive in international law it ultimately needs to purge the possibility of relativity in the essence of the claim. Should one prove that "social progress and better standards of life in larger freedom" has no essence or stable meaning, then the Preamble of the UN Charter and the object and purpose of the UN are reduced to demagogy. The moment one demonstrates that a certain type of bias or discrimination (gender, race, economic, political, cultural, etc.) is inherent part of "social progress"; the moment the statement is proven to privilege certain segments of the affected group and denigrate others; then one opens Pandora's Box and weakens the authority of a claim that defines a major project of internationalist reform. For progress to work as a label to caption one's reformist agenda, it must demonstrate a certain property that 'speaks itself' and trumps relativist criticism in a decisive manner. Otherwise it would not be 'true' progress but the ephemeral prevalence of a partial, ideological project. Progress can only be proclaimed if one axiomatically

---

[50] R. Barthes, 'Introduction to the Structural Analysis of Narratives', in R. Barthes, *Image, Music, Text* (1977) 79-124, at 79.

accepts a meta-narrative that declares closure or end to contestation.[51] In this sense, narratives of progress are not different from narratives of regression or decline/declension.[52]

Let me demonstrate this by turning to yet another example, the account of progress that introduces Shaw's classic textbook on public international law.

> "In the long march of mankind from the cave to the computer a central role has always been played by the idea of law – the idea that order is necessary and chaos inimical to a just and stable existence. Every society, whether it be large or small, powerful or weak, has created for itself a framework of principles within which to develop. What can be done, what cannot be done, permissible acts, forbidden acts, have all been spelt out within the consciousness of that community. Progress, with its inexplicable leaps and bounds, has always been based upon the group as men and women combine to pursue commonly accepted goals, whether these be hunting animals, growing food or simply making money. Law is that element which binds the members of the community together in their adherence to recognized values and standards. [...] And so it is with what is termed international law, with the important difference that the principle subjects of international law are nation-states, not individual citizens."[53]

It could be argued that one should not read too much in this text that is merely the overture to a student textbook and not a treatise on human history. Some degree of over-generalization is permissible for reasons of economy and is rhetorically necessary in order to situate the topic within a wider context. Indeed, the essence of the author's account of progress

---

[51] For a most characteristic example, see the neo-conservative idea that the turn to liberal democracy at the end of the Cold War heralds the 'end of history', ending ideological struggle and declaring the triumph of political and economic liberalism. See F. Fukuyama, *The End of History and the Last Man* (1992).

[52] Narratives may use a similar form of determinism when speaking of regression or decline instead of progress. See for example de Lapradelle (Progrès), *supra* note 8, at 139-152; or, more recently, E.A. Posner, 'The Decline of the International Court of Justice', in S. Voigt, M. Albert and D. Schmidtchen, eds., *International Conflict Resolution* (2006). See also C. Landauer, 'The Gentle Civilizer: Declension Narratives in International Law', presented in the 3rd Birkbeck Workshop on Critical Approaches to International Law (Birkbeck, London, 16 May 2006) (on file with the author).

[53] M.N. Shaw, *International Law* (2003) at 1.

(whether it is right or wrong) is not at issue here. The text is interesting however because it is an example of how progress can be entwined with international law writing. The excerpt speaks of human progress, the nature of human society and the role of law and, indeed, international law. It adopts a formal idea of progress that is catalytic for the production of meaning in the rest of the passage. The first sentence immediately situates the reader within the context of a historical evolution of humankind: a story about how things were before, how things are today, and what is the distance traveled; or, to put it differently, a story with a well-marked beginning, middle, and end-phases. In Shaw's excerpt, humanity has had a "long march from the cave to the computer", leading to the present day. With a single strike the reader is summoned and placed inside a concrete and clearly defined context: a historical continuum (humanity's development) and a social group (a universal community of human beings). The reader is also informed that humanity's progression (*our* progression) was long and arduous ("long march"). It has resulted, however, into definite progress. On the one hand, it has evolved from technologically primitive life ("the cave") to modern technological advancement ("the computer"); on the other, from a primitive social state ("chaos") to an advanced social state ("order"). In Shaw's text this statement receives no further elaboration and is taken as self-explanatory: our modern era *is* a much better time for humanity than its primitive past because of these advances.

Law, we are also told, has played a "central role" in this transformation. This central role was performed "always" and in "every society, whether it be large or small, powerful or weak". The idea of law that Shaw alludes to is universal, perennial, and transcendental. Law embodies the idea of order and is the element that binds the community of humans together and enables progress. Progress has "always been based upon the group as men and women combine to pursue commonly accepted goals". International law is finally introduced in the closing sentences as something similar to law at large, with the same effects and sharing the same history. The founding difference is that nation-states and not individuals are its principal subjects. At the end of Shaw's passage the student is assured that the history of humanity unequivocally demonstrates that law existed in every society and has always done well. In this account of progress, the "I" of the author is absent. Shaw adopts the posture of a dispassionate, neutral, objective chronicler that merely records events as they "are", from a seemingly external point of view.

Regardless of whether one agrees with Professor Shaw, one may wonder whether the transformation occurred *really* or *only* along the lines described. This is a crucial question: if the objectivity of the account is disrupted, and if a multiplicity of alternative histories of equal plausibility is allowed, then the background for his approach to the international law of today should be more nuanced, since different lessons should be learned from the past. If one was able to demonstrate, for argument's sake, that life in today's world is not necessarily 'better' than the one in a previous era, one would then have to adopt a more ambivalent posture towards the social function of international law than the one nurtured in Shaw's text. The book would have to explain, for example, how international law might be either a sword or a shield, depending on the context. It might also have to list international law's failures or examples of cases in history when international law was part of the problem instead of part of the solution.

Additionally, one may also wonder about the epistemic basis on which such an account of human progress has been constructed as well as its po-litical, cultural, ideological, gender, race, class and other orientations. Again, regardless of whether one agrees with the specific choices of each author, one could say that no compendium of historical records can be compiled without an external point of view that offers itself as a filter, which helps distinguish events worth being recorded from others that are not. A simple list of events, listed by date or genre, is never sufficient to describe what happened and, besides, what is an appropriate event to include such a list? As historian and philosopher Hayden White writes,

> "the capacity to envision a set of events as belonging to the same order of meaning requires some principle by which to translate difference into similar-ity. In other words, it requires a subject common to all of the referents of the various sentences that register events as having occurred".[54]

One can begin to ask what has been left out in Shaw's account of progress. What are the alternative accounts which have been set aside? What has been fore-grounded and what has been relegated to the background? What alternative accounts does his history compete with? Finally, one may won-

---

[54] H. White, 'The Value of Narrativity in the Representation of Reality', in H. White, *The Content of the Form. Narrative Discourse and Historical Representation* (1987) 1-25.

der whether it is a 'good' or a 'bad' thing to limit oneself to a single account of how humankind and international law have reached the present point.

After reading Shaw's passage the reader hits the road running. She is introduced to international law with the conviction that this body of rules and its supporting scientific discipline has always been a progressive agent for humanity. History's sadder moments are not attributed to international law, are explained away, or entirely kept out sight. It is this overt/covert claim to progress that legitimizes, for the purposes of his introduction, the 'goodness' of the study of public international law.

Using progress as a notion that 'speaks itself' raises some good questions about the way in which one perceives reality and translates it into legal argument. First, can progress really ever 'speak itself'? Or, is the meaning of progress always defined by concrete epistemic or other choices (e.g., ideological, political, cultural, personal, etc.) that are open to the critique of relativism? Second, if meaning is based on such choices, can progress ever be universal or will it necessarily always involve power relations and an ideological struggle, during which some will gain and others will lose? Third, if progress cannot 'speak itself', why does one need to use progress in a way that speaks itself in order to be able to articulate a convincing argument about international law? Why does the profession have to resort to third person accounts of how things are in order to be taken seriously? Fourth, could one see progress talk not as a descriptive exercise but as a powerful rhetorical strategy of legitimation? Finally, if progress talk legitimizes and de-legitimizes, includes and excludes, how aware are we of the exclusions of our own progress narratives?

These are very important questions. By investigating how meaning about progress is produced in international law one may be able to understand how our accepted professional rhetorical strategies remove from sight the ideological dimensions of legal argument, while at the same time performing a deeply ideological function. To put it in crude terms, if progress talk in international law, aside from the legitimate expression of subjective conviction or aspiration, proves to be an ideological strategy, one may be forced to reconsider some well-rooted assumptions present in our founding narratives about the nature of international law, such as the ideas that international law is a formal discourse with no gender, religion, culture, ideology, economic theory, and so on. One will suddenly be confronted with uncanny exclusions kept away from sight. One may also be able to understand better the structure of concrete legal debates that use the idea of progress as part of their rhetorical apparatus. It may also help understand how specific relationships of power and exclusion are meted out in specific contexts through legal discourse. The above considerations constitute the starting point of this enquiry.

## 1.3    CRITIQUE AND THESES: PROGRESS AS THE PRODUCT OF NARRATIVES

A notion of progress that 'speaks itself' is in tension with recent developments in the humanities and social sciences. The thesis that meaning is actively produced by text as opposed to being merely recorded by text ('speaking itself') constitutes a principal tenet of some of the most influential intellectual movements of the 20th century. Any attempt to draw here a synopsis of the theoretical origins of this proposition would be Sisyphean, if only because intellectual movements evade (and often detest) reduction to a standard set of theses, and for good reason. The purpose of the quick review that follows is only to situate the reader in the intellectual tradition that forms the background of this enquiry.

The claim that meaning is actively produced by (as opposed to being recorded in) by text stands in unison with a variety of writings in linguistics, social theory, history, anthropology, philosophy, and law. The movements of structural linguistics, structuralism, post-structuralism, deconstruction, post-modernism, social constructionism (all within or without inverted commas) have given rise to an enormous body of literature which shares some key starting points and parts company on others. Starting points include the idea that the world should not be treated as objective truth: knowledge and representations about how the world is 'out there' are not mere reflections of the world but products of certain ways of categorizing the world – they are products of discourse. Truth is a discursive construction. The origins of the thesis that our access to reality is always through discourse and language can be traced to the movement of structural linguistics that followed the work of Swiss linguist Ferdinand de Saussure at the beginning of the 20th century.[55] De Saussure argued that the linguistic sign

---

[55] See F. de Saussure, *Course in General Linguistics* (edited by Charles Bally and Albert Sechehaye, translated by Roy Harris, 1983). For important commentaries to Saussure's work

(words, expressions, etc.) is a "double entity" made up of two different components, namely the signifier (form) and the signified (content, meaning). The relationship between the two is 'arbitrary'. Arbitrary means in this context that the meaning we attach to words is not inherent in the form of the sign (sound, spelling) but is the result of social conventions according to which we associate specific meaning with specific forms. According to de Saussure, the meaning of signs is determined by their relationship to other signs. Language is possible because each sign has a fixed position relative to other signs. Language is thus seen as a network or structure of signs. This structure is related to the social context in which is operates and therefore changes from time to time. De Saussure distinguished two levels of language, *langue* and *parole*. *Langue* is the abstract structure of language, the network of signs that has been internalized by the users of the language that give meaning to signs, whereas *parole* is the actual use of language, the utterances of people when speaking. Such utterances can only be understood by reference to the *langue*, for it is the structure of the language that makes specific statements meaningful. The relationship between language and reality is therefore 'arbitrary' in the sense that there is no natural reason why a particular sign should be attached to a particular form – it is the *langue* that determines these relationships.

Structural linguistics at the beginning of the 20th century and the movement of structuralism later on claimed that meaning is produced through linguistic, cultural, and other 'structures' that vary from person, language or culture.[56] Following the above insight, the way we understand the world is culturally and historically specific, the product of interchange between people, cultures, society. Different systems of knowledge determine what is true or not in their own way. As such, our understanding of the world is relatively contingent. Following de Saussure and structuralism, post-structuralist work took structuralist insights a step further and claimed that the structures identified by structuralists are further subverted and de-stabilized

---

see J. Culler, *Saussure* (1976); R. Harris, *Reading Saussure: A Critical Commentary on the Cours de linguistique générale* (1987).

[56] In addition to Saussure, the works of Émile Benveniste, Roman Jacobson, Claude Lévi Strauss, Roland Barthes, Jacques Lacan, and early works of Michel Foucault and Julia Kristeva are associated with this movement. For some useful reviews of the structuralist movement, see J. Sturrock, *Structuralism* (1993); J. Sturrock, *Structuralism and Since: From Lévi Strauss to Derrida* (1981).

by the texts themselves, thus denying any possibility of systematic knowledge.[57] Post-structuralism takes from stucturalism the idea that signs derive
meaning not from a direct relationship to reality but from internal relations
within the network of signs. Post-structuralism however rejects the view
that language is stable. Signs are no longer fixed in a permanent relationship to one another but their relative position changes according to the context in which they are used. Thus words can even acquire opposite meaning
in their use. For post-structuralists, *langue* continues to perform the same
function as Saussure claimed but always in an ephemeral, inconsistent state.
The structure of language, for the post-structuralists, changes with language
use. Authors such as Michel Foucault further linked this insight about language with power. Foucault took previous insights on narrativity and language to demonstrate how knowledge and power presuppose each other.[58]
Foucault explained that within a certain situation of language use there are
rules that determine which statements may be acceptable as meaningful
and which statements are pushed outside the four corners of what is permissible. Discourses therefore impose limits on what gives meaning. Different
discourses struggle for supremacy in the determination of meaning or truth.
Following Foucault, post-modern work has famously expressed incredulity
towards meta-narratives or other discursive formations that claim to be decisive.[59] This is an anti-foundationalist and anti-essentialist strand of thought
which rejects the so-called foundationalist view that knowledge can be
grounded on a meta-theoretical, decisive, or transcendental base.

   The practice of the imposition of the form of a narrative on truth or
reality has been described in the social sciences as "narrativity" or

---

[57] The work of Jacques Derrida, Gilles Deleuze, Jean Baudrillard, Fredric Jameson,
and later work of Roland Barthes, Michel Foucault and Julia Kristeva is considered representative of the post-structuralist turn. See generally J. Culler, ed., *On Deconstruction: Theory
and Criticism after Structuralism* (1983).

   [58] See especially M. Foucault, 'Truth and Power', in C. Cordon, ed., *Power/Knowledge
– Selected Interviews and Other Writings 1972-1977* (1980); M. Foucault, *Discipline and
Punish: The Birth of the Prison* (1977, translated by Alan Sheridan, originally published in
French in 1975).

   [59] Post-modernism is usually associated with the work of Jean-François Lyotard, Jacques
Derrida, Richard Rorty, Jean Baudrillard, and Pierre Bourdieux. See J.F. Lyotard, *The
Postmodern Condition: A Report on Knowledge* (1984, translated by G. Bennington and
B. Massumi, originally published in French in 1979); F. Jameson, *Postmodernism or, the
Cultural Logic of Late Capitalism* (1991).

"narrativizing discourse".[60] In his seminal work Hayden White describes narrativizing discourse as "a discourse that feigns the world speak itself and speak itself as a story".[61] White writes:

> "Unlike that of the Annales, the reality represented in the historical narrative, is 'speaking itself', speaks to us, summons us from afar (this 'afar' is the land of forms), and displays to us a formal coherency to which we ourselves aspire. The historical narrative, as against the chronicle, reveals to us a world that is putatively 'finished', done with, over, and yet not dissolved, not falling apart. In this world, reality wears the mask of a meaning, the completeness and fullness of which we can only imagine, never experience. Insofar as historical stories can be completed, can be given narrative closure, can be shown to have had a plot all along, they give to reality the odor of the real. This is why the plot of a historical narrative is always an embarrassment and has to be presented as 'found' in the events rather than put there by narrative techniques."[62]

Following White's work, the odor of truth, reality, or objectivity in narrative is mostly generated by the absence of all references to a narrator. Events are recorded as they appear, and they seem to present themselves to the reader without mediation by the author. The excerpt by Shaw earlier on, for

---

[60] For the purpose of economy in this introductory chapter, I use as representative of this body of literature the seminal work of philosopher and historian Hayden White. See White (Narrativity), *supra* note 54; and H. White, 'Historicism, History, and the Figurative Imagination', 14 *History and Theory* (1975) 48-67. Narrative and narrativity, however, have been among the most intensely debated topics in the social sciences for the best part of the 20th century. For some essential readings in support of the views taken in the present essay see Barthes (Introduction to the Structural Analysis of Narratives), *supra* note 50, at 79-124; C. Lévi-Strauss, *The Savage Mind* (1962, translation by G. Weidenfeld, and Nicholson Ltd., 1966), esp. Chapter 9; G. Lukács, 'Narrate or Describe', in G. Lukács, *Writer and Critic and Other Essays* (translated by A.D Kahn, 1971); J. Culler, *Structuralist Poetics: Structuralism, Linguistics, and the Study of Literature* (1975); G. Genette, 'Boundaries of Narrative', 8 *New Literary History* (1976) 1-13; O. Ducrot and T. Todorov, *Encyclopedic Dictionary of the Sciences of Language* (1979, translated by Catherine Porter, originally published in French, 1972) at 297-299; P. Ricoeur, 'Narrative Time', 7 *Critical Inquiry* (1980) 169-190. See generally R.H. Canary and H. Kozicki, eds., *The Writing of History: Literary Form and Historical Understanding* (1978). Cf. I. Berlin, 'The Concept of Scientific History', 1 *History and Theory* (1960) 11.

[61] White (Narrativity), *supra* note 54, at 2.

[62] White (Narrativity), *supra* note 54, at 21.

example, spoke of humanity's progress "from the cave to the computer" as a fact and not as a personal interpretation of facts. This is not a "bad thing". At the same time, the filter by which the author has chosen to represent certain events but not others is removed from sight or denied altogether. Reality acquires a plot, a structure of relationships that makes events meaningful and runs from the beginning through the end. The story recounted is complete, linear, and without gaps. Thus International law is assumed to have always contributed to progress, as a universal phenomenon, and these are self-evident 'facts' and not constructed or debatable fictions.

Does, however, international law present itself to observation in the form of such complete and coherent stories of progress, with proper beginnings, middles, ends, and causalities? Does our own everyday experience of international law agree with such linearity? Or does international law present itself rather in the form of a mere sequence of facts without concrete beginnings or ends, or even as a series of beginnings and ends that could be read in a number of different ways depending on who is talking? Is there something that is left out, that is excluded, when we speak about international law this way? How aware are we of these exclusions? Or, as White would ask, "is the fiction of such a world, capable of speaking itself and of displaying itself as a form of a story, necessary for the establishment of that moral authority without which the notion of a specifically social reality would be unthinkable?"[63] In other words, is the use of the progress narrative, with all of its exclusions, the only way to speak about international law with authority? Is the resort to coherent and complete stories a good or a bad thing? Could we answer this question without giving our own narrative account of the history of international law's epistemology, an account that would already prejudice the outcome of the story we would tell? Is there actually a way of understanding international law beyond such progress narratives?

Such questions were introduced in international law relatively recently. Starting at the end of the 1980s, different strands of scholarship that has become known under the rubrics of Critical Legal Studies,[64] New Ap-

---

[63] White (Narrativity), *supra* note 54, at 24-25.

[64] See, e.g., R.M. Unger, *The Critical Legal Studies Movement* (1986); A. Altman, *Critical Legal Studies* (1993); J. Boyle, *Critical Legal Studies* (1994); M. Kelman, ed., *A Guide to Critical Legal Studies* (1990).

proaches to International Law,[65] Feminist Approaches,[66] Third World Approaches to International Law (TWAIL),[67] and so on, have offered a major contribution to the understanding of the relationship between narrativity, politics, ideology and legal argument. In its diversity, this body of work has pointed to the structure of foundational doctrines and argumentative forms of the discipline in order to challenge the idea that they 'speak themselves', thus appropriating much of the language of the movements of structuralism and post-structuralism as described above.[68] Hence in debates about democracy or human rights, the politics of the idea of universality has been demonstrated.[69] Same with the darks sides of the 'virtue' of humanitarian action and the doctrines of *jus ad bellum* and *jus in bello*;[70] or the gender[71] and colonial bias[72] of international law doctrines; and so on. The findings

---

[65] E.g., D. Kenedy, *Of War and Law* (2006); A. Orford, ed., *International Law and Its Others* (2006); A. Anghie, *Imperialism, Sovereignty, and the Making of International Law* (2005); M. Koskenniemi, *From Apology to Utopia: The Structure of International Legal Argument* (originally 1989 – reissue 2005); D. Kennedy, *The Dark Side of Virtue* (2004); G. Simpson, *Great Powers and Outlaw States: Unequal Sovereigns in the International Legal Order* (2004); B. Rajagopal, *International Law from Below: Development, Social Movement, and Third World Resistance* (2003); A. Orford, *Reading Humanitarian Intervention: Human Rights and the Use of Force in International Law* (2003); Martti Koskenniemi, *The Gentle Civilizer of Nations: The Rise and Fall of International Law 1870-1960* (2002); K. Knop, *Diversity and Self-Determination in International Law* (2002); S. Marks, *The Riddle of All Constitutions: International Law, Democracy and the Critique of Ideology* (2000); A. Carty, ed., *Post-Modern Law: Enlightenment, Revolution, and the Death of Man* (1990); D. Kennedy, *International Legal Structures* (1987).

[66] E.g., C. Chinkin and H. Charlesworth, *The Boundaries of International Law: A Feminist Analysis* (2000); H. Charlesworth, C. Chinkin and S. Wright, 'Feminist Approaches to International Law', 85 *American Journal of International Law* (1991) 613; A. Wing, ed., *Global Critical Race Feminism: An International Reader* (2000).

[67] See, e.g., B.S. Chimni, 'Third World Approaches to International Law: A Manifesto', 8 *International Community Law Review* (2006) 3; M.W. Mutua, 'What is TWAIL?', 94 *Proceedings of the American Society of International Law Annual Meeting* (2000) 31-40; O.C. Okafor, *Re-defining Legitimate Statehood: International Law and State Fragmentation in Africa* (2000).

[68] On the intellectual roots of these moments, see D. Kennedy, 'Critical Theory, Structuralism, and Critical Legal Scholarship', 21 *New England Law Review* (1985-86) 209.

[69] See, e.g., Marks (Riddle), *supra* note 65; Simpson (Great Powers), *supra* note 65.

[70] See, e.g., Kennedy (Of Law and War), *supra* note 65; Orford (Humanitarian Intervention), *supra* note 65; Kennedy (Dark Sides), *supra* note 65.

[71] See, e.g., Chinkin and Charlesworth (Boundaries), *supra* note 66.

[72] See, e.g., Anghie (Imperialism), *supra* note 65; Knop (Diversity), *supra* note 65.

of this group of scholars cannot possibly be summarized and can only be described in their diversity.[73] While critical scholarship has not specifically dealt with the notion of progress in the form of performing genealogies or ontologies of the notion of progress, it has certainly done enough to disrupt the traditional perception that international law can be associated with progress in a decisive way. Most importantly, it has successfully imported to the study of international law a wealth of techniques and insights from other social sciences that enable horizons of research and possibility that are 'new' to international law argument and have unlocked alternative readings of the discipline's history. Twenty or so years after the strident entrance of critical scholarship in the field[74] the study of the ruptures, discontinuities and exclusions of international law has been fore-grounded by an ever-growing body of scholarship. While critique is a task that never ends, and critical readings and dismissals of the above critiques will further contribute to exploring relationships of narrativity and law, the foundation for critical readings of progress narratives in international law is now firmly established. When it comes to the relationship between international law and progress, Koskenniemi writes in the *Epilogue* to the 2nd edition of his *From Apology to Utopia*:

"Indeed it does not seem possible to believe that international law is automatically or necessarily an instrument of progress. It provides resources for defending good and bad causes, enlightened and regressive policies."[75]

Kennedy in *The Dark Sides of Virtue* writes of international law's narratives of progress:

"These stories give direction to our work, define what humanitarianism will next become. But they also reinforce the biases and the blind spots in our

---

[73] For some overviews, see D. Kennedy, 'A New Stream of International Law Scholarship', 7 *Wisconsin International Law Journal* (1988-89) 1; D.Z. Cass, 'Navigating the Newstream: Recent Critical Scholarship in International Law', 65 *Nordic Journal of International Law* (1996) 341; A. Carty, 'Critical International Law: Recent Trends in the Theory of International Law', 2 *European Journal of International Law* (1991) 66.

[74] T. Skouteris, 'New Approaches to International Law (NAIL) and Its Impact on Contemporary International Legal Scholarship', 10 *Leiden Journal of International Law* (1997) 415.

[75] Koskenniemi (From Apology to Utopia, 2nd edn.), *supra* note 65, at 513.

mental map of the terrain on which we work. They deceive us with promises that humanitarianism will be achieved in the final days, if we work now in our own interest, on our own tools, building our own institutions and strengthening our own professions. They reinforce an unwarranted faith in the upward humanitarian spiral of conversations about the legitimacy of government action carried on in our professional vocabularies."[76]

Despite the critical turn, the majority of international law texts continue to keep a cautious distance from the 'newstream' critique. The impact of critical scholarship on international law is a complex affair that may be too soon to properly evaluate. Critical work is frequently cited today and, in some cases, has become compulsory reading. Some of its proponents have become an accepted and celebrated part of the profession with much following. The questions that they raise are considered intriguing or challenging. There is little doubt that a substantial zymosis over these two decades has even 'mainstreamed' some of the newstream insights. At the same time, few scholars pick up the challenge to formally engage the argument on its merits.[77] Critical work is still on occasion dismissed for its alleged lack of commitment to concrete models of 'reconstruction' or inability to propose concrete alternatives.[78] Either way, as a partial consequence of the formal refusal to read law as text, in the sense of the intellectual traditions discussed above, the notion of progress has so far received little in depth attention in the dominant traditions of international law writing.[79]

The above-mentioned debates provide much of the background of this analysis, which seeks to explore the function of the notion of progress in international law debates. The objectives of this study, as explained in the Preface, must not be overstated but, instead, must be narrowly defined. The

---

[76] Kennedy (Dark Sides), *supra* note 65, at 353.

[77] For an assessment at the end of the 1990s, see T. Skouteris and O. Korhonen, 'Under Rhodes's Eyes: The "Old" and the "New" International Law at Looking Distance', 11 *Leiden Journal of International Law* (1998) 429.

[78] I. Scobbie, 'Towards the Elimination of International Law: Some Radical Skepticism about Skeptical Radicalism', 61 *British Yearbook of International Law* (1990) 339; N. Purvis, 'Critical Legal Studies in Public International Law', 32 *Harvard International Law Journal* (1991) 81, esp. at 116 et seq.

[79] See Section 1.1, *supra*. See also J.H. Nieuwenhuis and C.J.J.M. Stolker, eds., *Vooruit met het recht: wat geldt in de rechtenwetenschap als vooruitgang?* [Forward with the Law: What Counts as Progress in Legal Science?] (2006).

primary goal is to explain how meaning about progress may be produced in international law discourse. In other words, the objective is to investigate 'what is it' that makes certain events become associated or synonymous with progress in public international law. In this regards, the book puts forward three propositions that form the backbone of the analysis.

i.   *Progress as the product of narratives*: Although progress is a convenient rubric to describe international law events (arguments, developments, actions, and so on), it is a notion that is ultimately devoid of meaning unless placed in the context of a progress narrative.

ii.  *Progress narratives as politics*: Progress narratives are by definition non-objective. As such, they compete with (or exclude) other progress narratives. Traditional international law scholarship tends to deny or mask the non-objective character of its progress narratives.

iii. *Discourse analysis as action*: Although progress narratives may be a useful discursive form, the de-mystification of such narratives may be an equally productive and meaningful form of international law argument in itself, but one that gives access to a different horizon of action and intellectual possibility.

## 1.4    APPROACH, METHOD, OUTLINE

### 1.4.1    **Approach**

The analysis relies on three case studies as illustrations of three types of narrative of progress, namely international law *as* progress, progress *within* international law, and the combination of the two.[80] The term "case study" is used here as a term of art in order to describe the focused study of specific instances of legal discourse. It does not wish to evoke images of empiricism, where 'facts come first', or any other such imagery associated with the term in the parlance of the humanities or natural sciences. It certainly does not refer to the study of judicial decisions (case law) as such. The term is nevertheless useful in order to refer to the complete and autonomous examination of a specific instance of legal discourse, which consists

---

[80] See Section 1.1, *supra*.

of a close reading of an extensive but finite set of materials. This approach is used consciously and in lieu of the more customary international law genre of a scientific monograph. The latter usually refers to a systematic, autonomous, and exhaustive disquisition on a limited subject, based on a set of well-defined and determinate set of materials. The case study approach does not abandon the central academic endeavor of demonstrating the validity of intellectual propositions on the basis of research and reasoning. The difference is that arguments are tested only in the context of the cases under consideration. The choice of the approach is dictated by the potentially infinite breadth of the topic (the notion of progress in international law discourse) as well as the desire to ground the argument in concrete examples taken from the practice of international law. While the selection is obviously not random, the studies selected do not represent unique or exceptional moments of international law discourse. On the contrary, they are selected as examples of 'everyday' international law, as mundane stories, symptomatic of international law's everyday life.

## 1.4.2   Method

In terms of method, the case studies are performed by means of the interpretative or deconstructive technique that is often referred to as discourse analysis.[81] Discourse can be understood in simple terms as "a particular way of talking about and understanding the world (or an aspect of the world)".[82] In this colloquial sense, we speak of medical, political, economic, or legal discourse to refer to the different ways (the different vocabularies) in which a doctor, political scientist, economist, or jurist would speak in their professional language about the same topic. For our purposes it is

---

[81] For useful overviews, see L. Philips and M. Jørgensen, *Discourse Analysis as Theory and Method* (2002). See also B. Paltridge, *Discourse Analysis* (2007); M. Bloor and T. Bloor, *The Practice of Critical Discourse Analysis: An Introduction* (2007); J.P. Gee, *An Introduction to Discourse Analysis: Theory and Method* (2005); D. Schiffrin, D. Tannen and H. Hamiton, *The Handbook of Discourse Analysis* (2005); H. Widdowson, *Text, Context, Pretext: Critical Issues in Discourse Analysis* (2005); M. Hoey, *Textual Interaction: An Introduction to Written Discourse Analysis* (2001); N. Fairclough, *Critical Discourse Analysis: The Critical Study of Language* (Language in Social Life) (1995); G. Brown and G. Yule, eds., *Discourse Analysis* (1983); M. Stubbs, *Discourse Analysis: The Sociolinguistic Analysis of Natural Language* (1983).

[82] Philips and Jørgensen (Discourse Analysis), ibid., at 1.

perhaps more useful to resort to Michel Foucault's definition, whose "ar-
cheology" was a defining moment for discourse studies:

> "We shall call discourse a group of statements in so far as they belong to the
> same discursive formation; [...] [Discourse] is made up of a limited number
> of statements for which a group of conditions of existence can be defined.
> Discourse in this sense is not an ideal, timeless form [...] it is, from begin-
> ning to end, historical – a fragment of history [...] posing its own limits, its
> divisions, its transformations, the specific modes of its temporality rather than
> its sudden irruption in the midst of the complexities of time."[83]

The technique of discourse analysis has been developed in tandem with the
intellectual movements of structuralism, post-structuralism and
deconstruction. It originates from the initial idea that language is structured
according to different patterns that people's utterances follow when they
take part in different domains of social life (see Section 1.3, *supra*). These
patterns set limits as to what may and may not be meaningfully said and
they produce determinations of what is true and false. Discourse analysis,
in simple terms, could be described as the analysis of the structures within
a discourse that produce meaning. In our case, our investigation is a study
of the structures within specific international law discourses that produce
meaning about progress.

Discourse analysis also claims that discourses are forms of social action
that play a big part in producing the social world, including knowledge,
identities and social relations.[84] Therefore, within a particular world-view,
some forms of action are considered as natural or possible, whereas others
are ousted beyond the realm of mere possibility.[85] Understanding the structure of discourse helps one understand the limits of action accepted as natural, normal, universal, possible, progressive.

It would be misleading, however, to try to understand discourse analysis
as a strict unitary method. There are numerous types or theories of dis-

---

[83] M. Foucault, *The Archaeology of Knowledge* (1972) 117.

[84] Different approaches to discourse analysis part company with regard to the extent to
which reality is constituted or constitutive of discourse. For a useful map of the different
approaches, see Philips and Jørgensen (Discourse Analysis), *supra* note 81, at 18-21.

[85] This is one of the main tenors of Foucauldian discourse analysis. See in particular,
Foucault (Archaeology), *supra* note 83, at 3-40 and 107-117.

course analysis. Jacques Derrida's 'deconstruction',[86] Chantal Mouffe's and Ernesto Laclau's discourse theory,[87] Norman Fairclough's 'critical discourse analysis',[88] Michel Foucault's 'archaeology'[89] and later 'genealogy',[90] Fredric Jameson's Marxian analysis,[91] Julia Kristeva's reading of social practices,[92] are only some examples. Instead of a single unitary method, discourse analysis can also be seen as a set of techniques questioning the basic assumptions that a text (a project, a statement, a method, a system of classification, a set of arguments) has taken for granted in order to produce meaning and appear coherent. Discourse analysis therefore seeks to trace the mechanisms that enable the production of meaning, by reference to the structure of a discourse. While discourse analysis performs a deconstructive reading of a text, it accepts that it is itself a text that could be deconstructed in a similar manner. In that sense, the reading of the specific case studies by means of discourse analysis that follows has no claim to truth nor does it hope to provide final answers. Discourse does not only point to structures that produce meaning but also draws on the close relationship between the text and the social context in which it was produced. Its task is partly to explain how discourse participates in the creation of relationships of power and domination. This makes it a very interesting method for approaching the question of progress in international law discourse.

The method applied in the following chapters does not attach itself strictly to one of the types or theories of discourse analysis just mentioned. This does not mean, however, that everything goes. The analysis that follows

---

[86] See, e.g. J. Derrida, *Of Grammatology* (1997).

[87] E. Laclau, 'Discourse', in R. Goodin and P. Pettit, eds., *The Blackwell Companion to Contemporary Political Philosophy* (1993); E. Laclau and C. Mouffe, *Hegemony and Socialist Strategy: Towards a Radical Democratic Politics* (1985); E. Laclau and C. Mouffe, 'Post-Marxism without Apologies', in E. Laclau, *New Reflections on the Revolutions of Our Time* (1997).

[88] N. Fairclough, *Critical Discourse Analysis. The Critical Study of Language* (1995).

[89] See Foucault (Archaeology of Knowledge), *supra* note 83, esp. Part II, which discusses his notions of discourse and his methodology. See also M. Foucault, *The Order of Things: An Archaeology of the Human Sciences* (1966).

[90] Foucault (Birth of the Prison), *supra* note 58.

[91] F. Jameson, *Marxism and Form* (1972); F. Jameson, *The Prison-House of Language* (1975).

[92] J. Kristeva, *Desire in Language: A Semiotic Approach to Literature and Art* (1980); K. Kristeva, *Revolution in Poetic Language* (1984).

consists of four inter-related 'moments' that are common to most of the styles of analysis described above. Much of discourse analysis, especially the one performed by linguists, is formidably technical, formalistic, and therefore unsuited for direct application in international law. The idea was to use a technique that, although consistent with the aims of discourse analysis, would be also meaningful to international law research and in sync with international law writing styles.

Accordingly, the first 'moment' of the analysis identifies the horizon of the discourse that will form the field of the analysis. It identifies the group of statements or events belonging to the same discursive formation and announces the point of unity between them. The three case studies that comprise the main body of the present research are examples of three such discourses. Along these lines, later chapters speak of "interwar international law discourse", "sources discourse", or "tribunals discourse" to refer to sets of materials that form, in each case, the horizon of the field of the analysis. This operation is arbitrary, in the sense that it creates unity or continuity between a range of texts by means of a seemingly random (overt or covert) origin. The fact that different discourses could be identified, or the fact that the limits of each discourse could be drawn differently, however, does not undermine the claim that meaning within such discourses is conditioned by the existence of discursive structures or rules that circumscribe the limits of permissible statements.

The second 'moment' of the method is the identification of the structures within a discourse that enable statements to appear as true. This operation, which could be called the 'structuralist moment', looks at the texts that form the field of analysis and asks a wide range of questions about the ways in which meaning is produced. To fly the structuralist flag full-mast, it looks for important 'events' (words, terms, statements, notions) and 'structures' (systems of rules) that allow the production of the meaning.[93] I use the term 'vocabulary of progress' to caption the conglomerate of discursive 'structures' that enable the production of meaning about specific 'events' ("progress") within each discourse.

The third 'moment' of the analysis assesses the claim of progress narratives to 'speak themselves'. This operation, which could be called the 'post-

---

[93] See Section 1.3, *supra*. The pairs of signifier/signified, parole/langue, and event/ structure form the classical vocabulary of structural linguistics, with origins in the work of de Saussure's classic word at the beginning of the 20$^{th}$ century.

structuralist moment', borrows from the practices of post-structuralism and deconstruction. It aims to demonstrate that, although vocabularies may be the structures that produce meaning about progress in each discourse, the vocabularies themselves are not stable – they do not have transcendental meaning. To use an example: if the opposition of "democracy" and "absolutism" may be the basis of a vocabulary that determines what is progressive (democratic) and regressive (absolutist), the 'post-structuralist moment' of discourse analysis demonstrates that neither democracy nor absolutism are terms which possess a fixed or stable meaning. The moment that a vocabulary is proven unstable, its claim to objectivity or truth is subverted. As a consequence, the capacity of the progress narrative to 'speak itself' is subverted in turn.

Finally, a fourth 'moment' of the analysis identifies the benefits of looking at discourses this way. It points to the possibilities of action that are enabled, their impact, and to ways in which such action can be seen in itself as progressive or regressive in turn.

## 1.4.3   **Outline**

The three chapters that follow are each devoted to a case study. Chapter 2 turns to the first category of progress narratives of our typology (see Section 1.1, *supra*), namely narratives of international law *as* progress. It is devoted to the lifework of an individual international law scholar in order to bring to the fore the central role that the notion of progress performs in his argument. It sketches an intellectual portrait of Stelios Seferiades, a Greek jurist of the interwar (1918-1939) period who emerged as one of the most important figures of his generation. The work of Seferiades is singled out not as example of a unique relationship between progress and international law but rather as symptomatic of a closely-knit relationship between the two. Seferiades is interesting not because of his exceptional commitment to progress. Instead, the study of his lifework is meant to demonstrate how the notion of progress may perform a discreet but catalytic role in creating legitimacy for any international law reformist project. The chapter performs an intellectual portrait of Seferiades: while it reviews the complete academic work of our hero, it situates his ideas about international law in their personal, historical and political framework in order to foreground the ever-present role of the progress narrative in his work. The chapter conducts an analysis of the international law discourse in the writings of Seferiades. It identifies the notion of progress as a structure that produces meaning within that discourse, by legitimizing and de-legitimizing doctrinal solutions and policy outcomes. The chapter looks at the lifework of Seferiades comprehensively, from his publications to the relationship between his scholarship and everyday life and, in particular, his identity as a scholar-statesman and political refugee. Without revealing too much at this stage, the chapter argues that his writings consistently fall back on a narrative of progress that rationalizes and organizes his argument, setting a historical and ideological framework while explaining to the reader what are the limits and potentials of international law. This narrative of progress is centered on the opposition of the notions of democracy and absolutism. By means of a historical account of humanity's evolution, Seferiades decisively associates democracy with internationalism and progress, while absolutism is associated with introvert sovereignist politics and regression. His proposals for internationalist reform are deeply intertwined with this opposition. The study demonstrates however that, despite its overpowering rhetorical effect, the narrative of democracy and absolutism far from 'speaks itself'. Far from a descriptive account of how human progress has been achieved, the narrative doubles as a powerful ideological device for the legitimation/de-legitimation of a series of political and legal initiatives. Progress, far from a formal and self-explanatory concept, is a structure that enables the production of meaning about what is right and wrong. The study, however, goes a step further: it explains that democracy and absolutism are 'unstable' notions that continue to subvert themselves within the work of Seferiades. In the name of democracy, our hero goes as far as to defend legal measures that move dangerously close to his self-proclaimed 'absolutist' ideological opponents.

Chapter 3 turns to the second category of progress narratives of our typology, a narrative of progress *within* international law. It turns away from the lifework of individual scholars to engage a public international law doctrine and, indeed, one of the most of foundational international law doctrines, namely the doctrine of the sources of international law. The horizon that forms the field of discourse analysis is the literature on the sources of international law during the interwar period (1918-1939). The emergence of the doctrine of the sources in the wake of the establishment of the Permanent Court of International Justice was welcomed at the time as a great

moment of disciplinary progress in international law's methods and techniques (progress within international law). Similarly to Seferiades, Chapter
3 claims that arguments about progress associated with the doctrine of the
sources fell back on a narrative that recounted international law's flaws and
identified specific priorities for disciplinary improvements as a *conditio
sine qua non* for preventing catastrophes, such as the Great War, from occurring again. This narrative told a before/after story and associated the
"new" international law of the interwar period as progression in the discipline by means of two sweeping rhetorical moves, termed 'standardization'
and 'formalization'. The narrative tells a story about how the 'new', post-
1920 doctrine of the sources improved the legal quality of international law
by offering a determinate (closed, standard, technical, formal) set of sources
and in opposition to the indeterminate (open, fragmented, political, non-
formal) 'older', pre-1920 understanding of lawmaking. Upon closer readings of the texts, determinacy and indeterminacy prove to be 'unstable'
notions whose opposition was subverted by the interwar argument itself.
Progress in sources, far from 'speaking itself', was constructed by reference to terms such as determinacy, which simply relocated the problem of
indeterminacy to a different place within the doctrine instead of resolving
it. Chapter 3 sets out to explore the important function of the notion of
progress in reforming the doctrines and techniques of international law as a
discipline.

Chapter 4 turns to the third category of progress narratives, one that
portrays international law events as signifying both social progress (international law *as* progress) *and* internal disciplinary improvement (progress
*within* international law). The third case study is drawn from debates about
the future of the institutional structure of international law and, in particular, the well known debate about the proliferation of international courts
and tribunals. Similarly to the two previous chapters, Chapter 4 also argues
that the salience of the argument about the importance of proliferation relies heavily on a narrative of progress that performs a subtle but catalytic
discursive role. This narrative also tells a before/after story about international law's evolution. By means of an elaborate set of sub-arguments, assumptions, and metaphors, it frames the recent proliferation of international
judicial institutions as a development crucial for the achievement of important social goals (e.g. leading to more peace or justice) while improving
international law's condition as such (e.g. strengthening the fabric of the

law). Conducting a close reading of the relevant literature, Chapter 4 aims to underline the decisive relationship between the narrative of progress and the symbolic and financial investment in international dispute settlement during the past two decades. The chapter argues that the argument in favor of proliferation is based on two inter-related 'vocabularies of progress', well rooted in the scholarly traditions and professional communities in the two sides of the Atlantic. Both vocabularies, and despite significant difference in their conception of the role of law, its relationship to politics, and so on, shake hands in endorsing recent court-building as a progressive development for international law. This assessment is partly the product of historical narratives that present today's international law as the culmination of a long process of evolution, with a long way still to go. Like previous chapters, Chapter 4 seeks to demonstrate how the claim that proliferation of tribunals is "a good thing" is the product of the deployment of vocabularies of progress that, ultimately, fail to 'speak themselves'. On the contrary, in their partiality, they elide and exclude alternative histories of internationalism and, in the process, prevent a number of viable alternative solutions from gaining currency in international law debates. Far from being a neutral, self-explanatory concept, the notion of progress fulfils a crucial ideological role that is not acknowledged by the literature. By constructing a seemingly true and incontestable version of history, the debate leaves alternatives and critiques disempowered and marginalized.

The closing chapter of this enquiry (Chapter 5) has a dual objective. First, to test the intellectual propositions of this enquiry, as outlined above, in the context of the three case studies. Secondly, to situate these intellectual propositions in wider debates about international law today. Chapter 5 offers an explanation about how this type of discourse analysis of progress narratives, although it can itself be considered as "progressive" or "regressive", makes a difference with regard to the recipients or beneficiaries of the transformative potential of international legal discourse.

# Chapter 2
# INTERNATIONAL LAW AS PROGRESS –
# STELIOS SEFERIADES AND INTERWAR
# INTERNATIONAL LAW

## 2.1    INTRODUCTION

The first case study sketches an intellectual portrait of Stelios Seferiades (1876-1951), a classic figure in European international law during the interwar (1918-1939) period and, for many, the founder of the discipline of public international law in Greece.[94] This intellectual portrait, in addition to paying homage to the work of a neglected but fascinating scholar, doubles as a narrative device that allows a close examination of his 'vocabulary of progress': the discursive strategies used in his legal argument in order to legitimize the transformation of the pre-war discipline of international law into the modern international law of the interwar period.

Underlying this interest in the work of Seferiades is not a desire to identify errors or shortcomings in his scholarship. To be sure, that would be too simple a task, especially with the benefit of hindsight but would result in an inquiry of limited analytical value. Judging Seferiades with today's standards would inevitably involve applying today's knowledge to someone who reflected on international law nearly a century ago. Like David Scott, one would have to resist the temptation of essentializing today's personal experience as a standard of judging the salience of past intellectual or ideological projects.[95] Besides, a certain amount of truth and falsity, realism and illusion, and so on, must be credited to any argument that seeks to

---

[94] Although Seferiades was not the first scholar to teach international law at the University of Athens, he was the first to offer a systematic study in Greek. The work of Seferiades as a whole has received very little attention so far, with the exception of a posthumous collection of essays in his honour, containing only a brief introduction to his life and work. See G. Tenekides, 'Στυλιανός Σεφεριάδης, 1873-1951' [Slylianos Seferiades, 1873-1951] (in Greek), in S. Kalogeropoulos et al., *Mélanges Séfériadès* (1961) (2 volumes, with essays in Greek, English and French) at xv-xxiv. For a complete list of publications of Seferiades, see Falogeropoulos (Mélanges), ibid., at xxv-xxvi.

[95] Scott (Conscripts of Modernity), *supra* note 31, at 1-11.

explain why certain values or solutions are better than others. Without some form of preference or bias one would not be able to pass judgment on an issue or situation.

This paper pursues a different line of inquiry and probes the ways in which Seferiades and some of his contemporaries argued their case for the renewal of international law. The term 'vocabulary of progress' is used here to refer to the discursive strategies with which arguments buttress their power over others and seek to distinguish themselves from their ideological opponents. In other words, this analysis does not concern truth or falsity in legal argument but the strategies that enable arguments to *appear* true, false, progressive, conservative, and so on. This line of inquiry leads one to pose a number of very different questions about the work of a scholar than the 'what did he do wrong?' type of investigation. Rather, it considers how Seferiades argued his case for the renewal of international law: What was his idea of progress? Did this idea 'speak itself'? Did he privilege any ideals in the process? Were other ideals denigrated? What was at stake in his plea for the transformation of the law? Who were his ideological opponents? What effects were produced? Who was the beneficiary of these effects? And so on.

Why should one be interested in the writings of a scholar in this manner? Although 'progress' is a convenient rubric to caption one's reformist agenda, it will be demonstrated that progress does not have a natural or obvious meaning out of context or, in any case, without reference to other terms that are equally equivocal. One person's progress is another's regression. To understand the meaning of progress in a particular debate, one would have to look not at the etymology of the term but rather at the historical and political discourse in which the term is employed. 'Progress' does not acquire concrete meaning without a background story, an explanation of how things were before and how they ought to become, and why. Progress, in that sense, is not an essence but a narrative. And this essay makes the narrative itself the target of its inquiry.

Why use the intellectual portrait of an interwar scholar from the periphery of Europe as the heuristic for this case study? Not only because one may understand, in hindsight, Seferiades's contribution as having a catalytic role in the development of international law doctrines and institutions that we consider important today. A much more symbolic function is envisaged for our scholar in this inquiry. The story of Seferiades appeals to contemporary consciousness as the story of an archetypal figure of our discipline, representing much of international law's efforts to reinvent itself. This is not because Seferiades is exceptional, rather the opposite. In a way, Seferiades 'did it all', and he 'did it well'. His legal and political credentials as a liberal internationalist would be considered impeccable even today. He advocated disarmament and the obligation to resolve international disputes peacefully; he argued the primacy of international law over national constitutions; he believed that democratic governance could lead to peace between nations; he fought for the right of individuals to stand before international tribunals; he sought to demystify the doctrine of state sovereignty; he promoted the notion of the nation as the basis for the formation of an international community; he subscribed to the sociological jurisprudence of the time; he believed in the importance of the role of public international lawyers in the reconstruction of the post-war international community. Certainly, one might disagree with some of his lateral views: whether, for instance, foreign nationals should be subjected to mixed (internationalized) tribunals because of what he considered to be structural bias of domestic courts towards foreigners; or whether within a monist conception of law the national judge should nevertheless apply national law which has not been amended to comply with international obligations. Some of these choices might even be conceded to him for historical or other reasons. But few would disagree that Seferiades had his heart and his politics 'in the right place'.

Moreover, Seferiades published widely and excellently, addressing issues of the highest political currency. His work is still cited today as a source of authority, and copies of his classic textbook[96] still figure prominently on the bookshelves of Greek international lawyers. The facts of his life leave no doubt that he engaged with international law with greater skill and devotion than might be expected of anyone. Although he shared the international law stage in Greece with another outstanding scholar, Nicolas Politis, who merits attention in a separate essay, Seferiades became Professor of International Law at Athens University and created the first complete set of

---

[96] S. Seferiades, *Μαθήματα Διεθνούς Δημοσίου Δικαίου* [Courses on International Public Law] (in Greek), Volume 1, *Το εν Ειρηνη Διεθνές Δημόσιον Δίκαιον* [International Public Law of Peace], 1920; Volume 2, *Διεθνεις Διαφοραί και Συγκρούσεις* [International Disputes and Conflicts], 1928-1929.

reference works in Greek, thus becoming a founding figure of the international law profession in that country.

Seferiades was not your proverbial ivory tower scholar either. He served the dual function of statesman and academic, rising to prominence in both realms. He was able to exercise considerable influence over institutional, political and scholarly developments on the national and international level, including the negotiation of the text of the Treaty of Versailles and other instruments of extreme national importance for Greece. For a large part of his professional life he was a close associate and advisor of Eleftherios Venizelos, the legendary Prime Minister who dominated Greek politics between 1910 and 1936. Seferiades publicly aligned himself with the liberal movement and became a staunch supporter of modernist political reform in Greece, advocating constitutionalism, democratization and the codification of fundamental rights and liberties. He advised the Greek government in times of monumental importance for the future of the nation. A curriculum vitae for Seferiades would include functions such as Professor, Dean of the Faculty of Law and Rector of the University of Athens, delegate at the Paris Peace Conference, Judge *ad hoc* of the Permanent Court of International Justice, member of the *Institut de Droit International*, three times lecturer at the Hague Academy of International Law, member of the Greek *Conseil d'Etat*, legal advisor to the ministry of Foreign Affairs, among others. In addition, Seferiades wrote fine romantic poetry, translated many works from Ancient to Modern Greek, and was the father of one of the most important poets of his generation, Giorgos Seferis (Seferiades), a jurist and diplomat himself and Nobel Prize laureate for literature in 1965.[97] All in all, an exemplary international lawyer, liberal intellectual, and more.

Against this background, and perhaps not surprisingly, the story of Seferiades appeals to that same contemporary consciousness as the story of a tragic figure of internationalism. Seferiades did not see his lifework come to fruition. His dream of lasting peace in the context of the League of Nations was shattered by the traumatic developments of the 1930s. On the

---

[97] As a consequence, the student of Seferiades can benefit from a number of biographies of Giorgos Seferis where a useful amount of information can be collected about his father. Among those biographies, the ones that stand out are R. Beaton, Γιώργος Σεφέρης – Περιμένοντας τον Αγγελο [George Seferis – Waiting for an Angel. A Biography, Greek translation] (2004); I. Tsatsou, Ο Αδελφός μου Γιώργος Σεφέρης [My Brother Giorgos Seferis] (in Greek) (1974).

home front, the 1936 dictatorship put an abrupt end to the interwar hope of a democratically governed Greece and signaled the marginalization (and even persecution) of many liberal intellectuals. At the dusk of his career, Seferiades found himself unable to comprehend the reasons for the failures of the liberal reform project of the interwar period. In one of his last publications, he pleaded for the 'moral armament' of the new generation as the last resort against what seemed to be the inevitable outcome of the boiling European front.[98] Dates could not be more telling. His last essay on international law was published in 1939, submitted for publication just before the outbreak of the War.[5] World War II signaled an end of his academic writings and his complete withdrawal from professional life. During his last twelve years (his passing came in 1951), he was largely preoccupied with his literary interests, withdrawn to his Paris banlieue apartment.

Did interwar internationalism 'fail'? If so, why? The explanation to be found in the writings of Stelios Seferiades appears to be quite an intuitive one even to contemporary ears: liberal reform in international law, the story goes, failed because of the resistance of 'absolutism' as a system of domestic governance and as an approach to international politics as well. As he writes in one of his texts:

"Public law, domestic or international, and total absolutism are mutually exclusive concepts, concepts that cannot temporally co-exist."[99]

The view that international law is incompatible with autocratic ideologies of different sorts (absolutist, totalitarian, Nazi, fascist, dictatorial, fundamentalist, and so on) has survived 20th-century mainstream international law writing and re-surfaces each time international lawyers discuss what to do with situations like Yugoslavia, Afghanistan. Iraq, terrorism, failed states, humanitarian intervention, and so on.[100] For Seferiades and his contempo-

---

[98] S. Seferiades, *Ο Ηθικός Οπλισμός* [Moral Armament] (in Greek) (1935).

[99] S. Seferiades, Το Μέλλον του Διεθνούς Δημοσίου Δικαίου [The Future of International Public Law] (in Greek) (1919).

[100] Debates about the compatibility of international law with non-democratic systems of governance have been popular in international law writing since the interwar and post war periods: see, e.g., S.E. Edmunds, *The Lawless Law of Nations: An Exposition of the Prevailing Arbitrary International Legal System in Relation to Its Influence upon Civil Liberty, Disclosing It as the Last Bulwark of Absolutism against the Political Emancipation of Man* (1925); G. Schwarzenberger, *International Law and Totalitarian Lawlessness* (1943).

raries, progressive efforts to reform international law were prevented from attaining their full potential because of the existence of an 'absolutist' approach to politics that resisted – and often waylaid – progress in international law and institutions. For Seferiades, the opposition of absolutism v democracy and the role of these two concepts in achieving progress was a historical reality beyond doubt or contestation, one that 'spoke itself'.

Thus this first case study addresses the narrative of progress that underlies the legal argument of Stelios Seferiades. To this end, Section 2.2 introduces the international law writings of Seferiades and outlines the basic argumentative strategies that comprise his narrative of progress and its 'vocabulary''. More specifically, it delineates the role of the opposition of the notions of absolutism and democracy in this context. Section 2.3 describes the discursive functions of the narrative of progress within the context of his international law argument or, in other words, the way in which it is presented as 'speaking itself' while at the same time participating in an ideological discourse of inclusion and exclusion. Section 2.4 digresses to interwar Greece to situate Seferiades and his scholarship within the political landscape of the time and, in particular, the political movement of 'bourgeois modernization'. Sections 2.5 and 2.6 look closely into the writings of Seferiades to explain the foundational relationship between his narrative of progress and his international law arguments. It rereads his ideas about the basis of obligation in international law as an example of how his 'vocabulary of progress' is reflected in his doctrinal prescriptions for the reform of international law. A final section suggests some directions for a critical reassessment of the work of Seferiades and the concept of progress in international legal argument.

---

These debates have become reinvigorated since the end of the Cold War. See, e.g., M. Reisman, 'Islamic Fundamentalism and Its Impact on International Law and Politics', in M.W. Janis and C. Evans, eds., *Religion in International Law* (2004) 357; A.-M. Slaughter, 'International Law in a World of Liberal States', 3 *European Journal of International Law* (1995) 503; F. Tesón, 'The Kantian Theory of International Law', 92 *Columbia Law Review* (1992)53; G.H. Fox and B.R. Roth, eds., *Democratic Governance and International Law* (2000). For a critical review of such debates see Marks (Riddle of All Constitutions), *supra* note 65; and Simpson (Great Powers and Outlaw States), *supra* note 65.

## 2.2    THE NARRATIVE OF ABSOLUTISM V. DEMOCRACY

Let us then begin at the beginning. What is the reform project that Seferiades seeks to impress upon public international law? In November 1919, with the echo of the Paris Peace Conference in his ears, Seferiades delivers his long overdue inaugural speech as Professor of Public International Law at the University of Athens on the topic of 'The Future of International Public Law'.[101] This speech should have been delivered four years earlier, in 1915, when he was first elected Professor. The dissolution of the liberal government of Venizelos by King Constantine in 1915, however, prevented his appointment due to the connection of Seferiades with the Liberal Party of Venizelos (Κόμμα Φιλελευθέρων). Seferiades had to wait until the next liberal government in order to be able to assume his duties. Thus in 1919, standing before the friendly audience of his students, he reads out an evocative speech about the professional responsibility of the jurist in the reconstruction of the international community in the wake the Great War.

The *Future of International Public Law* is Seferiades's first attempt to engage international law on such a level of abstraction and his first international law publication in Greek. The language is direct and emotional, the tone intense, exuding the feeling of urgency and responsibility of a man standing before a crucial historical moment, when things shall be made or broken. Seferiades commences his speech in grand style. He predicts that the future of international law would be similar to that of Ancient Greek art in the aftermath of the wars of the 5th and 4th centuries BC: although the wars nearly decimated the monuments of all that had been achieved, the same monuments somehow became the 'life-giving beginning' for the production of the finest masterpieces of all times in the years following the wars.[102] Same with international law after the Great War:

"Thus embarking on our current enquiry, we believe that it is possible to assert that the elements of international law which existed till our day, and which were nearly extirpated by the recently terminated cataclysm, will create an international law superbly corresponding to the meaning and purposes

---

[101]    Seferiades (The Future of International Public Law), *supra* note 99.
[102]    Seferiades (The Future of International Public Law), *supra* note 99, at 5.

of our discipline, when rejuvenated and reshaped by the influence of a wider perception and new ideas."[103]

His intellectual project is therefore the reconstruction of international law. The idea of reconstructing international law was a common trope in inter-war liberal scholarship on both sides of the Atlantic and Seferiades was at home with it. With Le Fur, Brierly, Scelle, Lapradelle as his oft-cited authorities and in some cases as his personal friends, Seferiades had no trouble agreeing with Alejandro Álvarez that "the task that is now necessary is the reconstruction of this law".[104] Brierly spoke of a "need of rehabilitation";[105] Politis called for "la reconstruction du droit international sur de nouvelles bases",[106] and so did Nippold and Hudson and a long list of others.[107] These writers presented reconstruction as a major, all-encompassing project of re-conceiving international law in its totality, from its theoretical foundations to institution building, the codification of new law, and the creation of new doctrines. Álvarez went as far to discern a fully-fledged professional movement of reconstruction.[108] In a symbolic way, the critical event enabling the transition from the 'old' to the 'new' for these scholars was the Great War itself.[109] The atrocities offered the surface against which the new interna-

---

[103] Seferiades (The Future of International Public Law), *supra* note 99.

[104] See Álvarez (The New International Law), *supra* note 27, at 38.

[105] J.L. Brierly, 'The Shortcomings of International Law', in H. Lauterpacht, ed., *The Basis of Obligation in International Law and Other Papers by the Late J.L. Brierly* (1958) 68. For Brierly's ideas on the matter, see the excellent intellectual portrait of the scholar by C. Landauer, 'J.L. Brierly and the Modernization of International Law', 25 *Vanderbilt Journal of Transnational Law* (1993) 881.

[106] N. Politis, 'Le Problème des Limitations de la Souveraineté et de la Théorie de l'Abus des Droits dans les Rapports Internationaux', 6 *RCADI* (1925) 1, at 5.

[107] O. Nippold, *The Development of International Law after the World War* (1923) 4, at 25, who sought future "reconstruction" of international law. For the project of the reconstruction of international law, see also Chapter 3, *infra*.

[108] Álvarez writes: "[W]e may conclude that there exists a movement for the reconstruction of International Law. And in view of the crisis through which International Law is now passing, it is the duty of all international associations to study this great problem of the reconstruction of the law of nations and to agree as to the best method of realizing it"; see Álvarez (New International Law), *supra* note 27, at 40.

[109] See, e.g., B. Schmitt and H. Vedeler, *The World in the Crucible 1914-1919* (1984) 455; Nippold (The Development of International Law After the World War), *supra* note 107, at 25; See generally also H. Barnes, *World Politics in Modern Civilization* (1930); and W. Langsam, *The World Since 1914* (1933). For a fascinating treatment of the international

tionalist movement could be projected and catalyzed the creation of a new internationalist sensibility: a 'wider', open-minded conception on which the new international law will be founded.[110]

The *Future of International Law* is an important text for our purposes not only because of its sensibility and timing but also because it introduces the nuts-and-bolts of Seferiades's narrative of progress. First, and very importantly, Seferiades fervently argues the existence of a fundamental incompatibility between absolutist political ideology and the very existence of international law. International law, he pronounces in the speech, will never exist as long as states continue to suppress democratic development, either on the national or on the international level.[111] *Secondly*, he stresses the need for the definition of a progressive agenda for reconstruction based on ideas of liberal democracy. The key to progress is the consolidation of an international community of democratic states.[112] *Finally*, Seferiades nominates public international lawyers as crucial agents for this change, nationally and internationally.[113]

Let us take a closer look at this three-fold argument (critique of absolutism; international community of democratic states; the international lawyer as agent of change) and how, in particular, the three components are made to fit together into one coherent syllogism about progress in public international law. To do so we will perform a parallel reading of three crucial texts by Seferiades, which squarely address the question of the foundation and nature of public international law and the role of absolutism and democratic governance in this context. Aside from the *Future of International*

---

law's approach to the war and the birth of interwar institution, see D. Kennedy, 'The Move to Institutions', 8 *Cardozo Law Review* (1987) 841. See also the excellent account of the birth of "modern" international law in N. Berman, '"But the Alternative is Despair": Nationalism and the Modernist Renewal of International Law', 106 *Harvard Law Review* (1993) 1793.

[110] Alejandro Álvarez wrote that with the end of the war: "Almost overnight there came into being a new psychology, a new mentality, a new ideology, the fruit of new circumstances and environment, as well as of new political, philosophic and social concepts; they repudiate many ideas and doctrines which were until then accepted without question"; see Álvarez (New International Law), *supra* note 27, at 37. See also F.P. Walters, *A History of the League of Nations*, Vol I (1952) 16.

[111] Seferiades (The Future of International Public Law), *supra* note 99, at 5-12.

[112] Seferiades (The Future of International Public Law), *supra* note 99, at 13-17.

[113] Seferiades (The Future of International Public Law), *supra* note 99, at 26.

*Public Law*, the same argument is elaborated in his other two major generalist texts, his textbook in Greek titled Μαθήματα Διεθνούς Δημοσίου Δικαίου [*Courses on International Public Law*][114] and his 1930 Hague Academy Courses on *Principes généraux du droit international de la paix*.[115] Mindful of their different audiences and contexts, the three texts adopt slightly different tones and styles. The texts in Greek are engaged and polemical, taking sides not only in the international scholarly debate about international law but also in the Greek political scene of the time. The Hague Academy Course, in contrast, is more descriptive, avoiding unnecessary political puns in favor of a more poised, scholarly and legalist tone. All three texts, however, share a common narrative device: a historical account of progress of the human society, which enables the author to draw conclusions about the nature of international relations at large, and subsequently translate this knowledge into guidelines about the reconstruction of public international law.

All three texts reiterate one of the grand narratives of modernity, the nature of man.[116] In a burst of ontological statements and a style worthy of a 19th century treatise on socio-economic theory, Seferiades presents his account of human nature. Man is a social being, he declares.[117] He joins fellow men in forming communities, due to the realization that life within a community yields benefits to all. With Kant and Rousseau as his regular authorities, Seferiades assures the reader that each individual human being is endowed with special characteristics and comparative advantages that are indispensable for the well being of society at large. Society vests all men with equal rights, the exercise of which, however, often results to conflicts with rights of fellow men. There are two ways of resolving such conflicts, he argues. First, there is the solution that is frequently resorted to in the primitive stages of human development, namely the forcible enforce-

---

[114] Seferiades (Courses on International Public Law), *supra* note 96.

[115] S. Seferiades, 'Principes généraux du droit international de la paix', 34 *RCADI* (1930-IV) 177, at 181-487.

[116] Seferiades (The Future of International Public Law), *supra* note 99, at 5 et seq.; Seferiades (Courses on International Public Law), *supra* note 96, at 7-15 and 47-107; Seferiades (Principes généraux du droit international de la paix), *supra* note 115, at 182-204 and 216-291.

[117] Seferiades (Courses on International Public Law), *supra* note 96, at 7-8; Seferiades (The Future of International Public Law), *supra* note 99, at 5-6; Seferiades (Principes généraux du droit international de la paix), *supra* note 115, at 182-184.

ment of rights, or "the law of force", as he calls it.[118] Human nature, however, could never satisfy itself with such a violent state of being! It, therefore, soon devised a second way, according to our author: the concept of law, a set of rules based not on brutality but devised for the purpose of regulating the rights and obligations of the members of the community.[119] With the passage of time, individuals formed families, communities, tribes, nations, polities, in order to better protect themselves and their common interests. The writings of Adam Smith, David Ricardo and James Stuart Mill are the unmentioned but obvious sources of his understanding of the workings of the comparative advantage on a global scale and the contribution of international trade for increasing the wealth of nations. For, due to environmental, geographic, cultural, and other reasons, Seferiades contends that these social formations developed their own characteristics that could be helpful to the well being of the entire humankind. Similarly to the laboratory example of individuals operating in the scale of a small local community, states participating in the international community are endowed with equal rights and obligations.[120] The rules stipulating the extent of the rights and obligations of states comprise the object of study of the science of international law.[121] These rules can be ascertained in the workings of society by the contemporary lawyer through scientific observation, with the use of other social sciences that systematically study human behavior, such as history, political science, sociology, economics, and geography.[122]

Rules defining rights and obligations for citizens in their relations with each other appear immediately after the emergence of such relations. But these rules are not always rules of law. For a rule of law to exist, there needs be a society of natural or moral persons that desires peaceful co-existence. Such meaning has to be attributed to the saying of *ubi societas, ibi jus*. If there is society, law will be there, Seferiades proclaims. And in order to be able to find International Public Law, we need to find ourselves before a

---

[118] Seferiades (Courses on International Public Law), *supra* note 96, at 7-8.

[119] Seferiades (Courses on International Public Law), *supra* note 96, at 8; Seferiades (Principes généraux du droit international de la paix), *supra* note 115, at 182-184.

[120] Seferiades (Principes généraux du droit international de la paix), *supra* note 115, at 182-184.

[121] Seferiades (Courses on International Public Law), *supra* note 96, at 9; Seferiades (Principes généraux du droit international de la paix), *supra* note 115, at 183.

[122] Seferiades (Courses on International Public Law), *supra* note 96, at 30-33.

society of nations, that is to say, before polities recognizing mutual rights, and most importantly, mutual obligations on the basis of equality.[123]

Seferiades warns that the formation of an international community is not an easy matter. Certain conditions are essential for it to exist. States must be prepared, for example, to appreciate the benefits of co-existence and, as a consequence, make concessions to each other and undertake common responsibilities.[124] This presupposes a certain coincidence of views, values and principles among the different states participating in the international community.

> "C'est qu'en vérité, l'existence et par suite l'application, des règles du droit international présupposent une certaine similitude de mœurs et des conceptions juridiques entres les peuples dont ce droit est appelé à régir les rapports."[125]

The history of mankind teaches us, he suggests, that institutions similar to contemporary international law have come to existence only whenever such a common conception of morality and similarity of social institutions existed, such as in Ancient Greece or Ancient China.[126] The period of the Roman Empire or the Middle Ages, on the contrary, was a period of formidable regression ("un formidable renversement")[127] because of the absence of such a shared conception.

> "The spirit of international law assumes an internationalist sensibility, that is to say, a modesty of desire, voluntary limitation of ambition, favoring justice over interest. Most importantly, it must be guided by the fair and clear vision of the common interest of states. Without such a spirit there can be no perception of international law."[128]

---

[123] Seferiades (The Future of International Public Law), *supra* note 99, at 5-66.
[124] Seferiades (Courses on International Public Law), *supra* note 96, at 8, 47 and 99.
[125] Seferiades (Principes généraux du droit international de la paix), *supra* note 115, at 211.
[126] Seferiades (The Future of International Public Law), *supra* note 99, at 6.
[127] Seferiades (Principes généraux du droit international de la paix), *supra* note 115, at 234.
[128] Seferiades (Courses on International Public Law), *supra* note 96, at 15.

This explains why international law took so many centuries to develop, he observes. International law "presupposes a superior civilization".[129] Until the beginning of the 20th century there were practical reasons, such as the lack of technological advances in communication, which prevented the development of this sensibility.[130] There was a "psychological" reason as well. Until recently, there was no common feeling of equality between states and, most crucially, the "maturity" to realize the need to foster such equality. For Seferiades, with the exception of the enunciation of these principles in the French revolution and small brave steps taken here and there international politics were governed by a Hobbesian perception of the world, where power and self-interest reigned paramount. In direct analogy to human societies, the closer the ties connecting two or more groups or individuals, the more similar were conceptions of ethics and social structures they would need in order that their bonds lasted.[131] Not any kind of common political institutions or morality fosters the creation of community and rules of law.[132] Here Seferiades shakes hands with many of his Western European contemporaries in postulating the ideal of an international community based on a Eurocentric idea of civilization.[133] He explains that for an international community to exist, it logically flows that nations need to share basically three elements: analogous moral principles, analogous political institutions, and a shared internationalist spirit. Without these three, disagreements between states would be of such nature that the system would break down.[134]

"Between 1648 and the end of the 19th century, the blood-stained armies of Europe and their diplomatic contests only sought to secure crowns and

---

[129] Seferiades (Courses on International Public Law), *supra* note 96, at 10.

[130] Seferiades (Courses on International Public Law), *supra* note 96, at 10.

[131] Seferiades (The Future of International Public Law), *supra* note 99, at 14.

[132] Seferiades (The Future of International Public Law), *supra* note 99, at 6-12.

[133] See, e.g. H. Wheaton, *Elements of International Law* (1936) 15-16, at Para. 1; L. Oppenheim, *International Law: A Treatise*, Vol. I (1920) 8-10, at Para. 7. See generally N. Tsagourias, 'The Will of the International Community as a Normative Source of International Law', in I.F. Dekker and W.G. Werner, eds., *Governance and International Legal Theory* (2004) 97-113; G. Abi-Saab, 'La "communauté internationale" saisie par le droit. Essai de radioscopie juridique', in Boutros Boutros-Ghali *Amicorum Discipulorumque Liber* (1998) 81.

[134] Seferiades (The Future of International Public Law), *supra* note 99, at 7; Seferiades (Courses on International Public Law), *supra* note 96, at 33.

thrones. To be sure, the contests of that time for political equilibrium in Europe have nothing to do with *the open-minded and splendid conception of the public international law of morality which we espouse this very day.*"[135]

With the passage of time, and culminating with The Hague Peace Conferences and the Treaty of Versailles, man managed to develop the 'splendid and open-minded conception' needed for the reconstruction of international law. Oscillating between descriptive and prescriptive language in the text, Seferiades suggests that this conception consists of three tenets/conditions, "not different from those any human society relies upon".[136] First, there is the principle of interdependence. Bonds of interdependence, without which the existence of an international community is impossible, connect polities around the world. Interdependence has to be realized and sustained through the development of legal principles and doctrines. Then there is the principle of compulsory settlement of international disputes on the basis of justice, which is a natural corollary of the principle of interdependence.[137] And finally, the principle of "homogeneous domestic structure", without which it will be impossible for nations to comprehend the possibility of interdependence.

> "Especially in recent times, all those who studied attentively the means by which an international community governed by rules of law would be possible, teach without reservation that a viable establishment of such a community is not possible unless it comprises *democratic* states [...], regardless of whether they are headed by Kings or ordinary citizens. Because indeed public law, domestic or international, and *total absolutism* are mutually exclusive concepts, concepts that cannot possibly co-exist."[138]

Seferiades avoids too frequent a use of the terms 'democracy' or 'democratic'. The terms are used in various passages as adjectives alluding rather abstractly to a representational system of governance inspired by Enlightenment ideas and in opposition to absolutism, but not to a clearly defined

---

[135] Seferiades (The Future of International Public Law), *supra* note 99, at 7 (emphasis added).

[136] Seferiades (The Future of International Public Law), *supra* note 99, at 9.

[137] Seferiades (The Future of International Public Law), *supra* note 99, at 11 et seq.

[138] Seferiades (The Future of International Public Law), *supra* note 99, at 15 (emphasis added).

model of democratic polity.[139] This is hardly surprising: Seferiades, like his audience, is a jurist writing during the interwar period and not a political philosopher of the 21st century. Traditionally international law writing did not concern itself directly with term democracy, a situation that has been reversed only recently.[140] Rather the contrary holds true: It would be a mistake to essentialize today's experience with democratic discourse as the angle through which the argument of Seferiades should be read. Anyway, the fluid political scene in Greece at the time did not permit even strategic public commitment to a strictly defined system of governance, especially with regard to the sensitive matter of the future role of the Palace and the King.[141] Seferiades, however, does sketch out with a broad brush a system of governance, which he openly calls democratic, and without which internationalism and international law appears to be impossible. With Rousseau and Kant as his authorities,[142] his system possesses many of the classical characteristics of liberal democracy: division of powers, rule of law, legislature elected by the population, representative government, a compulsory system of adjudication, liberty, equality – but also the realization that individuals must accept rights and obligations common to all.

> "The more common the characteristics of domestic law that connect two peoples, the more lasting their international law bonds will be, based as they are on a firmer ground. States governed by absolutist rules of domestic public law find it difficult to accept being subjected to international rules, the same rules that would be accepted by polities governed constitutionally. History in its entirety teaches us the correctness of this perception."[143]

Seferiades remarks that in order to be governed by truly representative institutions, states need to have "settled" pending self-determination questions on their territory, so that the governments of these states truly represent their populations: in all cases where international associations have been successful, Seferiades asserts, people "of the same race" have populated

---

[139] Seferiades (The Future of International Public Law), *supra* note 99, at 8, and 14-15.
[140] On this point see S. Marks, 'International Law, Democracy, and the End of History', in Fox and Roth, eds., *supra* note 100, at 532-566.
[141] See Section 2.3, *infra*, for a discussion on this point.
[142] Seferiades (The Future of International Public Law), *supra* note 99, at 14-15.
[143] Seferiades (Courses on International Public Law), *supra* note 96, at 33.

states.[144] One can read here the echo of his concern about the Greek populations of Turkey. But his examples in the text are Alsace and Lorraine. It
would not be possible for any association of human beings to be successful,
he claims, if important matters remain pending and if the existence of good
faith between them is questioned.[145] Finally, states to accept the principle
of compulsory resolution of international disputes on the basis of rules of
law.[146]

In the antipodes of this "open minded and splendid conception" of international law, Seferiades postulates an opposite sensibility, which could be
historically traced to the Middle Ages and the early origins of international
law. The Treaties of Westphalia and Utrecht, he claims, were not treaties
concerned with the interests of nations, but rather deals securing the interests of emperors and kings. They were "des règlements interroyaux", as he
calls them, using a French neologism in the Greek text:

> "The Treaties of Westphalia and Utrecht, which brought together to a peace-
> ful negotiation after long-lasting wars the representatives of the powerful
> polities of Europe, are considered by public law jurists as the landmarks that
> laid progressively the foundations of later public international law. Unfortu-
> nately these foundations, at least for the most part, have nothing to do with
> law. They are not arrangements dealing with the interests of nations but ar-
> rangements between emperors and kings. They are, if you would permit me to
> create a new expression, inter-royal arrangements (des règlements interro-
> yaux)."[147]

Similarly to the use of term democracy, Seferiades does not make frequent
use of the term absolutism. Again, one can point to epochal reasons for this
choice, some related to the Greek political situation of the time. Recent
appraisals in political theory deny the term absolutism any determinacy or
even any historical accuracy.[148] Misleadingly or not, in mainstream politi-

---

[144] Seferiades (The Future of International Public Law), *supra* note 99, at 14 and 16-17.

[145] Seferiades (The Future of International Public Law), *supra* note 99, at 14.

[146] Seferiades (The Future of International Public Law), *supra* note 99, at 9 and 23.

[147] Seferiades (The Future of International Public Law), *supra* note 99, at 6.

[148] See, e.g. N. Henshall, *The Myth of Absolutism: Change and Continuity in Early
Modern European Monarchy* (1992) at 1-6 and 199-214. Henshall argues that standard descriptions of absolutism are misleading on account of a very myopic understanding of the
role of consultation and delegation of powers in their system of governance and the nature
of their economic policies and objectives.

cal theory, absolutism is today normally associated with the type of government of *Ancien Régime* states (especially France, Russia, Spain, and Prussia)
and connotes, in its more colloquial sense, a despotic, dynastic form of
governance that encroaches on subjects' rights and privileges.[149] Absolutism is seen as autocratic. The term describes a system in which the only
legitimate source of power is the monarch, or agencies dependent solely on
the monarch, and where consultation is shunned in favor of a centralized
decision-making process, eschewing the vestiges of a representative form
of government. Seferiades appears to be using the term abstractly, in this
general meaning of non-democratic, autocratic governance, both nationally and internationally: on the one hand, the idea of the absolute power of
the state in international law (e.g. unlimited exercise of sovereignty, self-
limitation, etc.); on the other, absolutism as a political concept of non-rep-
resentative domestic governance.

It is hard to tell whether Seferiades was aware of any historical reap-
praisals of absolutism that may have entered the debate of political theory
at the dawn of the Nazism and Fascism in the 1930s. It is clear, however,
that the image of a coherent philosophy of autocratic governance with roots
in the monarchic past of Europe was perfectly suited to his argument and
was in sync with mainstream accounts of history of the time.[150] In his international law writings Seferiades carefully sketches out a political sensibility that is constantly present in European history since the Middle Ages,
privileging the interests of the monarch or hegemon over those of the people;
and those of the sovereign state over the international community of states.
The Hague Peace Conferences of 1899 and 1907, for example, crucial as
they were for the consolidation of basic principles of law and the concept of
the international community, would have been so much more successful,
he claims, had it not been for the resistance of regimes such as that of Germany, refusing to accept the principles of disarmament and compulsory

---

[149] See, e.g., M. Beloff, *The Age of Absolutism* (1954), esp. at 11-27.

[150] Whatever it meant to be a liberal or even a republican in modern Europe, it meant
repudiating the age-old belief that monarchy is the best form of government. This often
necessitated the re-writing of history, with the accusation of "absolutism" associated with
practices of European monarchy. For an excellent collection of essays on this topic, see
M. van Gelderen and Q. Skinner, eds., *Republicanism: A Shared European Heritage* (2002),
esp. Vol. 1, Part I, at 1 and 9-84.

arbitration of disputes.[151] International law was confronted with this sensibility not only in 1648 but also throughout its history, from the ancient times until the present, and he mentions many examples. The 1814 Congress of Vienna, for example, when the plenipotentiaries of the Great Powers decided to divide the continent "purely in order to ensure the balance of power", instead of the prevalence of the rules of justice. The outcome of the Congress of Vienna "had nothing to do with the interests of nations: dynastic interests governed the division of lands".[152] The establishment of the *Sainte Alliance* in Paris one year later had the same objectives: the creation of an alliance of hegemonic rulers for the sole purpose of suppressing any popular revolutionary movement capable of challenging the decisions of the Congress of Vienna. The long historical narrative that follows includes numerous events recounted in the same light, from the Greek revolution in 1821 to the Greek-Turkish war of 1897.[153]

> "The outcome of these Congresses is not a community but rather an association of Great Powers, or rather of their hegemons, aiming at the limitation of any democratic activity without which the existence of an international community and of public international law is impossible."[154]

The Treaty of Versailles is the first true example of a new conception that manages to reverse the tides of resistance to internationalism.

> "Par ailleurs, l'idée que la société interétatique, pour pouvoir être régie par des règles de droit communes, doit être compose d'Etats ayant de mœurs politiques analogue et une conception similaire de la morale, se rencontre plus accentuée encore dans les textes adoptes par la commission française qui, le 8 juin 1918, présenta les principes sur lesquels pourrait être constituée la Société des Nations. D'après ces principes, en effet, dans le sein de la Société des Nations a établir, ne devaient pouvoir être admises que 'les Nations constituées en Etats et *pourvues s'institutions représentatives*'."[155]

---

[151] Seferiades (Courses on International Public Law), *supra* note 96, at 88 et seq.; Seferiades (The Future of International Public Law), *supra* note 99, at 10.

[152] Seferiades (Courses on International Public Law), *supra* note 96, at 63.

[153] Seferiades (Courses on International Public Law), *supra* note 96, at 55-102.

[154] Seferiades (The Future of International Public Law), *supra* note 99, at 8.

[155] Seferiades (Principes généraux du droit international de la paix), *supra* note 115, at 222-223.

So, what does the future hold for international law within his historical narrative of absolutism v. democracy? And how will his vision of a liberal international law be attained? The Treaty of Versailles and the establishment of the League are, for Seferiades, the "for centuries long-awaited cornerstone of the future progress of international law".[156] He is quick to caution his readers not to expect too much for now: they should not imagine the 1919 Paris Conference as able to instantly overpower the preexisting regime.[157] For the future of international law to be peaceful, hard work and substantial reform would be needed. In the closing section of the *Future of International Public Law* Seferiades answers the question of the outlook for the discipline by pointing to his audience.[158] It is ultimately the duty of public international lawyers to educate the general public, and especially the youth, and to do everything within their means to disseminate the new internationalist spirit that endorses the idea of a community of democratic states.

On the doctrinal level, Seferiades sees a number of principles, already articulated in the Covenant of the League of Nations, that require further elaboration and development:[159] the principle of compulsory adjudication of international disputes before international arbitral or judicial institutions; the "forcible imposition of the principles of law" through a system of collective forcible action against outlaw states; the abolition of what he describes as the "immoral" principle of neutrality. Finally, albeit less importantly, one needs to add the careful codification of new doctrines and principles of public international law. The creation of professional associations such as the American Society of International Law and the *Institut de Droit International* is crucial for the purpose.[160] The future of international public law, he emotionally proclaims at the end of his lecture, ultimately depends on the extent to which the internationalist spirit will become disseminated and accepted widely, by society and political institutions alike. It is especially up to the youth, students of international law and others alike, to protect the rights and obligations of their country. Not on the basis of "empty rhetoric" but on the basis of international law.[161]

---

[156]  Seferiades (The Future of International Public Law), *supra* note 99, at 18.
[157]  Seferiades (The Future of International Public Law), *supra* note 99, at 19.
[158]  Seferiades (The Future of International Public Law), *supra* note 99, at 22 et seq.
[159]  Seferiades (The Future of International Public Law), *supra* note 99, at 22-23.
[160]  Seferiades (The Future of International Public Law), *supra* note 99, at 26.
[161]  Seferiades (The Future of International Public Law), *supra* note 99, at 27.

## 2.3    THE FUNCTION OF THE VOCABULARY OF PROGRESS

This otherwise inconspicuous historical narrative in the argument of
Seferiades about the nature of man and the contest between absolutism and
democracy performs an extremely crucial discursive function. To begin with,
the narrative is presented as 'speaking itself'. The world begins in a primitive state of being, where life was nasty, brutish and short. Guided by Reason and, much later, the spirit of Enlightenment, slow and arduous progress
has yielded the advances of civilization. International law, and especially
the post-1919 "new international law", is the crown jewel of this advancement. In engaging history and the grand narrative of the Enlightenment in
such a manner, Seferiades situates international law at the apex of the long
process of maturity of human perception of society.

In a strange way, however, such lessons from history do precisely the
opposite of what they claim: they *de-historicize* his account of the nature of
international law, which is made to appear natural, universal and unequivocal. In this self-referential way, his account of the nature of international
law *becomes* the nature of international law. Seferiades assumes that which
requires demonstration and presents history in terms of a stark opposition
between absolutism and democracy, in which polar opposites appear as the
only options. The result is an argumentative vicious circle. This process, as
Terry Eagleton has described it, "involves a specific ideology creating as
tight a fit as possible between itself and social reality, thereby closing the
gap into which the leverage of the critique could be inserted".[162] Social
reality is redefined by ideology to become co-extensive with itself, in a way
that occludes the possibility that ideology may have constructed the reality
by the use of narrative account. Along these lines, Seferiades's historical
account performs a number of important functions in his international law
argument.

*First*, the concepts of democracy and absolutism are 'naturalized'.[163] Instead of being described as historically and culturally specific notions, they

---

[162]  T. Eagleton, *Ideology – An Introduction* (1991) 58.

[163]  The terms "naturalization" and "dissimulation" used in the next few paragraphs are
borrowed and adapted from the partly over-lapping discussions of "ideological modes and
strategies" that can be found in Eagleton, *supra* note 162; Marks (Riddle of All Constitutions), *supra* note 65, at 18-25; J.B. Thomson, *Ideology and Modern Culture: Critical So-*

are dehistoricized and de-politicized. They appear as forces of nature that somehow simply exist in a world out there as traits of humanity, like the propensities to drink, to eat, to maximize our individual interest, and so on. Scholars of ideology critique have identified this discursive strategy as 'naturalization', "whereby existing social arrangements come to seem as obvious and self-evident, as if they were natural phenomena belonging to a world 'out there'".[164] Along with other grand narratives about the eternal struggles between passion and reason, evil and good, now we have yet another one: absolutism and democracy. Along with the naturalization of these concepts as formal categories, on a more concrete level comes the naturalization of their content and meaning. If the concepts are no longer trenches of ideological contestation but real and tangible elements of the human habitat, their meaning can somehow be found in the social nature of man. The two notions acquire an essence that is not a product of the discursive framework in which they are employed but is somehow eternal, and delightfully unequivocal. The essentialization of the terms not only removes from view the problem of linguistic indeterminacy, but it also occludes the character and significance of heterogeneity – the complexity of social processes in which such concepts have thrived and constituted the banners of ideological opposition. Absolutism thus becomes a concrete, coherent mode of governance, despite the substantial differences that may have distinguished British, Prussian and Greek monarchies from each other. Likewise democracy is presented as a coherent global standard without internal ruptures or discontinuities. In this story Pericles, Kant and Wilson can be pictured as having advocated the same thing. As Eagleton caustically puts it, with such accounts of history "[o]ne just has to accept that twelfth-century French peasants were capitalists in heavy disguise, or that the Sioux have always secretly wanted to be stock-brokers".[165]

The de-historicized esentialization of the two opposite notions allows them to "speak themselves". It reduces the necessity to explain in detail the assumptions behind one's political agenda or to subject them to scrutiny. If my political agenda is derived from the concept of democracy, and if de-

---

*cial Theory in the Era of Mass Communications* (1990); and S. Žižek, 'Introduction: The Spectre of Ideology', in S. Žižek, ed., *Mapping Ideology* (1994) 1.

[164] Marks (International Law, Democracy, and the End of History), *supra* note 140, at 22. See also Eagleton (Ideology), *supra* note 162, at 58-61.

[165] Eagleton (Ideology), *supra* note 162, at 59.

mocracy stands on the side of progress, then my agenda is progressive. The logical error here is obvious. It would be enough for me to prove that I contribute to democracy in order to gain legitimacy, without really having to enter into investigations of the notion of democracy (what does it really mean? what are its limits?) or the potentially adverse (even 'un-democratic') consequences of my project. Together with democracy and absolutism a whole set of derivative terms are essentialized, acquiring their meaning in a descending manner from the normative concept: justice, nation, good nationalism v. bad nationalism, people, rights, liberties, rule of law, and so on. The naturalization of the terms also brings about a new field of expertise: the knowledge of how to extract a project of international governance out of the social nature of man. This is the field of expertise that Seferiades carves out for himself and the new international law jurists of the interwar period. The liberal intellectuals are the repositories of the new knowledge, managing authoritatively its content, its political vocabulary and its agenda, under the rubric of the new international law. Here Seferiades assumes one of the fundamental postures of 'sociological jurisprudence' of the interwar period: Law is the product of society, and in order to be able to improve this law one has to scientifically study the workings of society to derive the norms that should govern it.[166]

*Second*, naturalization formalizes the relationship between absolutism and democracy into a fixed opposition. It postulates that the dichotomy of the two is a stable one, or at least sufficiently stable for one can ask what is the role of the one versus the other in history. The two opposites cannot be flipped. Metternich is an absolutist dictator but Her Majesty's colonial administrations have served the purpose of civilizing the colonial subjects. The 1917 policy of the government of Venizelos to lay off thousands of civil servants loyal to Monarchy is to the service of democracy and progress whereas a similar policy regarding civil servants of liberal political persuasions by royalist governments a few years later is described as a terrible absolutist measure.[167] The concepts themselves acquire meaning through

---

[166] For interwar 'sociological' jurisprudence, see also see Section 3.3, *infra*.

[167] W. Edgar, 'The 1917 Cleansings: Their Importance for the Reformist Agenda of Eleftherios Venizelos' (in Greek), in O. Dimitrakopoulos and T. Veremis, eds., *Μελετήματα Γύρω απο τον Βενιζέλο και τιν Εποχή του* [Studies on Venizelos and His Era, in Greek] (1980) 519-550.

their opposition. Absolutism *is* the Other of Democracy. This is a totalizing teleology. The history of the world can be recounted through this polarizing prism, where there is no room for nuance. You are with us or against us. The Treaty of Westphalia was a legal instrument exemplifying the absolutist sensibility; the Hague Peace Conferences were an ambivalent fight narrowly won by the forces of progress; and the Paris Treaty, redefining the borders of Europe, constitutes the capstone of progress in international law so far. The 'old' international law stands for regression; the 'new' international law stands for progress. Being a monist is a part of the open-minded and splendid conception of the world, regardless of the international norms that you may admit in your national legal order; being dualist means that you support an absolute conception of sovereignty; and so on. Along these lines, international law's victories and defeats can be recounted rather tautologically, in much the same way as the Manichaean struggle. The mystified binary opposition becomes the interpretative device to understand almost any social or political decision. This hides terrible interpretative pitfalls. For one thing, the manifestations of a phenomenon can be (mis)taken for its causes. Thus, the eruption of the Great War is explained as the product of the resistance of absolutist governments to democratic internationalism. Surely, historical analysis does support the argument that some absolutist regimes did undermine specific efforts in international organization. Identifying absolutism, however, as the main agent of the Great War is a slightly different matter. As demonstrated above, Seferiades in his writings mystifies the role of absolutist 'resistance': he vests it with mythical proportions and specific cultural and political traits. Resistance becomes a recurrent interpretative device in order to explain failures of the past and of the present – and to legitimate one's political agenda.

This is the moment in the argument of Seferiades when his commitment shifts radically: from a commitment to the humanist agenda of democracy to a commitment to the formalized interpretative device of absolutism versus democracy, the lens through which interpretations are made, judgments are passed, and agendas are legitimated. Resistance averts our attention from the incoherence or the lack of genuine transformative potential in interwar liberal argument itself.

*Third*, the naturalized, formalized opposition masks relationships of domination produced by the liberal project itself. Scholars of ideology critique describe this function as dissimulation, whereby "relations of domination

are masked, obscured, or denied".[168] The transfer of attributes belonging to
the one side can be displaced (transferred) to the other. Democracy is depicted as the force of Good, without considering the possibility of itself
creating injustice in the name of progress. The 1928 law passed by the
government of Venizelos penalizing with imprisonment 'communist beliefs' is undoubtedly to the service of democracy and progress.[169] This is
part of the "open-minded and splendid" conception of the new international
law that Seferiades has in mind which, one supposes, can be found also in
the mandate system of the League and its infamous Article 22, which placed
a sacred trust for the administration of former colonies in civilized states.
The same splendid conception of international law envisages wars liberat-
ing "unredeemed" fellow nationals abroad with a view to "settling" self-
determination questions in third states that are not ethnically homogeneous.
Dissimulation is the effect of obscuring relations of domination created by
the advocacy of the democratic agenda, with measures such as the above,
leaving no doubt about the compatibility of the project with progress. Finally, dissimulation also resituates the causes of the failure of the internationalist project outside the project itself. Since the democratic project stands
on the side of progress, regression has to be attributed not to the project
itself but to external factors that have resisted or undermined it.

The naturalizing, dichotomizing, and dissimulating effects of the narrative of progress of Seferiades are not shortcomings or errors in his writing.
Every historical account inevitably naturalizes something and privileges
and occludes something else. My analysis here aims to demonstrate how
such argumentative strategies perform deeply ideological functions in legal
argument and present claims as unproblematic. The reader of Seferiades,
for example, having read only the historical account of the opening fifty
pages of his textbook, is already assured that the "new international law" of
the interwar period is progressive compared with the past. The reader has
been "summoned from afar" and is already convinced that the science of

---

[168] Marks (International Law, Democracy, and the End of History), *supra* note 140,
at 20.

[169] This is the infamous Law 4229/1929, which has stayed in history under the nick-
name 'Ιδιώνυμον'. On the topic of Law 4229/1929, see G. Katiforis, *Η Νομοθεσία των
Βαρβάρων* [The Legislation of the Barbarians, in Greek] (1975) 64-76. See also N. Alivizatos,
*Οι Πολιτικοί Θεσμοί σε Κρίση 1922-1974: Όψεις της Ελληνικής Εμπειρίας* [Political Institutions in Crisis 1922-1974: Aspects of the Greek Experience, in Greek] (1982).

international law had to combat absolutism at every turn of its history and has helped bring peace to the world through its progressive democratization. The League of Nations and the teachings of public international lawyers *are* the contemporary agents of the uninterrupted flow of the dissemination of humanist ideals. The legal argument to follow, as long as it can be explained on the basis of the basic principle, is also situated on the side of progress. But one could also argue that these very argumentative strategies that produce the feeling of forward movement are also the veil that prevents the reader from understanding the inadequacies and shortcoming of the liberal project itself. The liberal international law project becomes co-extensive with progress, without internal ruptures or shortcomings. The legal argument is no longer acting in the service of the ideal of democracy but in the service of defending a narrative of progress, in which democracy versus absolutism can remain the central, interpretative device.

In a tragic twist of fate, the same narrative that 'speaks itself' brings Stelios Seferiades dangerously close to his ideological opponents. A few years later, and for the protection of the liberal project, Seferiades goes as far as proposing the censorship and punishment of individuals advocating ideas subversive to the liberal project. For Seferiades, there is no conflict between the "splendid and open-minded conception of law" that he advocated earlier and his suggestion for an International Press Court which would take journalists disseminating "false news" to trial.

In 1934 Seferiades inaugurated the new academic year as Rector of Athens University and delivered another fervent keynote on the topic of *The Moral Armament*.[170] The speech reverberates with the passion and zeal of the newly appointed Professor of International Law who, fifteen years earlier, inspired his students on the topic of the 'Future of International Public Law'. In 1934, however, Seferiades is anxious and no longer optimistic. The interwar reform has failed to yield a peaceful international community of states. Hitler's ascent to power, the progressive demise of the League of Nations, the election of yet another royalist government in Greece, and the ensuing marginalization of liberal intellectuals are his primary concerns. Seferiades asks his students to "arm" themselves with morality in order to stand against the "hatred" and "moral decay" that absolutist practices have brought about.[171] Moral armament is the last trench of resistance when

---

[170] Seferiades (Moral Armament), *supra* note 98.
[171] Seferiades (Moral Armament), *supra* note 98, at 3-4, 9 and 21.

states (such as Germany) or state institutions (such as the Greek pro-
monarchic government) engage in absolutist practices, and when international institutions cannot manage to achieve the limitation of the absolute
power of sovereign states. As a consequence, Seferiades proposes the "modernization" of the social sciences and the education of the public through
the teaching of "objective history" and objective knowledge; that is to say,
history and knowledge purified from the morals of absolutism.[172] He suggests that the objectivity of knowledge is controlled by international institutions and is disseminated through the school system and mass media. He
proposes three concrete plans of action in order to cultivate "moral armament". First, reform of the criminal codes of all nations, criminalizing 'subversive action' that threatens international peace and security, committed
either by individuals or groups of people.[173] Second, the creation of an
International Press Agency which will censor and prevent the release of
news misrepresenting reality for the purpose of destabilizing peace between
nations.[174] This agency should retain the right to put to trial journalists
engaged in such subversive behavior. Third, the education of youth and the
general public on the basis of "objective" history which, once more, will be
safe-guarded by international institutions.[175]

   The purchase of the narrative of absolutism v democracy as an interpretative device for Seferiades becomes even more apparent when situated in
the historical, political, and personal setting of the life of our hero. The
following paragraphs digress to the life of Seferiades and sketch out an
arresting correspondence between his international law writings and life
trajectory.

## 2.4   A Vocabulary Situated

Intellectual ruminations of liberal scholars during the interwar period in
Greece must be read in the context of the political project of "bourgeois
modernization" ("αστικός εκσυγχρονισμός"), launched by Prime-Min-
ister Eleftherios Venizelos in 1910 and pursued until the 1936 dictator-

---

[172] Seferiades (Moral Armament), *supra* note 98, at 5.
[173] Seferiades (Moral Armament), *supra* note 98, at 13 and 16-17.
[174] Seferiades (Moral Armament), *supra* note 98, at 14 and 18-19.
[175] Seferiades (Moral Armament), *supra* note 98, at 14 and 19-25.

ship and the final withdrawal of Venizelos from active politics.[176] The immense literature surrounding the personality of Venizelos bears testament to the momentous influence that the legacy of his era continues to exercise over contemporary Greek political consciousness.[177] In Greek history "Venizelism" represents the most ambitious, dynamic, and comprehensive attempt for the modernization of the country and the one that got the closest to achieving its declared objectives.[178] It marked some of the nation's most celebrated successes, such as the consolidation of its borders in their current form, and some of its most lamented disasters, such as the 1922 defeat of the Greek army and destruction of Smyrna (Izmir).[179] Its power emanated from an unprecedented in Greek political reality combination of nationalism and modernization in organic partnership. Bourgeois modernization was a political-ideological project aimed at transforming Greece into a modern, Western state. It aspired to effect changes on a variety of levels, from the economy to language, education, law, administration, architecture, urban planning, social welfare, defense, and so on. In that sense, it shared a lot with similar projects of nationalist modernization elsewhere, from Turkey to Africa, Latin America, and Asia.[180]

---

[176] For the project of bourgeois modernization, see, e.g., G. Mavrogordatos, *Stillborn Republic: Social Coalitions and Party Strategies in Greece, 1922-1936* (1983); G. Mavrogordatos and C. Hatziiosif, eds., *Βενιζελισμός και Αστικός Εκσυγχρονισμός* [Venizelism and Bourgeois Modernization, in Greek] (1988); O. Dimitrakopoulos and T. Veremis, eds., *Μελετήματα Γύρω απο τον Βενιζέλο και τιν Εποχή του* [Studies on Venizelos and his Era, in Greek] (1980).

[177] For an interesting interwar appraisal of the statesmanship of Venizelos, see V.J. Seligman, *The Victory of Venizelos: A Study of Greek Politics 1910-1918* (1920), esp. at 171-185.

[178] For an appraisal along those lines see G. Mavrogordatos, 'Venizelism and Bourgeois Modernization', in Mavrogordatos and Hatziiosif, *Venizelism and Bourgeois Modernization, supra* note 176, at 9.

[179] For a concise account of Greek interwar history, see R. Clogg, *Concise History of Greece* (2002) 46-141; and T. Vournas, *Ιστορία της Νεώτερης και Σύγχρονης Ελλάδας*, Vol. B: 1909-1940 [History of Later and Modern Greece, in Greek] (1977). For the destruction of Smyrna and the Minor Asia campaign, see A.A. Pallis, *Greece's Anatolian Venture – And After: A Survey of the Diplomatic and Political Aspects of the Greek Expedition to Asia Minor (1915-1922)* (1937); M. Housepian Dobkin, *Smyrna 1922: The Destruction of a City* (1971).

[180] See, e.g., J.M. Landau, ed., *Atatürk and the Modernization of Turkey* (1984). For mainstream accounts on the relationship between modernization and nationalism, see E. Hobsbawm, *Nations and Nationalism Since 1780: Program, Myth, Reality (Canto)* (1992);

Bourgeois modernization operated on two broad, interdependent levels. First, a nationalist plane, aimed at uniting the population under a new national identity. Venizelism sought the symbols necessary to forge nationhood on a new basis and found them in the idea of 'national fulfillment' (εθνική ολοκλήρωση), a set of irredentist ambitions concerning the liberation of 'unredeemed' (αλύτρωτοι) Greeks beyond the borders of the Greek state of the time, predominantly under Ottoman/Turkish domination and possessing strong historical, ethnic, and other ties with mainland Greeks.[181] The reuniting of Greeks on both sides of the Aegean Sea was a desire that resonated vibrantly across the Greek political and social spectrum and thus quickly became a central policy for Venizelos.

Second, there was a modernizing level as well. The project sought to reorganize society across Western, liberal lines, espousing secularism, pragmatism, economic efficiency, rational development, industrialization, and so on. It signified the transition from the pre-capitalist 19th-century economy, which was primarily based on agriculture, an inflated state apparatus, and state interventionism, to a capitalist, industrialized model of production, with all its social and cultural consequences. It necessitated linguistic reform; secularization of education; sanitization of public administration; interventionist urban planning to accommodate mass flows of factory workers; and, of course, a flexible political system to absorb the turbulence of the transition. In political terms, this meant the difficult task of reassessing the role of monarchy, which was, in more than one ways, associated with the pre-capitalist system. This in fact meant advocating the transition to a new constitutional model, monarchic or republican. It is in this context of political survival against monarchic institutions that the notion of absolutism as a social and political force resisting progress started having purchase for liberal intellectuals.

From its beginning in 1910, bourgeois modernization in Greece placed itself in the service of 'national fulfillment'. In return, 'national fulfillment' served modernization to its very end, offering indispensable political legitimacy for the project and a wide social basis.[182] The political power of

---

A.D. Smith, *Nationalism and Modernism, A Critical Survey of Recent Theories of Nations and Nationalism* (1998).

[181] For a chronicle of the changes in the Greek borderline, see the informative account of D. Dakin, *The Unification of Greece 1770-1923* (1972).

[182] Mavrogordatos (Venizelism and Bourgeois Modernization), *supra* note 176, at 11.

Venizelos stemmed from an uncanny multi-party alliance spearheaded by bourgeois entrepreneurs and powered by the emerging labor class and a landless rural population craving for social and political rights, the welfare state, and the redistribution of land.[183] Bourgeois modernization in Greece, not unlike other similar movements, was a flexible amalgam of secularism, realism, empirical rationalism, and nationalism. Key to its success was the ability to regularly shift between various objectives and components in order to forge temporary political alliances and guarantee stability. Paramount was its ability to reject for itself the denomination of an Ideology in uppercase, like 'Marxism' or 'Communism', but rather to present itself as a political program focusing on pragmatic, tangible political objectives, governed by the over-arching goals of national fulfillment and modernization, as values that were 'good for everyone'. The strong link between modernization and nationalism is key to understanding both the momentum and the incoherence of the project. The combination of the two often led to brave progressivism in legislation and social reform (rights of women, freedom of association, unionization, a system of free public education, urban planning, social welfare), which earned Venizelos and his governments the support of liberal intellectuals and a rapidly growing industrial labor class. Other times, it led to measures restricting fundamental rights and fostering nation building, which earned Venizelos the occasional support of the capital and the Palace. In spite (or because) of such contradictory strategies Venizelism, as a political-ideological movement developed a clear sensibility, style, and morals, which were liberal par excellence.[184] They included optimism, pragmatism, faith in education, and the usual strategies of rationalist planning, reconstruction, and piece-meal social engineering.

The most interesting example, at least for the purposes of this essay, of the opportunistic oscillation between conflicting positions is the relationship between liberalism and the institution of monarchy. Although republicanism, democratization, and constitutionalism were at the heart of its

---

[183] On the origins of the problem of land ownership and redistribution, see W.W. McGrew, *Land and Revolution in Modern Greece, 1800-1881: The Transition in the Tenure and Exploitation of Land from Ottoman Rule to Independence* (1985).

[184] See A. Ioannidis, *Ο αισθητικός λόγος στο μεσοπόλεμο ή η αναζήτηση της χαμένης ολότητας* [Aesthetic Discourse in the Interwar or the Quest for the Lost Wholeness, in Greek], in Mavrogordatos and Hatziiosif (Venizelism and Bourgeois Modernization), *supra* note 176, at 369.

political agenda, Venizelism was not necessarily, and not at all times, opposed to a system of constitutional monarchy. Recent assessments conclude that Venizelos and his governments considered Greece to be "unready" to become a Republic and that the King could perform useful stabilizing functions, at least as long as his behavior did not counter the project of bourgeois modernization.[185] Venizelos himself indulged on more than one occasions in extreme and unconstitutional political measures that he usually associated with his counterparts.[186] On two occasions (1909 and 1916-1917) he assumed power by means of an armed coup, and attempted another coup to "restore democracy" in 1935.[187] In early 1917 thousands of royalist civil servants were made redundant in a systematic effort of the government to "cleanse" the state apparatus from anti-liberal elements.[188] In 1929 Venizelos fielded an infamous law penalizing heavily the mere advocation of communist beliefs.[189] At the same time both the Palace and the King were depicted as agents of absolutism. In 1932, with the prospect of losing the forthcoming parliamentary election looming in the horizon, Venizelos used the accusations of absolutism and "not accepting the democratic system of governance" as one of the main campaign slogans against his royalist counterparts.[190] The Palace stood in the consciousness of interwar liberals as the political establishment that defended pre-modern, pre-capitalist political and social structures. It also stood for foreign interventionism, due to the foreign ancestry of King Constantine and the open sympathy of the latter towards the Central Empires at the beginning of the Great War. Venizelos called the King "a tool of our enemy, of our chief enemy the German" and an agent of autocracy and absolutism in Greece.[191] Venizelos

---

[185] V. Papakosmas, Ο Βενιζέλος και το Ζήτημα του Αβασιλεύτου Δημοκρατικού Πολιτεύματος 1916-1902 (Venizelos and the Question of the Republic, 1916-1920, in Greek), in Dimitrakopoulos and Veremis (Studies on Venizelos and his Era), *supra* note 176, 485-499, at 485.

[186] Papakosmas (Venizelos and the Question of the Republic), *supra* note 185, at 485-490.

[187] Vournas (History of Later and Modern Greece), *supra* note 179, at 368.

[188] Edgar (The 1917 Cleansings: Their Importance for the Reformist Agenda of Eleftherios Venizelos), *supra* note 167, at 519-550.

[189] Regarding Law 4229/1929, see *supra* note 169.

[190] See Vournas (History of Later and Modern Greece), *supra* note 179, at 348.

[191] E. Venizelos, 'The Internal Situation in Greece and the Amnesty of Political Officers, Speech of E. Venizelos in the Greek Chamber', 23 April 1920, A Literal Translation from the Official Report (pamphlet) (1920) at 17.

is responsible for Greece joining World War I on the side of the *Entente*, a decision that brought significant territorial gains to Greece in the region and renewed hopes for the creation of a "Greater Greece", including the "unredeemed" populations of Minor Asia. The Palace, on the contrary, insisted on a policy of neutrality during the war, which permitted accusations of allegiance to the Central Empires. Venizelos was quoted in a newspaper of the time stating that "the gap which divides me and my friends on the one hand, and King Constantine on the other, is as deep as the gap that divides the Allied Powers and the Central Empires. These are two entirely incompatible political conceptions".[192]

Seferiades's attraction to the liberal politics of Venizelos is not hard to understand in context. Stylianos Prodromou (Stelios) Seferiades was born in 1873 in the town of Smyrna (today Izmir, Turkey). Although not much is known of the family's occupation, it is clear that he belonged to the well off, newly established bourgeois class that constituted the economic heart of the city. Smyrna was at the time the most important international commercial port of the Ottoman Empire with the West and home to a vibrant Greek community dating back to the ancient Greek Ionian colonies.[193] Greeks on both sides of the Aegean considered the Greek population in Smyrna and the rest of Asia Minor to be 'unredeemed', as living under foreign rule. It is no wonder that Greek–Turkish relations became an important focus of Seferiades's work later on.

Seferiades studied law in Aix-en-Province, where he ranked top of his class in all three years of study. He received his doctorate title at the Sorbonne for a celebrated thesis on civil law in 1897.[194] Days after receiving his doctoral title he returned to Smyrna to practice law and settle down. Before long he married Despo Tenekidou, daughter of one of the richest and most influential families in town. Roderick Beaton describes Seferiades as a hand-

---

[192] Statement as published in daily newspaper "Πατρίς" ["Patris", in Greek], 22 May 1917.

[193] Estimates on the exact size of the Greek population range between 25-50 percent of the total population of the city. On the position of the Greek community in the commercial life of Smyrna, see E. Frangakis-Syrett, *The Commerce of Smyrna in the Eighteenth Century (1700-1820)* (1992), esp. at 43-118. See generally B. Braude and B. Lewis, eds., *Christians and Jews in the Ottoman Empire: The Functioning of a Plural Society* (1982).

[194] S. Seferiades, *Etude Critique sur la théorie de la cause (Ouvrage couronne par la Faculté de droit de Paris)* (1897).

some man, extrovert, a zealous idealist in matters of politics and the arts and uncompromising in his demands towards himself and his family.[195] In 1900 Stelios and Despo celebrated the birth of their first son Giorgos, later to become Nobel Prize laureate for literature in 1965, under the *nom de plume* of Giorgos Seferis.

Seferiades is not reported to have had any involvement with international law before 1912. He spent his time mostly with his family, practicing law, translating ancient Greek texts into Modern Greek, and writing (mostly romantic) poetry.[196] His only publications, aside from his doctorate, included poems published in local newspapers and a booklet on the regulation of the Smyrna stock exchange.[197] A set of events on the island of Samos in 1912 triggered his career shift to public international law. Samos was populated mostly by ethnic Greeks and enjoyed special autonomy within the Ottoman Empire. After a successful armed revolt in 1912, the local population declared the island independent. Seferiades was quick to offer his services to the French consul in Smyrna (as legal adviser and translator), who was acting as mediator between the Sultan and the independence movement. Seferiades became crucially involved in the negotiations that eventually led to the independence of the island from the Ottoman Empire and its unification with Greece in October 1912. He was present on the island at the local parliamentary session that declared independence.[198] Beaton concludes that Seferiades appreciated at the time that his first sortie into international affairs had led to the best possible outcome for his country and his own political beliefs.[199] In the course of the same year Seferiades published his first international law essay addressing the legality of boycottage under international law,[200] examining the legality of recent practices of the Ottoman Empire against Greeks in Minor Asia. This was the first in a long series of international law writings.

---

[195] Beaton (Waiting for an Angel), *supra* note 97, at 33; Tsatsou (My Brother Giorgos Seferis), *supra* note 97, at 19.

[196] The only collection of his poetry will only appear one year after his retirement from his academic life: S. Seferiades, Απο το συρτάρι μου, Ποιηματα 1895-1912 [From my Drawer, Poems 1895-1912, in Greek] (1939).

[197] S. Seferiades, *Les Jeux de Bourse en droit international privé* (1902).

[198] Documents confirming his presence have been discovered in the archive of the Seferiades family and are on file with the author.

[199] Beaton (Waiting for an Angel), *supra* note 97, at 51.

[200] S. Seferiades, *Réflexions sur le Boycottage en droit international* (1912).

Following the Samos incident, Seferiades abandoned his legal practice in Smyrna and moved with his family to Athens in 1914. The deteriorating relations between Greece and the new Turkish state made conditions for Greeks in Asia Minor more difficult than ever. This was not only the result of the First Balkan War, which yielded significant territorial gains to the Greek side at Turkey's expense, but was also a product of the political change brought about by the Young Turks revolution of 1908, the formation of the modern Turkish state, and the subsequent rise to power of Mustafa Kemal Atatürk.[201] Commenting on the impossibility of liquidating his property when leaving Smyrna, Seferiades published his second international law essay on the regime of immobile property in Turkey seen from the point of view of international law.[202] The slaughter and forced departure from Smyrna of the Greek population by the Kemalist army in 1922 has been registered as a traumatic experience for the entire family. Seferiades is reported to have lamented the loss of his homeland for the rest of his life, fervently hoping for its eventual liberation from Turkish rule.[203] It is conceivable that this burning desire for liberation of his homeland forged the link between his early attraction to liberal internationalism (since his Paris years) and his subsequent identification with the liberal project of bourgeois modernization.

His involvement in the Samos incident earned Seferiades a fine reputation in continental Greece which, combined with his studies in Paris, led to a successful nomination for a professorship in international law at the Faculty of Law of Athens University. Although international law had been offered as a subject since the end of the 19th century, this was the first time that a specific Chair on the subject was established.[204] His allegiance to the liberal politics of Venizelos, however, caused a major setback. Venizelos lost the 1915 election with a landslide to the royalists and the new political situation prevented Seferiades from assuming his position. As a consequence,

---

[201] For an account of the monumental influence of Atatürk's arrival on the Turkish political scene, see the recent biography of A. Mango, *Atatürk* (1999). For a brief account of the years 1908-1915 see also A. Mango, *The Turks Today* (2004) 15-25.

[202] S. Seferiades, *Le Régime immobilier en Turquie au point de vue du droit international* (1913).

[203] Tsatsou (My Brother Giorgos Seferis), *supra* note 97, at 24.

[204] See Tenekides, 'Introduction', in Kalogeropoulos et al. (Mélanges Seferiades), *supra* note 94, at xvi.

and in order to be able to cater for the economic needs of his family, Seferiades temporarily moved to Paris to practice law.[205] The following years signaled his rise to prominence, becoming one of the most important international law figures in Greece. While in Paris, he became personally acquainted with Venizelos and started advising him and actively participating in Greek foreign politics. The years following the return of Venizelos to power in 1917 found Seferiades representing Greece in a number of international *fora* and, most notably, participating in the Paris Peace Conference in 1919. The same year he finally received his overdue appointment as Professor of International Law at Athens University and returned to Greece to be reunited with his family.

Seferiades spent the following years traveling between Athens, Paris, and other European capitals for the needs of his private practice and defending Greek causes. Amongst his different functions, one has to single out his appointment as member of the "National Commission for Unredeemed Greeks" ("Εθνική Επιτροπεία Αλυτρώτων Ελλήνων"), established by Venizelos in 1918. He later became Legal Advisor to the Greek ministry of Foreign Affairs and received a number of international appointments, such as member of the Permanent Court of Arbitration (1920), Greek delegate at the Assembly of the League of Nations (1920 and 1924), chair of the League Assembly sub-committee on the revision of the Paris Pact (1921), Greek Agent at the Mixed Arbitral Tribunals (1922-1923), Judge *ad hoc* before the Permanent Court of International Justice (PCIJ).[206] The *Institut de Droit International* invited him to join its prestigious ranks in 1925, where he remained member until 1936. In 1920, 1925 and 1929 he published two editions of his major work – Courses on Public International Law, and taught at The Hague Academy of international law on three different occasions.[207]

---

[205] Beaton (Waiting for an Angel), *supra* note 97, at 58; Tsatsou (My Brother Giorgos Seferis), *supra* note 97, at 36-37.

[206] *Lighthouses* case between France and Greece, Judgment of 17 March 1934, PCIJ Series A/B, No. 62 (1934).

[207] S. Seferiades, 'L'échange des populations', 24 *RCADI* (1928-IV) 307; S. Seferiades, 'Principes généraux du droit international de la paix', *supra* note 115; S. Seferiades, 'Le problème de l'accès de particuliers aux juridictions internationales', 51 *RCADI* (1935-I) 1.

## 2.5    BOURGEOIS MODERNIZATION AND INTERNATIONAL LAW

There is a striking correspondence between important political stakes for bourgeois modernization in Greece and the writings of Stelios Seferiades. In previous sections we pointed at the relationship between the vocabulary of absolutism and democracy on the one hand and the project of bourgeois modernization on the other. The narrative of absolutism and democracy served the dual function of recounting simultaneously the history of international law and the political history of Greece. This narrative of progress privileged a liberal-democratic rhetoric on both the domestic and international planes. While Seferiades spoke of international law and Greek participation in the *Entente* and the League of Nations, he also primed the Venizelist project of liberal-democratic reform on the domestic level. Although his textbooks were, on the face of it, addressed to an audience of public international lawyers, they also participated in a wider political debate about the future political system of governance in Greece and partisan political contestation.

In this light one can read his generalist texts also as an effort to convert the project of bourgeois modernization into legal doctrine. This is important ideological work that involves 'translation' into different discursive levels. First, it requires the carving out of a world-view in which the historical narrative and the founding assumptions of the project can be sustained. The historical argument discussed in Section 2.2 above belongs to this category of work. Second, it involves the construction and elaboration of legal doctrines that operationalize these assumptions into a coherent and functional legal system, from the question of the basis of obligation in international law to sources, subjects, responsibility, primary rules, standards, and the setting up of techniques that explain away inconsistencies and restore the system when failures occur.

Seferiades's textbook, *Courses on International Public Law*, can also be read as a performing this kind of 'translation' work for the liberal project. See for example how he squares the difficult question of the basis of obligation in international law with his liberal idea of an "international community of democratic states of coherent domestic structure". How was international law to be created in a world where many states were not democratic?[208] To tackle the problem of the basis of obligation in international

---

[208] Seferiades (Courses on International Public Law), *supra* note 96, at 38-43.

law Seferiades produces the doctrine of a three-track international law, postulating different types of legal relationships between states depending on
their degree of democratization. The argument, which may not sound to-
tally unfamiliar even to contemporary ears, goes as follows. The existence
of nations whose governance and culture do not share the model of Euro-
pean-type liberal democracy prevents such states from becoming equal part
of the international community. This is a matter of "pure logic" for our
author.[209] There are nations whose history has demonstrated that their 'morality' is different or inferior to that of 'civilized states'. Such states are
unable to comprehend and respect the system of international law, he claims.
As a consequence, only states exhibiting a 'European' democratic civilization enjoy the full privileges of being part of the international community,
even if they are located outside Europe, such as the USA and Japan.[210]
Japan is included on account of the "most splendid perception" of the doctrines of morality of the civilized world of its people and "their will, which
within very few years achieved the re-shaping of the condition of their society in accordance with the most admirable [European] models".[211]
    The world is thus divided into three categories of states: a) civilized
states, which ought to respect the rules of international law in their mutual
relations, in all circumstances and with no exceptions; b) semi-barbaric
states, that is to say states that have adopted some democratic principles but
by no means fully or consistently (such as Turkey and China), and towards
which civilized states should respect, on the basis of reciprocity, only those
rules of international law that semi-barbaric states themselves have consented to; and c) savage states, towards which civilized states have abso-
lutely no legal obligation and are bound only by rules of general morality
(such as respect of life, honor, property and the like).[212] In other words,
international law is of universal scope but not "pan-ethnic": it only concerns states that are part of the international community – only states with a
European culture.
    Seferiades realizes the need to establish a secondary set of principles as
well in order to elucidate some of the gray areas in his model.[213] What

---

[209] Seferiades (Courses on International Public Law), *supra* note 96, at 38.
[210] Seferiades (Courses on International Public Law), *supra* note 96, at 39.
[211] Seferiades (Courses on International Public Law), *supra* note 96, at 39.
[212] Seferiades (Courses on International Public Law), *supra* note 96, at 42-43.
[213] Seferiades (Courses on International Public Law), *supra* note 96, at 41-43.

happens when a civilized state persistently objects to the rules of international law? What if a group of civilized states decides to collectively deviate from "general international law", such as the "American International Law" movement that Alejandro Álvarez and others proposed?[214] How does one deal with "non-democratic" states of European civilization (such as Germany) or "democratic" states of non-European civilization? Seferiades builds his theory of the basis of obligation in international law revolving round this doctrine of a three-track international law. In an argument that could be called simultaneously "ascending" and "descending" (to use Koskenniemi's well-known metaphor[215]) Seferiades seeks the basis of obligation in the consent of states while, at the same time, resorting to peremptory normative safety valves that guard against the ever-present threat of absolutism. The basis of obligation is the "mutual consent" of states of European civilization ("consentement mutuel"), which may be express or tacit.[216] Public international law is based on the "gradual coincidence" of the volition of many such states. When this mutual volition is united, it forms a superior volition ("volonté supérieure"), from which individual states may not deviate.[217]

There are, however, limits. The Judge, for one thing, must not apply rules stemming from this superior volition if for some reason the rules have ceased to be in conformity with the morality of European civilization.[218] He terms the system of this morality as "international public order", in analogy to the public order of domestic legal systems.[219] Seferiades has "absolutist" European states in mind, such as Germany, and "semi-barbaric" states, such as Turkey. One can hear the echo of Greek sovereign interests of the time (e.g., in securing the rights of the Greek minority in Minor Asia) in the contestation that the volition of such states is canceled out by certain mandatory norms of the international public order. As long as these states do not endorse a democratic system of governance and 'European' morality they

---

[214] A. Álvarez, *Le Droit International Américain. Son fondement – Sa Nature* (1910).

[215] Koskenniemi (From Apology to Utopia), *supra* note 65.

[216] S. Seferiades, 'Aperçus sur la Coutume Juridique internationale', 43 *Revue Générale de Droit International Public* (1936) 129; Seferiades (Courses on International Public Law), *supra* note 96, at 11 and 28.

[217] Seferiades (Aperçus sur la Coutume), *supra* note 216, at 172.

[218] Seferiades (Aperçus sur la Coutume), *supra* note 216, at 189-194.

[219] Seferiades (Aperçus sur la Coutume), *supra* note 216, at 192.

shall remain outsiders to the law-making process. Similarly, a group of civilized states may not collectively deviate from "general" international law and form a system of their own, such as "American" International Law. This would fragment the system "unacceptably", Seferiades contests, and would in fact violate "general" international law if it involves existing rules.[220] There is only one international law, and this is the "general" international law formed along the lines of mutual consent described above.

So, if we reconstruct the matrix of legal relations in the new international law of Seferiades, we would have to concede the following categories of legal relations:

- The mutual consent of states of European civilization, when united, forms a superior volition that constitutes the basis of obligation in international law.
- Civilized states become bound by rules of international law only by expressing their consent (expressly or tacitly).
- Civilized states have the duty to respect rules of international law at all times, but only in their conduct towards other civilized states.
- Semi-barbaric states may change their status into civilized through the acceptance of rules of international law and by implementing the necessary changes in their domestic structure, such as establishing democratic institutions or settling pending questions of self-determination.
- Civilized states ought to respect international obligations towards semi-barbaric states only on the basis of reciprocity (on the basis that the latter have accepted the same rules.
- Civilized states ought to respect only basic principles of general morality towards savage states.
- Although different standards may be applied between civilized and non-civilized states, civilized states have to apply general international law between each other, and not 'American' international law or law of any other origin or denomination.
- Civilized states (such as Germany) with absolutist governments remain fully bound by international law obligations, since they were initial members of the international community. Their volition cannot create new rules if these rules contradict the international public order.

---

[220]  Seferiades (Courses on International Public Law), *supra* note 96, at 42.

- The persistent objection of civilized states towards specific rules of international law results in the non-binding effect of such rules.
- The mutual consent of semi-barbaric or savage nations may never create rules of international law or principles that general international law will take into account.

## 2.6   How to Explain Away Sovereign (In)Equality

The conception of a three-track international law may sound patronizing today, at least to some contemporary ears. It does appear, however, as a perfectly logical and legitimate world-view when seen through the lens of the narrative of progress that Seferiades adheres to throughout – and this is precisely the point. The opposition of absolutism v. democracy sets the framework for determining the limits of what is a permissible argument and what is not, naturalizing some and excluding others. Since 'absolutism' has undermined progress since the beginning of time; and since the European model of democracy exemplifies progress; it is perfectly 'logical' for Seferiades, and at the time, that non-democratic states must not derive unjust benefits from a system that they have not supported. Reciprocity is to be enjoyed only by those who commit to the rights and obligations that international law stipulates. Inequality is thus naturalized and normalized as a logical consequence of the relative position of each state on the democracy v. absolutism spectrum.

On this basis, Seferiades constructs a number of exceptions in order to explain away the unequal relationship that needs to exist between civilized and semi-barbaric states. Such an unequal relationship applies, not surprisingly, to the legal relations between Greece and Turkey as well, since the former is postulated as democratic while the latter as semi-barbaric. This logic explains the legitimacy of capitulation agreements and various privileges and concessions that foreign nationals enjoy on Turkish soil. The same holds for the institution of mixed tribunals: if Turkey's legal system does not provide the necessary procedural guarantees for foreign nationals, the latter should be subjected to either mixed tribunals or to their own national law directly.[221] On a global scale, the idea of a three-track international law

---

[221] Seferiades (Le problème de l'accès de particuliers), *supra* note 207.

explains the Mandate system of the League, which is understood as the holy duty of civilized states to pass on their lights to savage states that became "pre-maturely independent".[222] The list of such exceptions can go on indefinitely.

The numerous specialized writings of Seferiades continue the 'translation' work of the project of bourgeois modernization into public international law doctrine. They deal with politically sensitive issues of the time, often by means of the lens of exceptionalism justified on account of the seemingly unequal relationship between civilized and non-civilized states. Unlike his generalist work, most of his specialized publications are written in French. They use the habitual scholarly genre of academic monograph on doctrinal or institutional matters. Yet, similarly to his generalist work, much of the specialized work can also be read as falling back on the familiar by now progress narrative of democracy and absolutism. They can also be read as articulate defense of the rights of the Greek population on Ottoman/Turkish territory or the policies of Venizelos. A strong parallel can therefore be drawn between important political issues of the time and the thematography, timing, and tenor of his academic work. A few examples will illustrate the point.

*Réflexions sur le boycottage*
The first international law publication of Seferiades is a monograph on boycottage.[223] The book, published in 1912, is framed as an academic monograph "reflecting" on the question of the legality of boycottage under international law and on the conditions for its exercise. The argument doubles as a legal condemnation of a major boycottage of Greek products that took place a year earlier in Turkey, with serious economic and social repercussions for the Greek population. This first monograph of Seferiades is a passionate plea for the illegality of boycottage under international law. The main argument is that, while in theory international law permits boycottage as long as it occurs by private individuals without state involvement ("pure boycottage"), it is ultimately a phenomenon that cannot occur on a large scale without the acquiescence, collusion, or active involvement of the state apparatus. The problem with boycottage, Seferiades remarks, is not only

---

[222]  Seferiades (Courses on International Public Law), *supra* note 96, at 101.
[223]  Seferiades (Réflexions sur le boycottage), *supra* note 200.

INTERNATIONAL LAW AS PROGRESS

the financial loss incurred by the boycotted state. It is more the fact that the nationals of the boycotted state who happen to be domiciled in the territory of the boycotting state (see, for example, Greeks domiciled in Izmir or Istanbul) become targeted as well. Their livelihood is threatened; they are discriminated against and often persecuted. All this amounts to unequal treatment of foreign nationals prohibited by international law.

Legal ('pure') boycottage is imaginable in exceptional cases only, when consumers by themselves and without state involvement decide to abstain from purchasing products of the boycotted state. But if state organs participate in or encourage the boycottage, the host state has the responsibility to prevent and punish such behavior. Seferiades considers it unlikely that states would ever prevent or punish their own nationals if the boycottage happens to be politically convenient. State involvement in boycottage becomes apparent in states such as Turkey, Seferiades claims, where governmental institutions do not represent the will of the people – a reference to absolutism. In addition, the population consists of many different ethnic groups, including majority populations of the ethnic origin of the *boycotted* state. It is hard to imagine a successful boycottage that is not supported by the state apparatus, since it would require individuals to act against their own interests, Seferiades concludes. Since the distinction between permissible and non-permissible boycottage is open to abuse, an absolute prohibition is a better guarantee of the rights of individuals.

The argument employs historical and legal analysis with references to a troop of boycottage incidents, including the 1910 Greek-Turkish case. In this account, the history of diplomatic relations is retold as a continuous fight for the maintenance of an equilibrium of power: while some states use aggression to further their interests, others resort to other economic, diplomatic, political or coercive measures to restore the equilibrium. Boycottage is one of these measures. It is the consumers and importers within national legal orders that materialize the boycottage with their actions, albeit often with the encouragement of states. Individuals must be mindful of what is a justified reason for a boycott and who is a legitimate target. Each individual should choose whether to participate or not since by means of participating one could be in fact causing injustice (discrimination against foreign nationals) through the use of otherwise permissible means. A boycottage can be favorable for the boycotting economy as well, as its market share will increase. States should therefore be internationally responsible for the actions of their own consumers or importers, since states have the means to prevent or punish discriminatory behavior from taking place.

Every right, for Seferiades, carries a corresponding obligation. State prerogatives can only be exercised while taking into consideration a state's correlative responsibilities under international law, within and outside its *domaine reservé*. Personal liberty, for example, requires conscious behavior towards the rights of the other, say, the alien. The dichotomy between the self and the other can be transposed from the micro-social level to the interstate level as well. In no case should legitimate rights of individuals be infringed by governmental measures. The violation of the principle of equal protection between nationals and aliens, on the one hand, and between civilized nations on the other, necessitates the reparation of damages inflicted upon individual victims. Unfortunately, and this is a subject to which Seferiades will return to in later essays, there is no recognition of individual legal personality and responsibility on the international level, where only nation states participate. Boycottage invariably has the effect of the violation of rights of aliens and should be attributed to the state.

### Le régime immobilier en Turquie

One year later comes the second international law publication of Seferiades, a disquisition on the laws regulating ownership of immobile property by foreign nationals in Turkey.[224] There can be little doubt that this monograph was also inspired by the difficulties that Seferiades and numerous other Greeks encountered when trying to liquidate their property and flee to Greece in the aftermath of the 'Young Turks' movement. Turkish law of the time imposed substantial limitations on the rights of foreigners over immobile property, particularly with regard to ownership, sale, and inheritance. As a consequence, and despite owning substantial assets in Smyrna, the Seferiades family only managed to bring to Athens a tiny fraction of their wealth. This forced Seferiades to practice law in Paris for several years in order to support his family in Athens. In *Le Régime immobilier* Seferiades, who had native knowledge of the Turkish legal system as a law-practitioner in Smyrna, assumes the posture of the academic commentator, elaborating his argument in 243 pages. His analysis is comprehensive, examining the history of Ottoman and Turkish property law, international agreements in

---

[224] Seferiades (Le régime immobilier en Turquie), *supra* note 202.

force concerning foreign nationals (especially the system of capitulations), and relevant practice. Seferiades concludes that property questions relating to foreign nationals in Turkey should be regulated either on the basis of the law of their nationality or be resolved by international or 'mixed' (consisting of national and foreign judges) tribunals.

Already in the opening page of the book Seferiades opposes two different conceptions of property, quite reminiscent of the familiar progress narrative of absolutism and democracy. First, he identifies an "outdated" conception of collective ownership, associated with autocratic and primitive systems of governance. This conception he finds common to all primitive, ancient and feudal legal systems and, as of late, to the Ottoman Empire and the new Turkish state as well. This conception is originally based on conquest and occupation: the conquering state is free to appropriate and distribute at will the property of the defeated nation to its own nationals as spoils of war and depending on their individual contribution to victory. This conception of property, Seferiades claims, is outdated and irreconcilable with the democratic conception of human society and economy that was favored by Enlightenment thought, which is now supported by international law. In the antipodes, Seferiades identifies a modern conception of property, one of individual ownership, which is in line with the Enlightenment values and democracy. This protects the rights of ownership of the individual, regardless of the outcome of a war or the identity of the occupying power. In other words, individuals retain their right to property regardless of whether their territory has been occupied by a foreign state. The consecutive Balkan wars and the transfer of sovereignty between different occupying powers over cities such as Smyrna (Izmir) is the recent historical context.

Seferiades claims that the Ottoman system was based on the first conception of collective property. He finds that progress did occur during the last centuries, primarily due to diplomatic pressure and international agreements between the Sublime Porte and the European allies. Capitulation agreements guaranteed the property rights of aliens as long as the latter respected the laws of Turkish public order. This 'assimilation' of rights of aliens with those of the Turkish population, however, implied also the regulation of personal matters, such as succession and marriage, by Ottoman law and not the law of the nationality of the alien, causing overlap and confusion. Although capitulation agreements between the Ottoman Empire and the European states have led to a progressive granting of property rights to foreigners, he found that the legal regime was unclear and created interminable conflicts. The overlapping legal orders of capitulations and Ottoman law, ownership and other private law relations, such as family law and succession of rights to property, has lead to endless disputes as to the applicable law and its precise content. Some of the treaties provided European states with the right to intervene in order to protect the property rights of their nationals. Others granted unalienable property rights for Greek citizens within Turkish territory. Ottoman law, however, prevented the sale of this property or even prohibited full ownership.

In addition, one had to account for the fact that Turkey was not a democratic state, Seferiades adds. As an absolutist, non-Christian, pre-modern state, prejudice against foreigners was a common phenomenon in its legal system. One had to read the unclear existing legal framework also in the context of such a biased court system. Hence, disputes created due to overlapping legal regimes regarding the property of aliens were hard to resolve by means of local national courts. The Ottoman real property regime, full of contradictions and incoherence, and its practice of injustice through tribunals that imposed politically pre-determined judgments, did not guarantee a fair trial to aliens. He therefore proposed two different internationalized solutions. One would be to establish arbitral tribunals consisting of international judges who would only apply the capitulations or other international agreements. So, for example, an arbitral tribunal based in The Hague, as envisaged in the 1913 Treaty of Peace between Turkey and Greece, or international commissions, would be appropriate solutions in that regard. Another solution would be the creation of a system of "mixed" domestic courts. For Seferiades, a bench consisting of judges of different nationalities would resolve the problem of bias and prejudice. In addition, the judgments of such courts would contribute to progressive legal reform. By reference to his over-arching conception of a three-track international law and the wider narrative of progress of democracy and absolutism, this solution appears perfectly logical.

*Le problème de l'accès des particuliers aux juridictions internationales*
Judicial bias against aliens was the focus of yet another monograph in French, entitled *The Problem of Access of Individuals to International Jurisdic-*

*tions.*[225] Slightly different versions of this paper were presented both at the Institut de Droit International and The Hague Academy of International Law.[226] The tone of this paper too is academic but his concern for the rights of the Greek minority in Minor Asia reverberates throughout the text. The argument is quite simple and builds on the two previous papers. The rights of all individuals to life, freedom, and propriety are to be protected by their state of domicile, without discrimination on grounds of nationality, language, race, or religion. There is a "legitimate suspicion" according to Seferiades that the judicial system of certain states is biased against certain minorities or aliens. Individuals in such situations are in a predicament. The control exercised by the state over the national judge often leads to violations of basic procedural principles of fairness and impartiality. Seferiades suggests instead the transfer of such cases to international courts. While absolute impartiality, Seferiades concedes, is almost impossible to achieve, international courts are less invested in national politics. In addition, the appointment of judges *ad hoc* of the nationality of the applicant can help guarantee fair trial. Seferiades justifies this proposal further on the grounds of the growing importance of the international legal personality of corporations and of shareholders of corporations. Seferiades laments the fact that the traditional view about international dispute settlement continues to accept legal standing only for states before international courts. For Seferiades this "Vattelian fiction" is a barrier to justice that needs to be abolished once and for all. His paper ultimately calls for the recognition of legal standing for individuals before international courts in cases where there is a "legitimate suspicion" of bias against them in a domestic legal system.

### Les tribunaux de prises en Grèce

Seferiades uses the argument of bias also in cases of property seized in times of war, which is the subject of another essay on Prize Tribunals.[227] This time his argument is a critique of the Greek system of justice. But it

---

[225] Seferiades (Le problème de l'accès des particuliers), *supra* note 207.

[226] Seferiades (Le problème de l'accès des particuliers), *supra* note 207.

[227] S. Seferiades, 'Les Tribunaux de Prises en Grèce – Leur Constitution, Leur Fonctionnement et Leur Jurisprudence', 23 *Revue Générale de Droit International Public* (1916) 31.

may not come as a surprise to the reader that the critique is directed against judgments adopted as a consequence of political decisions taken by royalist governments of the time. The personal experience that Seferiades gained while litigating Greek commercial shipping interests during the early years of the Great War should be credited for his interest in the subject.[228] In *Les Tribunaux de prises en Grèce* Seferiades challenges the legality of the judgments of Greek tribunals dealing with the confiscation of contraband goods during the Balkan Wars of 1912-1913. Greece had not become party to the different 1907 Hague Conventions regulating the status of merchant vessels during hostilities (e.g., Conventions V, VI, VII, XI, and XII), nor to the 1909 London Declaration Concerning the Laws of Naval War. As a consequence, Greek domestic courts were bound in the matter by domestic law and international customary law only. Greek Prize courts, according to Seferiades, applied a restrictive interpretation of the customary right of the freedom of navigation of neutral commercial ships. On many occasions Greek authorities seized commercial and valuable materials, among other reasons in order to finance their own war efforts, but the owners were not properly compensated. Seferiades castigates this practice. Once more, he turns to the international plane to suggest that an international court would be a much more fair, impartial and independent judge of the legality of the seizure of such vessels.

*Chronique sur l'arrestation*

It is also worth noting his 1916 *Chronique sur l'arrestation*.[229] This brief note is a clear defense of the acts of the government of Venizelos. Seferiades explains why the arrest of the German and Austro-Hungarian consuls by the British and French occupying forces in Thessaloniki was in accordance with international law and not in violation of consular law. What is not mentioned in the paper is that, during the early years of the War, Britain and France exercised all their political influence to provoke the resignation of the Greek royalist government, which favored a stance of neutrality during the Great War. In the meantime Venizelos, who advocated Greek participa-

---

[228] This can be inferred from the account in Tsatsou (My Brother Giorgos Seferis), *supra* note 97, at 36-37.

[229] S. Seferiades, 'Chronique sur l'arrestation des consuls d'Allemagne, d'Autriche-Hongrie etc. a Salonique', 23 *Revue Générale de Droit International Public* (1916) 84.

tion in the war on the side of the *Entente*, prepared with the support of France and Britain an armed revolt that brought him back to power.[230]

### L'échange des populations

The essay on the exchange of populations is written in the aftermath of the Balkan wars and in the wake of the 1922 defeat of the Greek army in Asia Minor and the destruction of Smyrna.[231] The ethnic cleansing and displacement of most of the Greek population by the Kemalist army must have left a lasting mark on Seferiades. The 1923 Lausanne Convention Concerning the Exchange of Greek and Turkish Populations that resulted is central to his analysis. By means of introduction, Seferiades begins by contending that the relation between state and man is characterized by reciprocal recognition and respect. Although public international law purports to regulate mostly interstate affairs, states have obligations towards individuals as well. States, as social institutions consisting of individuals, should protect the individual's rights to life, freedom, religion, and so on. These rights perform a crucial constitutional function in national legal orders and constitute goals that policies should serve and not undermine. The protection of such human rights should remain applicable in times of warfare as well, since it is not persons but states that make war. For Seferiades, law-making treaties (because of their orientation towards serving interests of the international community as a whole) create rights for individuals which are more durable than those created by treaties-contracts, which in his view serve mostly sovereign interests. International agreements, international courts and even, in some cases, intervention, guarantee the respect of human rights. Now, the dissolution of the Ottoman Empire, in his view, had to be followed by international treaties that would protect the rights of minority groups or aliens within the newly created states. Through public international law, the protection of the individual can be effected deliberately within national legislations, as non-discriminatory application of human rights contributes to global peace and human dignity. In addition, governments should conserve the wealth that their populations represent, since without this wealth there is no state. In this light, international treaties on the exchange of populations must guarantee that at after the transfer populations shall have exactly the same rights and liberties as autochthonous populations.

---

[230] Vournas (History of Later and Modern Greece), *supra* note 179, at 178-200.
[231] Seferiades (L'échange des populations), *supra* note 207.

*La question du rapatriement des 'Marbres d'Elgin'*
A few years later, Seferiades will align himself with Greek foreign policy
interests in yet another essay on the so-called 'Elgin marbles'.[232] The facts
are quite well known. Between 1801 and 1812 a British diplomat by the
name of Thomas Bruce, the 7th Earl of Elgin, had a number of marble stat-
ues and other objects removed from the Acropolis in Athens and had them
transported to the British Museum in London. Elgin acted under controversial permission by the Ottoman authorities, which occupied Athens at the
time. In his article, Seferiades does not disagree with the "civilizing mission" of the Western world (*mission civilisatrice*), which often involves the
safeguarding of the art of mankind. Indeed, advanced conservation methods may protect antiquities from the eventual disregard and decay that may
occur under "barbaric rule", as he found that the case was in Greece at the
time, under Ottoman occupation. Seferiades pleads the existence of a rule
of customary international law that obliges states to repatriate antiquities
when the initial reason for their removal is no longer valid, especially when
the new state is in good position to conserve its own antiquities.

   The decline of Venizelism in the mid-1930s coincided with the progressive withdrawal of Seferiades from active duty both as a statesman and
academic. Following the 1936 dictatorship, which led to the persecution of
many liberal intellectuals and the definite end of the bourgeois modernization movement, Seferiades retired from the University in 1938. Thereafter
he moved to his old apartment in a Paris banlieue, where his family only
visited him occasionally. He never published in international law again and
the remaining years of his life were devoted to his literary interests, leading
to the publication of a collection of his own poems.


## 2.7   THE INTERNATIONAL LAWYER AS ORGANIC INTELLECTUAL

This chapter has sketched out an intellectual portrait of Stelios Seferiades
and, in the process, it has used the term 'vocabulary of progress' in order to
refer to the argumentative strategies in his work that gave purchase to his

---

[232] S. Séfériadès, 'La question du Rapatriement des "Marbres d'Elgin" considérée plus
spécialement au point de vue du Droit des Gens', *Revue de Droit International*, Tome X
(1932) 52-81.

narrative of progress and, more concretely, to his prescriptions about the reconstruction of public international law. The opposition of absolutism and democracy was one of these argumentative strategies, straddling political agendas and priorities on both the national and international level. On the national level, it was in tune with the strategy of bourgeois modernization to portray monarchy as an agent of foreign interventionism and autocratic governance. On the international level, it paved the way for faith in the establishment of the League of Nations and the 'sociological jurisprudence' of the interwar period, while conveniently explaining away Greek irredentism in Asia Minor and the exceptionalism of Greek foreign policy towards Turkey. Altogether, the progress narrative of absolutism and democracy reinforced the self-perception of interwar liberal intellectuals as internationalist and progressive by situating them on the right side of a long historical tradition of struggle for social progress.

The same vocabulary of progress, however, became the veil that prevented Seferiades from speaking of the dark sides of the liberal project and the inherent limitations of its transformative potential. Seferiades blamed absolutism for the failures of democratization of Greece and of the 'new international law' of the interwar period. To make matters worse, he went so far as to defend, in the name of progress, measures and doctrines that could be viewed as being dangerously close to those of his 'absolutist' ideological opponents. The vocabulary of absolutism and democracy, far from a descriptive concept of how human progress has been achieved, became of powerful ideological device for the exclusion of a series of political and legal initiatives. Far from a formal and self-explanatory notion that 'speaks itself', progress doubles as an ideological device to legitimize one's argument.

In addition, Seferiades identified himself and his fellow liberal international lawyers as experts in the technique of deriving a project of international governance from the social nature of man. He presented the international lawyer as a scientific observer of human history, devoted to the task to defending humanist values through his scholarship. Indeed, from a scholarly point of view, his work was outstanding. His texts were thoroughly researched, written in fine style and celebrated for their accuracy and attention to detail. His publications became the basis of the nascent discipline of international law in Greece. In dialogue with colleagues in Europe and elsewhere, he helped build faith in the new international law of the interwar period in the task of reconstructing doctrines and institutions. He helped construct a comprehensive vision of public international law with universal application, with doctrines applicable to all states and in an infinite number of circumstances. At the same time, a decisive correlation may be traced between his universalist ideas and local-personal ideological stakes. His international law work was re-read as 'translating', at least in many instances, personal/collective ideological stakes into a workable universalist vocabulary about international law. Specific political goals high on the agenda of the liberal Greek governments of the time and the personal life of our hero were presented as indispensable components in the process of reconstructing international law in the aftermath of the Great War. Democratization of states, self-determination of minorities, discrediting monarchy as a system of governance, the protection of the rights of the Greek minority in Anatolia, the characterization of Turkey as a 'semi-barbaric' state, all became part and parcel of a progress narrative. His international law reform, a universalist vocabulary *par excellence*, was simultaneously a personal stake.

And there is nothing 'wrong' with all that. Is the closely-knit relationship between personal/collective ideology and universalist prescriptions problematic? Does it undermine the value of his otherwise excellent scholarship? Is this troubling news for the overall quality of our international law scholarship – if one assumes that the story of Seferiades is not unique? Should this relationship be castigated or could it be embraced and placed at the heart of a 'new' reading of the history of the discipline of public international law? To answer these questions I propose an image of the public international lawyer that is quite different from the one that Seferiades carves out for himself and his peers in his own writings. To do so, I resort to Antonio Gramsci's well-known essays on the role of the intellectual in the organization of culture.[233]

Gramsci argued in his work that every social group, created in the sphere of an operation indispensable for economic production, "creates with it, organically, one or more layers of intellectuals, which vest it with homogeneity and consciousness of their proper function, not only in the economic

---

[233] Antonio Gramsci's views on the topic can be found in the essays written during his long years of imprisonment, the relevant selection of which was published posthumously in Italian in A. Gramsci, *Gli Intellettuali e L'Organizzazione della Cultura* [Intellectuals and the Organization of Culture, in Italian] (1949).

field but also in the social and political one'.[234] For Gramsci 'organic intellectuals' are a crucial component in the production of culture. Gramsci's
representation challenges the classical image of the intellectual as a technician, whose influence is derived from specialist knowledge and talent. For
Gramsci, the latter qualifications are only "external and ephemeral instiga-
tors of affections and passions" ("motrice esteriori e momentanea degli affetti
e delle passioni")[235] and not the true basis of their role. It is rather their
active involvement in practical life as constructors, organizers, and "permanent persuaders" (propagandists) of new ideas that should be fore-
grounded in our understanding. These functions recast the intellectual from
a technical laborer into an instructor, an educator, a political cadre
("dirigente").[236] Thus, intellectuals are therefore not mere observers of our
social reality. With their work they 'organize' human masses and 'guarantee' their consent to and their confidence in the dominant class. Their important role rests precisely in creating the basis for a new and comprehensive
world-view, which is organically related to the dominant ideological group.
They are servants ("commessi") of the dominant group for the performance
of what he famously calls "interconnected, subaltern functions of social
hegemony and political governance".[237] The capitalist businessman,
Gramsci brings the example, brings along the industrial technician, the political scientist, the designer of a new educational system, of a new legal
system.[238] Gramsci sees a division of labor between intellectuals in this
process, similarly to the prescriptions of classical economic theory. On the
top of the pyramid will be the creators and theoreticians of the various
sciences, natural and social, of philosophy, of art, etc. In the lower ranks
one will find the administrators and disseminators ("amministratori e
divulgatori") of the accumulated intellectual wealth.[239] Different special-
ties of organic intellectuals (including jurists) become necessary, depending on the social context.

   Gramsci's idea of the organic intellectual is useful because it offers a
more complex understanding of intellectuals, such as public international

---

[234] Gramsci (Gli Intellettuali), *supra* note 233, at 3.
[235] Gramsci (Gli Intellettuali), *supra* note 233, at 7.
[236] Gramsci (Gli Intellettuali), *supra* note 233, at 7.
[237] Gramsci (Gli Intellettuali), *supra* note 233, at 9.
[238] Gramsci (Gli Intellettuali), *supra* note 233, at 3.
[239] Gramsci (Gli Intellettuali), *supra* note 233, at 10.

lawyers, who are pictured as having their technical-professional work closely conditioned by personal/collective ideological struggles and projects. This image contests the assertion that the law professional is (or should be) autonomous from the dominant socioeconomic class and the hegemonic political discourses; the classical conviction that the task of the jurist is precisely to help harness politics to the direction of the 'rule of law', the latter being an apolitical, non-ideological ideal. Albeit different, Gramsci's image presents the intellectual as equally and terribly important in the production of culture, as translator and converter of ideology into a coherent world-view and the necessary doctrinal and institutional machinery for its implementation.

Along these lines, I would like to suggest an alternative assessment of Stelios Seferiades as an organic intellectual, operating simultaneously in more than one ideological debate. In the context of the Greek political scene, for example, Seferiades can now be viewed as having actively participated in the defense of the bourgeois modernization project and drawn legitimacy from it. As a French-educated, bourgeois sophisticate from Smyrna, his scholarship bore the credentials of cosmopolitan knowledge and personal-historical experience. Seferiades truly believed in the capacity of international law to bring about change at the local level through democratic reform. In the service of these ideas, he offered the scientific vocabulary that the political movement of bourgeois modernization needed in order to bolster its purchase with its own ideological opponents in Greece. Seferiades gave legitimacy to the project by neatly placing it along a historical continuum of social progress. His universal narrative of progress and its international law vocabulary of progress rationalized foreign policy choices and placed it in the service of European foreign policy goals. Aside from his involvement in Greek politics, Seferiades participated in a separate scene: a worldwide, scientific, international law movement for disciplinary reconstruction in the aftermath of the Great War. He joined forces with friends and scholars in Paris, Geneva, London and elsewhere, in proposing a European conception of public international law based on a democratic community of states. As a Sorbonne-educated jurist, he enjoyed the confidence of the professional elite of scholars of the centre. As a sophisticate from the periphery of Europe, he furnished the new international law with some of the universal legitimacy that it needed.

## 2.8   Conclusions

In the case study on Stelios Seferiades, the opposition of absolutism and democracy was demonstrated to form the backbone of a historical narrative of international law *as* progress. Seferiades tells a story according to which democracy and internationalism have served for centuries as catalysts for progress in social organization. In the antipodes, absolutism and sovereignism have been the source of social regression and misery. For a historical account of this sort to be convincing, it was presented as objectively true, as 'speaking itself'. Seferiades does exactly that and recounts a story that is linear, complete, universal, and diachronic. In his writings, the opposition of democracy and absolutism is 'naturalized' and 'formalized', as the case study explains. The notions of democracy and absolutism acquire fixed and stable meaning and they are defined in opposition to each other. Absolutism *is* the Other of Democracy, a totalizing teleology. The history of the world can be viewed through this polarizing prism, where there is no room for alternative explanations. The historical narrative spans the entire course of history, from ancient times till our day, and is applicable to different parts of the world, creating a complete reality which allows no room for doubt: the road of democracy and internationalism appears to be the only path to progress. The notion of progress acquires its meaning through this historical narrative, which determines the range of permissible statements within the discourse. Thus the binary opposition becomes the interpretative device to understand almost any social or political decision. His generalist and specialized writings fall back on this narrative consistently in order to draw meaning as to what should be done. Internationalized solutions and exceptionalism towards less democratic states are favored on that basis.

The case study went, however, a step further and demonstrated that neither democracy nor absolutism had a stable meaning in the (same) texts of Seferiades. The two notions were de-historicized and de-politicized: they were made to appear as forces of nature that somehow simply existed in an absolute form, as traits of humanity. Seferiades presented the dichotomy of the two as a stable one, or at least relatively stable, to the extent that one could ask what is the role of the one versus the other in history. The essentialization of the terms performed a crucial role in the production of meaning. Not only did it remove from view the problem of linguistic indeterminacy but it occluded the character and significance of heterogeneity, namely the complexity of social processes in which such concepts have thrived and constituted the banners of ideological opposition. Absolutism thus became a concrete, coherent mode of governance, despite the substantial differences that may have distinguished different types of monarchies from each other; and democracy is presented as a coherent global standard without internal ruptures or discontinuities.

Such a use of the narrative was crucial for the persuasive effect of the writings of Seferiades. The use of the opposition of absolutism v democracy was a narrative technique that placed Seferiades safely and at all times on the side of progress, even when his argument would fail even its own standards of what is progressive. The opposition, far from having a stable content, was rather a trope or style of argument that helped vest with legitimacy a liberal ideological-personal project and jump over the ruptures and discontinuities of the experience of reality. The perception of progress was produced by the instability and iterations of the vocabulary rather than its stability. These iterations allowed the claims of Seferiades to be placed at all times on the side of progress (e.g., democracy), even when the claims were in logical contradiction with his own definition of progress at a different point in the text. Despite this incoherence, the vocabulary was nevertheless able to discredit his opponents as regressive (e.g., absolutist).

Ultimately, however, Seferiades did not control his own vocabulary. His work, instead of pursuing a political-ideological agenda, became devoted to the defense of the narrative itself. This strategy prevented Seferiades himself from realizing the contradictions of the bourgeois modernization project and the reasons for its failure. Failure was attributed to an external enemy (regression, absolutism) and not to the instability of the opposition itself.

# Chapter 3
# PROGRESS *WITHIN* INTERNATIONAL LAW –
# THE DOCTRINE OF THE SOURCES AS PROGRESS

## 3.1    INTRODUCTION

Following the typology of narratives that was introduced in Chapter 1,[240] the first case study discerned in the writings of Stelios Seferiades an example of a narrative of international law *as* progress. International law itself, by means of its association with democracy, and by its opposition to sovereignism and absolutism, was seen as the agent of social progress. This second case study continues the exploration of the over-arching theme of the function of the notion of progress in international law discourse by moving to yet a different plane of argument and a different horizon of analysis. It turns to the second 'style' of narratives of our typology, namely narratives of progress *within* international law. By this expression I refer to accounts in legal literature that present specific intra-disciplinary developments in techniques, doctrines, processes, institutions, and so on, as evidence of growth in the science of international law as working pure. To exemplify the point, Chapter 3 tells the intriguing story of one of the most celebrated of international law doctrines, the doctrine of the sources of international law. Like in the previous chapter, this second case study looks at 'what is it' that made the doctrine of the sources appear as an element of progress in international law-making methods and techniques.

In its colloquial sense the term 'doctrine' signifies a corpus of taught beliefs, principles, or positions within a given system of knowledge.[241] In international law, the term doctrine has several meanings and may connote

---

[240] See Section 1.1 *supra*.

[241] See, e.g., *Webster's Third New International Dictionary of the English Language* (2002) 666 giving the following meanings to the term: "something that is taught or held or put forth as true and supported by a teacher or school or sect"; "a principle or position or body of principles in any branch of knowledge"; "a principle of law established through past decisions and interpretations"; "a formulated theory supported or not controverted by evidence, backed or sanctioned by authority and proposed for acceptance"; *Black's Law Dictionary* (2004) 518, describes doctrine as a "legal principle that is widely adhered to".

a single principle, norm, rule, idea, belief, or a set of inter-twined principles, norms, rules, ideas, or beliefs, related to international law. Although no clear dividing line can be drawn between the various uses, a quick inventory reveals several distinct meanings in international law parlance. Thus, by doctrine one may refer to the writings of qualified publicists on a certain matter.[242] Other times we speak of the Monroe Doctrine,[243] the Bush Doctrine,[244] or the Human Security Doctrine,[245] to refer to a political dogma or a set of policies that may (or may not) become operationalized by means of international law instruments or institutions. In technical international law talk, we also speak of the legal doctrines of *uti possidetis*,[246] precedent,[247] Joint Criminal Enterprise,[248] indirect expropriation,[249] responsibility to protect,[250] and so on, to refer to a norm or a set of interrelated norms, standards, or rules regulating a specific international law problem. In the following pages I speak of doctrine as understood in the last technical-legal sense, of a regulatory approach to a legal question that has become crystallized into a finite set of inter-related and binding norms.

Along these lines in international law the 'doctrine of the sources' typically designates an agreed upon set of abstract forms (criteria, tests of validity, boundary conditions, categories) that determine two essential aspects of the normativity of international law rules: law-creation (how is interna-

---

[242] A. Carty, 'A Renewed Place for Doctrine as a Source of International Law in Times of Fragmentation', in R. Huesa Vinaixa and K. Wellens, eds., *L'influence des sources sur l'unité et la fragmentation du droit international* (2006) 239-261.

[243] A. Álvarez, *The Monroe Doctrine: Its Importance in International Life of the States of the New World* (1924).

[244] M. Buckley and R. Singh, *The Bush Doctrine and the War on Terrorism: Global Responses, Global Consequences* (2006).

[245] M. Glasius, *A Human Security Doctrine for Europe: Project, Principles, Practicalities* (2006).

[246] H. Ghebrewebet, *Identifying Units of Statehood and determining International Boundaries: A Revised Look at the Doctrine of 'Uti Possidetis' and the Principle of Self-Determination* (2006).

[247] M. Sellers, 'The Doctrine of Precedent in the United States of America', 54 *American Journal of Comparative Law* (2006) 67.

[248] A. Cassese, 'The Proper Limits of Individual responsibility under the Doctrine of Joint Criminal Enterprise', 5 *Journal of International Criminal Justice* (2007) 109.

[249] V. Heiskanen, 'The Doctrine of Indirect Expropriation in Light of the Practice of the Iran-United States Claims Tribunal', 8 *Journal of World Investment & Trade* (2007) 215.

[250] B. Delcourt, 'The Doctrine of the "Responsibility to Protect" and the EU Stance: Critical Appraisal', 59 *Studia Diplomaticade* (2006) 69-93.

tional law made) and law-ascertainment (how do we distinguish between legally binding and non-binding norms). For scholars and practitioners today, the starting point for any discussion on the sources doctrine is the wording of Article 38(1) of the Statute of the International Court of Justice (ICJ). Article 38(1) ICJ reflects with minor modifications Article 38 of the Statute of the Permanent Court of International Justice (PCIJ),[251] and reads as follows:

> "1. The Court, whose function is to decide in accordance with international law such disputes as are submitted to it, shall apply:
> a. international conventions, whether general or particular, establishing rules expressly recognized by the contesting states;
> b. international custom, as evidence of a general practice accepted as law;
> c. the general principles of law recognized by civilized nations;
> d. subject to the provisions of Article 59, judicial decisions and the teachings of the most highly qualified publicists of the various nations, as subsidiary means for the determination of rules of law."

The drafters of the PCIJ Statute back in 1920 neither intended nor foresaw that, soon after its adoption, Article 38 would become the expression of a new conception of the sources of international law. Within a few years the idea of a 'doctrine of the sources', in the contemporary sense of a finite list of abstract forms that determine law-creation and law-ascertainment, became introduced and consolidated as the standard approach to normativity.

---

[251] The PCIJ version of Art. 38 reads: "The Court shall apply: International conventions, whether general or particular, establishing rules expressly recognized by the contesting States; International custom, as evidence of a general practice accepted as law; The general principles of law recognized by civilized nations; Subject to the provisions of Art. 59, judicial decisions and the teachings of the most highly qualified publicists of the various nations, as subsidiary means for the determination of rules of law. This provision shall not prejudice the power of the Court to decide a case *ex aequo et bono*, if the parties agree thereto." There are four minor differences between the PCIJ and the ICJ versions of the text: a) the chapeau of Art. 38 of the PCIJ version ("The Court shall apply") was moved to the body of Para. 38(1) of the ICJ version; b) the phrase "whose function is to decide in accordance with international law such disputes as are submitted to it" was added to the text of Para. 38(1) of the ICJ version; c) Paras. 38(1) to 38(4) of the PCIJ version were converted into Sub-paras. 38(1)(a) to 38(1)(d) in the ICJ version. Finally, the two periods of Para. 38(4) of the PCIJ version were separated as Sub-Para. 38(1)(d) and Para. 38(2) of the ICJ version.

By the early 1930s, a previously divided literature started displaying great uniformity of views. The formative impact of Article 38 PCIJ on post-1920 theory and practice is hard to overstate.[252] Article 38 was heralded as an important moment of disciplinary progress. Commentators described it as "the solid bed of rock on which the fabric of international law has now to be built",[253] a development that ended an "embarrassing uncertainty"[254] about the sources of international law, and so on.

At the same time, the emergence and success of the doctrine of the sources is one of the great riddles of interwar international law. Surely, international law craved for reform in the aftermath of the Great War. But why the turn to sources? Why not institutions, processes, the judiciary? Although determinacy of legal obligations may appear an intuitive goal for the discipline today, was did appear as the way to go then? How can a provision describing the normative categories or primary rules to be applied by the PCIJ become "the solid basis of rock on which the fabric of international law has to be built"? The following pages attempt to solve the riddle by explaining 'what is it' that made (and in some cases still makes) sources discourse appeal to professional consciousness as a 'better' way of regulating international law making/ascertainment. Like in the previous chapter, the purpose is not to assess the 'progressiveness' of the event of the formation of the doctrine as such but, instead, to scrutinize the discursive structures that produced the perception of progress associated with the emergence of the doctrine.

An extraordinary amount of work has been published on the sources since 1920, with recent years being no exception.[255] This work has covered

---

[252] Several authors acknowledge this. See, e.g., C. Rousseau, *Droit International Public* (1970, Vol. I) 59; M. Sørensen, *Les sources du droit international: étude sur la jurisprudence de la Cour Permanente de la Justice International* (1946) 40.

[253] Williams (Aspects), *supra* note 11, at 38-39.

[254] H. Lauterpacht, *Private Law Sources and Analogies of International Law* (With Special Reference to International Arbitration) (1927) at 67-68.

[255] For some post-1989 book-length publications on the topic, see A. Boyle and C. Chinkin, *The Making of International Law* (2007); A. Orakhelashvili, *Peremptory Norms in International Law* (2006); C. Tomuschat and J.-M. Thouverin, eds., *The Fundamental Rules of the International Legal Order: Jus Cogens and Obligations Erga Omnes* (2006); R. Wolfrum and V. Röben, eds., *Developments of International Law in Treaty Making* (2005); M. Craven and M. Fitzmaurice, *Interrogating the Treaty: Essays in the Contemporary Law of Treaties* (2005); C.J. Tams, *Enforcing Obligations Erga Omnes in International Law* (2005);

the topic exhaustively. In addition, Critical scholarship during the last two decades has turned to the structure of sources argument, describing its limits and potentials as a form of argument.[256] The aim of this chapter is not to replicate the above-mentioned work. The hypothesis explored here, closely following the propositions of Chapter 1, is that the watershed of the doctrine of the sources can also be seen in the light of the role of vocabularies of progress in international law.

The backbone of the vocabulary of the sources is a story of forward movement and evolution. Interwar literature tells the story of 'old' international law, whose law-making processes were indeterminate and open-ended. Article 38 PCIJ was seen as able to resolve these problems and thus initiate a new era of talking about normativity, bringing determinacy and closure. Sources talk managed to capture the fantasy of an entire profession as a means of moving forward with the discipline. The idea was that, 'if only' one was able to devise a set of finite, universally applicable, formal categories of legal norms, one would be able to end the problem of indeterminacy. The case study demonstrates how this feeling of progress is generated by a vocabulary, a set of discursive structures. Similarly to Seferiades, however, this chapter demonstrates that the new doctrine was based on notions that

---

A. D'Amato, *International Law Sources* (2004); I.F. Dekker and H.G. Post, eds., *On the Foundations and Sources of International Law* (2003); R. Gaebler and M. Smolka-Day, eds., *Sources of State Practice in International Law* (2002); M. Koskenniemi, ed., *Sources of International Law* (2000); A. Aust, *Modern Treaty Law and Practice* (2007); M. Byers, *Custom, Power and the Power of Rules* (1999); B. Mulamba Mbuyi, *Introduction à l'étude des sources modernes du droit international public* (1999); O.A. Elias and C.L. Lim, *The Paradox of Consensualism in International Law* (1998); M.E. Villiger, *Customary International Law and Treaties: A Manual on the Theory and Practice of the Interrelation of Sources* (1997); V.D. Degan, *Sources of International Law* (1997); M. Ragazzi, *The Concept of International Obligations 'Erga Omnes'* (1997); J. Klabbers, *The Concept of Treaty in International Law* (1996); G.M. Danilenko, *Law Making in the International Community* (1993); K. Wolfke, *Custom in Present International Law* (1993).

[256] The work of David Kennedy and Martti Kosenniemi has been seminal in this regard. See Kennedy (International Legal Structures), *supra* note 65, esp. Chapter 1 ('Sources of International Law') at 11-107, reprinted in D. Kennedy, 'The Sources of International Law', 2 *American University Journal of International Law Review* (1987) 1-96; M. Koskenniemi, Editor's Introduction, in Koskenniemi (Sources), *supra* note 255, at xv-xxvii; M. Koskenniemi, 'The Normative Force of Habit: International Custom and Social Theory', 1 *Finnish Yearbook of International Law* (1990) 77; Koskenniemi (From Apology to Utopia), *supra* note 65, esp. Chapter 5 ('Sources of International Law') at 264-341.

were themselves neither stable nor determinate but they subverted themselves each time they were put to application. Legitimacy in sources discourse was produced not because Article 38 PCIJ Statute 'really' had the
capacity to decisively tell whether a certain norm was one of public international law. Legitimacy was produced instead via the *invocation* of the narrative concerning Article 38.

The study has defined interwar (1919-1939) literature on the sources as
the horizon of its analysis. Sections 3.2, 3.3 and 3.4 situate the adoption of
Article 38 PCIJ within the cultural and professional habitat of the movement of the "new international law" of the years between the two World
Wars. The chief aim of those sections is to explain how the need for law
making, and an ensuing doctrine of the sources, emerged as crucial part of
the reconstruction rhetoric. Section 3.5 tries to solve the riddle of the success of the doctrine of the sources in capturing the imagination of interwar
international law. It explains how the doctrine seemed able to bring clarity,
determinacy, and firm ground for public international law, while avoiding
the pitfalls of 19th century international law theory. Section 3.6 briefly digresses to some contemporary international law writings that illustrate the
continuing salience of the vocabulary of progress of the sources doctrine.
Section 3.7 looks behind the claims of the doctrine and assesses the limits
of its vocabulary of progress.

## 3.2    INTERWAR DISCOURSE ON THE SOURCES OF INTERNATIONAL
##        LAW AND THE QUEST FOR RECONSTRUCTION

In the years following World War I international law appears deeply im-
mersed in reflection about its future. An unusual number of publications of
the time address squarely the theme of the outlook, future, or prospect for
international law and pose openly the question of how to achieve progress
within the science.[257] In this spirit, Manley Hudson publishes in 1925 a

---

[257] See in chronological order, Seferiades (The Future of International Public Law),
*supra* note 99; L. Oppenheim, *The Future of International Law* (1921); Nippold (The Development of International Law After the World War), *supra* note 107; M.O. Hudson, 'The
Outlook for the Development of International Law' (An Address before the American Branch
of the International Law Association, New York, January 1925); Lauterpacht (Private Law
Sources), *supra* note 254; N. Politis, *The New Aspects of International Law: A Series of*

celebrated article titled *The Prospect for International Law in the Twentieth Century.*[258] The paper echoes Hudson's other publications of the time[259] and is written in the grand, evocative style typical of interwar scholarship.[260] The tone is engaging, intense, almost zealous, inviting international lawyers to join the author in a large-scale effort to redefine the goals of the science. Hudson sets out to answer the basic question of "what do we hope to be the contribution of the twentieth century to the progress of international law?"[261] To answer, he performs an anatomy of the problems plaguing international law, followed by suggestions for future action. This publication is illustrative of many of the standard tropes[262] of mainstream interwar scholarship and brings out the crucial role of the turn to law making and the doctrine of the sources. Hudson's article is examined here in some detail to help us flag out the main contours of interwar argument and the context in which the debate on the sources acquired its meaning.

Hudson begins with an appraisal of the influence of World War I on the development of international law.[263] The War is presented as a cataclysmic event that paradoxically produced two opposite effects. On the one hand, it put an abrupt end to the progress that was being achieved previously.[264] For

---

*Lectures Delivered at Columbia University* (1928); Álvarez (The New International Law), *supra* note 27; J.B. Scott, 'The Progress of International Law During the Last 25 Years', 25 *Proceedings of the American Society of International Law* (1931) 2; W. Simons, *The Evolution of Public Law in Europe Since Grotius* (1931); Hudson (Progress in International Organization), *supra* note 7; A. Álvarez, 'The Necessity for the Reconstruction of International Law – Its Aim', *Proceedings of the 4ᵗʰ Conference of Teachers of International Law and Related Subjects* (1930) 11; Brierly (Shortcomings of International Law), *supra* note 105.

[258] M.O. Hudson, 'The Prospect for International Law in the Twentieth Century', 10 *The Cornell Law Quarterly* (1925) 419.

[259] See *supra* note 257.

[260] See the discussion of the writings of Seferiades, Chapter 2, *supra*.

[261] Hudson (Prospect), *supra* note 258, at 420.

[262] The term trope is understood here in its meaning under literary theory, namely as a common motif, story or pattern in literary accounts. The term has a different meaning in linguistics, where it is used in the sense of a figure of speech, namely a deviation or modification of the meaning of a primary expression that is regarded as normal. See, e.g., Ducrot and Todorov (Encyclopaedic Dictionary of the Sciences of Language), *supra* note 60, at 275.

[263] Hudson (Prospect), *supra* note 258, at 421-423. This part of the argument is elaborated in great detail in Hudson (Progress), *supra* note 7, at 16-25.

[264] Hudson (Progress), *supra* note 7, at 6-15.

Hudson, pre-War progress consisted of an ever expanding and intensifying process of internationalization. Its main aspects were the emergence of new international organizations to handle sectoral issues of inter-state relations (notably telecommunications, transportation etc.) and the creation of new international agreements (what he later calls 'international legislation').[265] The failure of international law to prevent the War seems to have embarrassed deeply the jurists of the time.[266] On the antipodes, for Hudson, the War also gave rise to the more constructive realization that institutional and doctrinal structures needed to be reconsidered. Had the international community achieved more progress with international organization, Hudson writes, the War could have been prevented in the first place.[267] Eventually, the War managed to catalyze a 'new spirit' that allowed mankind to believe that progress was again possible and begin the reconstruction of the science of public international law.[268] Against the background of the War, Hudson invites a redefinition of the goals reconstruction. His reconstruction effort involves two distinct but parallel tasks. On the one hand, rethinking the philosophical foundations of international law. On the other, developing new methods of international law making.

"The War has left many specific problems which cry out to us for solution. They are so numerous, so varied, and so bewildering, their background is so new, so shifting and so complicated that even if the War had purified us as some people seem to believe, we could hardly summon the courage to face them without a pretty clear understanding of our situation and of the methods by which our work may be done. Two fundamental tasks lie at the threshold of our endeavor, therefore, and they must receive attention before our generation can entertain much hope of solving specific problems. The first task is the renovation of the philosophical bases of the law of nations; the second

[265] Hudson (Prospect), *supra* note 258, at 436 et seq.
[266] "Even in the excited periods of the war we lawyers were not immune from suspicion. Perhaps we were never quite absolved from guilt in connection with the lawless situation that inaugurated the war. There lurked in many people's minds a feeling that our failure to build a system of laws which no people would dare to violate had enabled particular peoples to play their role in causing the war. The Hague Conferences became most unpopular, and the man on the street came to be certain that international law had broken down." Hudson (Outlook), *supra* note 257, at 2.
[267] Hudson (Progress), *supra* note 7, at 16 and 18.
[268] Hudson (Progress), *supra* note 7, at 23.

task is the improvement of the method by which nations may consciously leg-
islate to enact international law."[269]

Hudson resolves his anxiety about how to cope with the quicksand of the
new terrain by rethinking of the philosophical foundations of international
law. These philosophical foundations required a 'divorce from religion'.[270]
Hudson cites frequently Elihu Root, Benjamin Cardozo, and Roscoe Pound
to demonstrate the need for legal scholarship to become emancipated from
theology, religion and any other mode of naturalist thinking. Any nexus
between one's approach to international law and Christianity, religion, the
law of nature, right reason, positive morality, or any such concept, is of
"doubtful utility".[271] Hudson includes in this category of naturalist thought
even those who consider consent, common consent, or any kind of "social
contract" as constituting the foundation of international law. For Hudson,
such concepts are a "mere substitute" of naturalist thought.[272] Foremost
among these concepts is what he saw as the absolute conception of sovereignty that prevailed in the past. The failure to develop a philosophy of law
divorced from naturalism bore negative consequences for international law,
Hudson claims. It prevented the development of an accepted theory of rights
and, in addition, it prevented international law from dealing with the circumstances that led to the Great War.[273] As a consequence, international
law needs to develop a new and sound philosophical basis. This will not be
an easy task, Hudson warns, but thankfully one that can take place over
time, with trial and error. What international law mostly needs is a direction
for enquiry rather than a complete set of answers. This direction can be
found in the study of human society. For Hudson, the law of nations must
seek contributions from history, political science, sociology, and keep pace
with the society that it serves. The international law of the twentieth century – Hudson cites again Pound and Cardozo to drive the point – "can only
result from 'a functional critique of international law in terms of social
ends'".[274] The starting point of the new way of thinking about public in-

---

[269] Hudson (Prospect), *supra* note 258, at 423 (footnotes omitted).
[270] Hudson (Prospect), *supra* note 258, at 423-436.
[271] Hudson (Prospect), *supra* note 258, at 428.
[272] Hudson (Prospect), *supra* note 258, at 429-430.
[273] Hudson (Prospect), *supra* note 258, at 430-431.
[274] Hudson (Prospect), *supra* note 258, at 435 and footnote 75.

ternational law is therefore the rejection of any theory or idea that prevents the science from being connected to its social basis.

Aside from rethinking the philosophical foundations of international law, the second urgent task is the elaboration of "new methods for the development of international law".[275] This second task should occur simultaneously with the first task and not wait for the development of a complete philosophical model before embarking on the practical reconstruction.

> "An attempt to construct a philosophy of law apart from its application in current life and affairs would almost certainly prove futile. It would result in the very unreality from which we seek to escape. Induction and deduction must proceed fairly evenly along parallel courses; we must live and move in a turgid stream of international events, and juristic development must ever follow its current. Time will not wait for any re-examination of the philosophical assumptions underlying our law of nations, and scant results would be yielded if it would. Our attention must be given to the methods of current development, therefore, at the same time that we are seeking to control its direction and purpose."[276]

The problem with the old sources of international law is that they were too dependent on sovereign will and thus they "negatived the possibility of promoting common action". The creation of the PCIJ changed all that and gave international law a new source of law (here Hudson refers to the inclusion of General Principles in the list of sources of Art. 38), which was "freed from the national character of court decisions in the past".[277] To make progress, international law needs to develop new methods of legislation ('international legislation') that would allow common action and common interests to be taken into account. The primary source in that direction is the codification of international law in the form of international agreements. The difference between the 'old' international law and this new form of law making is the joint participation of all states. This would allow the creation of rules that embody 'common interest'. To achieve the purpose of representing common interest and common action, these agreements should be the product of negotiation between many states along the lines of well-organized codification conferences.[278]

---

[275] Hudson (Prospect), *supra* note 258, at 436-459.
[276] Hudson (Prospect), *supra* note 258, at 436.
[277] Hudson (Prospect), *supra* note 258, at 437.
[278] Hudson (Prospect), *supra* note 258, at 441 et seq.

Finally, Hudson suggests that the reconstruction of international law has to be performed in a new spirit. In different parts of the text he reveals the properties of a new ethical posture to be adopted by the international lawyer. It involves pragmatism (solutions need to be based on the practical and contemporaneous needs of society and then be abandoned when they no longer serve the purpose), openness (detachment from any sort of fixed ideas, including the old philosophical traditions), communitarian spirit (thinking of the common interest instead of national interests), optimism, humility, but also boldness. In a characteristic passage he writes:

"New needs have come with the manifold changes in world society and new furrows may have to be plowed to meet them. We must have not only the patience and the detachment necessary to understand them, but also the boldness to make the departure which understanding may prompt us to undertake."[279]

## 3.3    TROPES OF RECONSTRUCTION

Interwar international law argument is a complex terrain. Rich and diverse stories can be told about the period and the various styles of argument that dominated professional communities on either side of the Atlantic. In that sense, interwar scholarship could not be adequately described by means of an epochal historical account that reduces that diversity into a flat common denominator. Without doubt, there are important scholars of the period, such as Hans Kelsen, Alf Ross, and others, whose work does not fit neatly within the picture. In addition, who can disagree that that the views of each author, like Seferiades in Chapter 2, are intertwined with personal-ideological projects and strategies and, in that sense, adding more layers in its interpretation. In this chapter, I merely wish to point to the existence of a specific discourse about the sources of international law, with recognizable patterns and structures of argument, which seems to revolve around specific anxieties as to what is "good" and "bad" international legal argument. The term 'sociological jurisprudence' is therefore used to refer to such recognizable patterns of argument of the interwar period.[280] The sociological

---

[279] Hudson (Prospect), *supra* note 258, at 422.

[280] What is referred to as interwar internationalist sociological style includes a broad alliance of scholars on both sides of the Atlantic who shared, despite many differences, a

'style' reflected to some extent voices in domestic law that demonstrated a similar rejection of foundationalism, conceptualism, and legal formalism.[281] Hudson's essay highlights some of the tropes of mainstream interwar argument that are relevant for our account of the sources. Despite their many differences, scholars of the sociological movement advocated in their writ-

---

similar style of argument. For the purposes of this analysis, the group would include Alejandro Álvarez, Léon Bourgeois, James Leslie Brierly, James Brown Scott, Léon Duguit, George Finch, Sir John Fischer Williams, Torsten Gihl, Manley Hudson, Joseph Kunz, Albert de Lapradelle, Hersch Lauterpacht, Sir Arnold McNair, Lassa Oppenheim, Nicolas Politis, Louis Renault, Georges Scelle, Stelios Seferiades, Charles de Visscher, and others. Voices that are partly or entirely in disagreement with this mainstream view continued to thrive, as will be explained below. See note 300 and accompanying text, *infra*. For the interwar sociological movement see Koskenniemi (Gentle Civilizer), *supra* note 65, at 266-412; D. Kennedy, 'International Law and the 19th Century: The History of an Illusion', 65 *Nordic Journal of International Law* (1996) 385; N. Berman, 'A Perilous Ambivalence: Nationalist Desire, Legal Autonomy, and the Limits of the Interwar Framework', 33 *Harvard International Law Journal* (1992) 353; E. Jouannet, 'La critique de la pensée classique durant l'entre les deux guerres: Vattel et van Vollenhoven: Quelques réflexions sue le modèle classique en droit international', in P. Kovacs, ed., *History in International Law: Historia ante Portas* (2005) 61-83; and E. Jouannet, 'Regards sur un siècle de doctrine française du droit international', 46 *Annuaire Français de Droit International* (2001) 1; S.J. Astorino, 'The Impact of Sociological Jurisprudence on International Law in the Interwar Period', 34 *Duquesne Law Review* (1996) 277; Landauer (Brierly), *supra* note 105; and the essays in F. Johns, T. Skouteris and W. Werner, eds., 'The Law and Periphery Series: Alejandro Álvarez', 19 *Leiden Journal of International Law* (2006) 875.

[281] For the relationship between international and domestic discourses in Continental Europe, see Koskenniemi (Gentle Civilizer), *supra* note 65, at 266-352. For the United States, primary candidate for such parallels would be the sociological jurisprudential movement exemplified by the writings of Oliver Wendell Holmes, Benjamin Cardozo, Roscoe Pound, and others. For the sociological movement in the USA, see G. Minda, *Post-Modern Legal Movements: Law and Jurisprudence at Century's End* (1995) at 13-43; see also the commentary of D. Kennedy and W. Fischer, *The Canon of American Legal Thought* (2006) at 19-26 and 47-51. The sociological movement is to be distinguished from the movement of American Legal Realism, of Karl Llewellyn, Wesley Hohfeld, Jerome Frank, Felix Cohen, Walter Wheeler Cook, Robert Hale, and others. Although American Legal Realism shared much of the claims of legal formalism made by the sociologists, they parted company in seeing the sociological movement as formalist in its own right, which failed, among other things, to take into account the complex and fluid nature of reality in rule interpretation and judicial decision making. The more radical strand of the realists went many steps further by seeking to expose the political context of both public and private law. For a classic account of American Legal Realism, see M. Horwitz, *The Transformation of American Law (1870-1960): The Crisis of Legal Orthodoxy* (1992); W.M. Fischer, M.J. Horwitz and T.A. Reed, eds., *American Legal Realism* (1993).

ings a pragmatic approach to law, which rejected what was described as the rationalist epistemology of 19<sup>th</sup> century thinking – the idea that law is a matter of formal reason, whose study can be exhausted in books and abstract logical argument. They favored a practical, functional understanding of truth and knowledge based on human experience and experimentation. They advocated a turn to the social sciences and scientific observation of society to retain the characterization of law as science, and despite their rejection of formalism.

Five narrative tropes, relevant to our purposes, are discerned in these interwar texts.[282]

### The war as the catalyst for reconstruction

*The first* trope is the use of the Great War as the surface against which the new beginning for international law could be projected. The War was seen as a catalyst and the starting point for reconstruction. Like Hudson, much of the interwar mainstream considers that the War, aside from putting an end to elements of progress previously attained, was a unique event that revealed the bankruptcy of the 'old' international law. Authors estimated that the prestige and credibility of international law was shattered by the atrocities committed in the course of the War and the repeated violation of legal rules so soon after the codification efforts of The Hague Peace Conferences of 1899 and 1907. International law's constraining ability was challenged, its ethical commitment questioned, its potential discredited.[283] At

---

[282] Hersch Lauterpacht, when discussing the work of James Leslie Brierly, identified five different "contributions" of Brierly to international law: "the rejection of positivism, the affirmation of the moral foundations of international law; the recognition of the individual as a subject of international law; the vindication of the unity of international and municipal law, and his criticism of the notion of the international sovereignty of the state"; H. Lauterpacht, 'Brierly's Contribution to International Law', 32 *British Yearbook of International Law* (1955-56) 1.

[283] Politis (Aspects), *supra* note 257, at 1; Herbert Smith wrote that "[u]pon the essential limitations of all such [pre-war] law-making the war itself threw vivid light. By this I do not mean that the rules so carefully drawn up were lightly broken or openly condemned, but that they were so dubiously worded that each belligerent might find in them authority for doing whatsoever he might desire to do"; H. Smith, 'International Law Making', 16 *Grotius Society Transactions* (1930) 93. Álvarez writes: "When the world war broke out, public opinion, overwhelmed and anguished by this event, and especially by the repeated violations of legal rules, believed that the law of nations had gone bankrupt, and many publicists shared this belief"; Álvarez (New International Law), *supra* note 27, at 36; A. Zimmern, *The*

the same time, in all its destructive effect, the Great War was seen as having created the space for the reconstruction of international law.[284] It awakened the legal profession, the story goes, and reminded it of its responsibility to take action.[285]

*The project for the reconstruction of international law*
A *second* trope is the urge to reconstruct international law in the ashes of the Great War. The theme of renewal, 'renaissance', rethinking, renovation, reconstruction of international law is central to interwar writing.[286] The idea was that international law should enter a new phase, a new step in its

---

*League of Nations and the Rule of Law 1918-1935* (1936) at 94-101; Walters, A History of the League of Nations, *supra* note 110, at 16.

[284] See, e.g., E.E.F. Descamps, 'Le droit international nouveau. L'influence de la condamnation de la guerre sur l'évolution juridique international', 31 *RCADI* (1930-I) 393; Álvarez (Necessity), *supra* note 257, at 2. Nippold warned that "[t]he science of international law is therefore not allowed to fold its hands idly, as it only too often has done. Instead of wearying itself with the Sisyphean labour of cleansing its own country of all guilt for violations of international law that may have occurred or instead of criticizing violations of international law on the part of enemies of its country [...] it will above all have to find its task in the deduction of useful applications from the lesson of this war for the future shaping of international law and in pointing out the way to nations for the future policy of international law"; Nippold (The Development of International Law After the World War), *supra* note 107, at 4. Politis writes: "A calmer, more dispassionate scrutiny of the situation brought the conviction that, far from being fatal to it, the trial that it [international law] had undergone, has been, in the end, a very good thing for international law; it had brought sharply into light certain changes which had already taken place [...]"; Politis (Aspects), *supra* note 257, at 1.

[285] E.g., Finch spoke of the "acid test of the World War in 1914" to which past conceptions of international law have submitted and proven insufficient; G. Finch, *The Sources of Modern International Law* (1937) 28. Nippold wrote that "this whole great war has really been nothing less than one great lesson for mankind"; Nippold (The Development of International Law After the World War), *supra* note 107, at 28.

[286] There is an abundance of sources advocating the necessity for a reconstruction of international law at the end of the war. Álvarez suggested that "the task that is now necessary is the reconstruction of this law", see Álvarez (New International Law), *supra* note 27, at 38; Brierly spoke of a "need of rehabilitation"; Brierly (Shortcomings of International Law), *supra* note 105, at 68. Politis writes: "Its [International law's] regeneration, bringing up to date, renovation, recasting on democratic principles and development"; Politis (Aspects), *supra* note 257, at 2; Nippold sought the future "reconstruction" of international law; Nippold (The Development of International Law After the World War), *supra* note 107, at 25.

evolution, and regenerate itself. Reconstruction was seen as consisting of two distinct moments: a "critical" and a "constructive" one.[287] The critical element was principally understood as a theoretical enquiry into the foundations and methods of international law, whereas the constructive part was seen as largely positive and practical, having to do with institutional and doctrinal modifications.[288] The literature was worried that a reconstruction project would run the risk of becoming overtly theoretical and therefore irrelevant. As consequence, theoretical work should be coupled with practical measures addressing the everyday, immediate needs of the international society.[289] The tasks of critique and construction therefore would need to take place simultaneously and in a complementary manner, even if this meant that some of the measures were only temporary.

*Critique of the philosophical foundations*
A *third* trope was the contention that "critique" has to begin by scrutinizing the foundations and methods of international law, as they existed before the War.[290] What was problematic with the foundations of the 'old' international law? International law, the story goes, had become too attached to theoretical constructions instead of observing the practice of states, became socially irrelevant and, thus, disempowered. Law became too separated from politics;[291] too dependent on national and sovereign political interest;[292] too invested in preventing war instead of fostering peace;[293] out of pace

---

[287] The division between a critical and a constructive component is widely reflected in the literature of the time. Álvarez (New International Law, *supra* note 27 at 41), for example uses the exact words to describe his project: "It includes two phases: that of criticism and that of construction". "[Le] travail de critique et de reconstitution du Droit International". Oppenheim argued that the new task for the science of international law is, first, to ascertain the existing rules and identify gaps in the existing law and, on that basis, then make de lege ferenda proposals for codification: Oppenheim (Future), *supra* note 257, at 57.

[288] Álvarez (New International Law), *supra* note 27, at 37 and 42.

[289] Álvarez (New International Law), *supra* note 27, at 40.

[290] See, e.g., J. Kunz, 'On the Theoretical Basis of the Law of Nations', 10 *Grotius Society Transactions* (1925) 115; W. Roemer, *The Ethical Basis of International Law* (1929); J.L. Brierly, 'Le fondement du charactère obligatoire du droit international', 23 *RCADI* (1928-III) 463.

[291] Álvarez (New International Law), *supra* note 27 at 37.

[292] Oppenheim (Future), *supra* note 257, at 17.

[293] Anonymous, 'The League of Nations and the Laws of War', 1 *British Yearbook of International Law* (1920-21) 109, at 115; A. Pearce Higgins, 'The Law of Peace', 4 *British Yearbook of International Law* (1923-24) 153, at 153.

with the evolution of the international society;[294] too rigid and detached from the practice of states.[295] Authors spoke of the need for the law to be able to accommodate "change" in international legal situations.[296] All these critiques led to the primary interwar concern, namely, the attachment of international law to theoretical rumination instead of pragmatic thinking, and especially to the traditions of naturalism and positivism, to which international law's failures were ascribed.[297] The critique was directed not against the two intellectual traditions as such, but against their extreme forms, which were presented in stark colors and in some cases even caricatured.[298] Authors were quick to confirm that they did not reject the essence of these traditions, which ought to be retained in a sensible way within legal argument.

The effect of the extreme conceptions of positivism and naturalism was three-fold. *First*, these conceptions made international law vulnerable to the so-called Austinian critique,[299] namely that international law is not really law proper because of the absence of a superior coercive authority. The Austinian challenge was empowered to challenge international law by the fact that neither of the two theories was able to adequately explain the basis of obligation. Extreme positivism[300] could not explain how law can be bind-

---

[294] Politis (Aspects), *supra* note 257, at 2-3.

[295] Álvarez (Necessity), *supra* note 257, at 2.

[296] T. Gihl, *International Legislation: An Essay on Changes in International Law and in International Legal Situations* (1937) at 77-135, suggests that international law has to find ways to include, handle and manage changes in international law and international legal situations. See also J.F. Williams, *International Change and International Peace* (1932), esp. at 1-5 and 15-20.

[297] The parallel rejection of the extreme forms of positivism and naturalism is one of the most common themes in interwar literature. See J.L. Brierly, *The Law of Nations – An Introduction to the International Law of Peace* (1936) at 1-18; Gihl (International Legislation), *supra* note 296, at 7-21; Williams (Aspects), *supra* note 11, at 59-75; Politis (Aspects), *supra* note 257, at 4-5. For an analysis of the positivist view only, see Lauterpacht (Private Law Sources), *supra* note 254, at 1-90; Oppenheim (Future), *supra* note 257, at 9-13.

[298] Álvarez writes that positivists "disdain systematic construction, general principles and theories, which seem to them abstract and dangerous things; they confine themselves to the study of concrete cases"; Álvarez (The New International Law), *supra* note 27, at 43.

[299] J. Austin, *The Province of Jurisprudence Determined* (1995), esp. Lectures I, V, and VI.

[300] The positivist works of Dionisio Anzilotti, Carl Bergbohm, Arrigo Cavaglieri, Georg Jellinek, Adolf Lasson, Heinrich Triepel, and, in later texts, Hans Kelsen, were the fre-

ing over entities whose essential nature is supposed to place them above the law. Similarly, naturalism in its extreme form[301] claimed that law binds because there is a moral duty to do so, while the principles of international law (e.g., equality, independence) could be inferred from the essential nature of the state. This understanding could not retain the autonomy of law from morality. When the basis of obligation in international law is declared to be an indemonstrable postulate, it presents itself as a mystery. It is no surprise, in this context, that international law of the time engaged in such vocal critiques of the traditional concept of sovereignty[302] and, for that matter, the PCIJ Judgment on the *Lotus* case.[303]

The *second* negative consequence was that, by consuming itself in the effort to meet the doubt of its deficiency and craft a credible theoretical model that could explain international law's existence to the skeptics, the science became detached from the everyday practice of international law, fell asleep at the wheel and failed to attend to the needs of the international community. Failure to understand the current needs of the international community distanced academic theory from the everyday practice of states. The body of norms of international law became superseded and ill equipped to attain the ends for which it was established.

The *third* (related) effect was that the extreme conceptions of positivism and naturalism legitimized reckless state behavior, leading ultimately to the causes of the Great War. Extreme positivism, in failing to provide an explanation about how international law can bind sovereign states against their will, became the pretext for the disregard of the rights of other states. By

---

quently cited examples of this view. For criticisms of this view see, in particular, H. Lauterpacht, *The Function of Law in the International Community* (1933) at 415 et seq.; Brierly (Le Fondement du caractère obligatoire du droit international), *supra* note 290, at 484 et seq.

[301] Samuel Pufendorf and Emer de Vattel were primary among the authors identified with this version of extreme naturalism.

[302] E.g., W.R. Bisschop, 'Sovereignty', 2 *British Yearbook of International Law* (1921-22) 122.

[303] *Lotus* case, PCIJ Ser. A, No. 10 (1927). For some criticism, see J.L. Brierly, 'The Lotus Case', in Lauterpacht (Brierly), *supra* note 105; L. Cavaré, 'L'arrêt du "Lotus" et le positivisme juridique', 10 *Travaux juridiques et economiques de l'Université de Rennes* (1930) 144; A. Steiner, 'Fundamental Conceptions of International Law in the Jurisprudence of the Permanent Court of International Justice', 30 *American Journal of International Law* (1936) 414.

the same token, in naturalism it was impossible to point to an authentic text for the law without a contesting interpretation, creating indeterminacy and the room to legitimize any contention of what is a natural right.

The answer was to be found in the rethinking of the philosophical foundations of the law and, more concretely, the basis of its obligation. The goal was to side-step the problem of high theory entirely, while at the same time being able to provide a convincing answer to the Austinian critique. The solution in these texts was a turn to pragmatism. For interwar scholars, international law exists as a social product, as a 'pure fact', which we have become conscious of through observation.[304] Concepts (and law) must represent reality. Despite different expressions and emphasis, many interwar authors shake hands in the contention that international law needs to liberate itself from the tyranny of finding an impregnable explanation about its basis of obligation and, instead, turn towards more useful enquiries. Those who contest international law's existence, the story goes, are mostly theorists. States and statesmen, who use international law in their everyday life, rarely deny its existence. If there is a final answer to be found on the question of the basis of obligation, it is for legal philosophy and not for international law to find it. For Álvarez, on the question of the basis of obligation the lawyer is entitled to take a pragmatic standpoint: "the international lawyer needs no special explanation of the obligatory force of international law, beyond the explanation, whatever it may be, of the obligatory force of law in general.[305] Torsten Gihl explains the legal phenomenon as the product of "complex forces actually at work".[306] If there should be an obligation to obey international law, this obligation should not come out of any theoretical acrobatism trying to force a coherent explanation on the basis of the concept of sovereignty or the law of nature. It must be moral in character.[307] In one of the most classical statements of this view, Brierly writes:

---

[304] For an analysis of how interwar literature dealt with the 'Austinian' question, see Kennedy (History of an Illusion), *supra* note 280.

[305] Álvarez had addressed the matter in a number of publications. In addition to the texts already mentioned, see also A. Álvarez, 'New Conception and New Bases of Legal Philosophy', 13 *Illinois Law Review* (1918-19) 167, at 179 and 181. For a review of Álvarez's idea of the basis of obligation, see W. Samore, 'The New International Law of Alejandro Álvarez', 52 *American Journal of International Law* (1958) 41. See also Johns, Skouteris and Werner (Alvarez), *supra* note 280.

[306] Gihl (International Legislation), *supra* note 296, at 19.

[307] Brierly (Fondement), *supra* note 290, at 546 et seq.

"There need to be no mystery about the source of the obligation to obey international law. The same problem arises in any system of law and it can never be solved by a merely juridical explanation. The answer must be sought outside the law, and it is for legal philosophy to provide it. The notion that the validity of international law raises some peculiar problem arises from the confusion which the doctrine of sovereignty has introduced into international legal theory."[308]

*Elaboration of methods for the development of the law*
A *fourth* trope in the literature is the contention that the "constructive" moment of the new international law should clarify the legal methods for the development of the law and by creating more determinate legal obligations. The term frequently used to refer to this activity was "legislation" or "international legislation"[309] and the method par excellence for its attainment was codification.[310] Although codification was used as a term of art across the literature, different ideas about codification were underlying this common vocabulary. Some saw codification as a scientific enterprise, to be executed by trained, independent international law professionals in their individual capacity. Others saw codification as an exercise to be performed by sovereign states in duly organized diplomatic conferences. Some suggested that codification should solely aim at the transcription into written form of norms that already existed as customary international law. Others

---

[308] Brierly (Law of Nations), *supra* note 297, at 44-45.
[309] Gihl (International Legislation), *supra* note 296, at 1; Hudson (Prospect), *supra* note 258, at 436 et seq.
[310] From the large body of literature on codification in the period, see F. Gahan, 'The Codification of Law', 8 *Transactions of the Grotius Society* 107 (1922); P.J. Baker, 'The Codification of International Law', 5 *British Yearbook of International Law* (1924) 38, at 40; C. de Visscher, 'La Codification du droit international', 6 *RCADI* (1925-I) 325; E. Root, 'The Codification of International Law', 19 *American Journal of International Law* (1925) 671; S. Cole, 'Codification of International Law', 12 *Grotius Society Transactions* (1927) 49; J.B. Scott, 'The Gradual and Progressive Codification of International Law', 21 *American Journal of International Law* (1927) 417; A. McNair, 'The Present Position of the Codification of International Law', 13 *Grotius Society Transactions* (1928) 129; F.-J. Urrutia, 'La codification du droit international en Amérique', 22 *RCADI* (1928-II) 81; J.L. Brierly, 'The Future of Codification', 12 *British Yearbook of International Law* (1931) 2; A. Álvarez, 'Impressions Left by the First Hague Conference for the Codification of International Law', 16 *Grotius Society Transactions* 121 (1931); Smith (International Law-Making), *supra* note 283; M. Sibert, 'Quelques aspects de l'organisation et la technique des conférences internationales', 48 *RCADI* (1934-II) 387.

favored the modification of existing rules in order to reconcile conflicting views and make agreement possible. Others suggested progressive development or even the development of entirely new rules. Jurists of a civil law background were thought of as more enthusiastic about codification than those of common law background, allegedly due to the fact that the former were more accustomed to codes.[311] It was scholars in the Americas, however, who got a head start with codification efforts.[312] General consensus was formed around the idea that codification, in the general sense of the creation of written texts containing binding international law rules, was the desirable way forward.[313] Another common denominator between the different angles was the conviction that codification should not aim at drafting a complete 'code' of public international law but rather at the gradual and progressive codification of areas 'ripe' for the purpose, either because of 'common purpose' to be found among states and/or already existing adequate practice and principles.[314] Elihu Root writes:

"As a declaration of war brings to the soldier the opportunity for which his life has been in preparation, so this call [for codification] from both sides of

---

[311] See, e.g., comments in McNair (Present Position), *supra* note 310, at 130.

[312] Two major codification projects dominated the 1920s in the opposite sides of the Atlantic. On the one hand, there was the codification effort commissioned to the American Institute of International Law by the Pan-American Union. This resulted in 30 codification projects that were discussed in Rio de Janeiro in 1927. The text of these projects was published in a Supplement to the *American Journal of International Law* (Special Number, 1926) at 300-387; and Codification du Droit International (Pan-American Union, 1925 and 1926). For a review of these efforts, see Scott (Gradual and Progressive Codification), *supra* note 310. On the other, there was the League of Nations. On 22 September 1924, the Assembly of the League adopted a Resolution whereby the Council was requested to convene a committee, later to be known as "Committee of Experts for the Progressive Codification of International Law", with the mandate to identify a list of subjects and areas ripe for codification. This effort led to the First Hague Conference for the Codification of International Law, which took place from 13 March – 12 April 1930. See the multi-volume publication by S. Rosenne, ed., *Conference for the Codification of International Law* [1930] (1975), esp. the Editor's Foreword, at viii-lvi; for another appraisal, see Álvarez (Impressions), *supra* note 310.

[313] Scott exclaims that "codification is the order of the day"; Scott (Progress), *supra* note 257, at 11; McNair speaks of a "desire", even a "craving" for codification; McNair (Present Position), *supra* note 310, at 130; Cole (Codification), *supra* note 310, at 51, speaks of "widespread demand".

[314] Oppenheim (Future), *supra* note 257, at 23-24; Scott (Progress), *supra* note 257, at 10; Williams (Aspects), *supra* note 11, at 54; Politis (Aspects), *supra* note 257, at 70-71.

the Atlantic presents the occasion for which all these societies, learned in international law, exist. It is for such an opportunity as this that they have been preparing, some of them for seventy years past. Now is their time to justify. Of course they will justify with ardor and devotion, and there will be no more avoidable delay, no more hesitation."[315]

A strong connection was forged between codification and the PCIJ.[316] It was the Advisory Committee of Jurists that drafted the PICJ Statute that submitted the first-ever official proposal to the League of Nations to begin a codification project.[317] In addition, and although many authors were quick to underline that the new international law should not emulate the structure of domestic legal systems, many saw that some version of the classical model of the division of powers of the liberal state should and could apply to international law as well. The establishment of the Permanent Court created, at least formally, the first international court with potentially universal appeal. The general view was that the new World Court should have some kind of 'world law' at its disposal. Codification was one of the ways to achieve rules of potentially universal application and a common, or universal international law.[318]

"We end as we started, in a wilderness of divergence and a conflict of right and duty and interpretation. The common law of nations requires a common code, and a common code is the result of a conference, discussion, agreement

---

[315] Root (Codification), *supra* note 310, at 684.

[316] The role of the PCIJ in the interwar equation is a complex topic that would require a separate study to do justice to its complexity. For an interesting recent assessment, see O. Spiermann, *International Legal Argument in the Permanent Court of International Justice: The Rise of the International Judiciary* (2005).

[317] See Rosenne (Conference for the Codification of International Law), *supra* note 312.

[318] Root (Codification), *supra* note 310, at 678-679. Scott writes: "The multilateral treaty is a recognition of a unity of interest on the part of the international community. The Permanent Court of International Justice is a recognition of the unity of the international community and of the necessity of a single and universal interpretation of each and every obligation arising under a treaty and the common law of nations"; Scott (Progress), *supra* note 257, at 9. Álvarez wrote that the solution to the theoretical uncertainty of the past may be the establishment of "uniformity of views concerning the most essential principles of international law"; Álvarez (New International Law), *supra* note 27, at 45; Oppenheim (Future), *supra* note 257, at 15-17.

upon the content, as well as the form of each of its articles, with an agency for their interpretation and application which, fortunately for us, exists at The Hague."[319]

The nexus between codification and progress in international law now begins to emerge. The contention was that the development of new rules to regulate previously unregulated areas of international practice would prevent future setbacks, what Brierly appositely called the "annexation" of matters within the domain of international law.[320] Not only would the presence of 'new law' regulate the conduct of states and limit their reserved domain. Law produced via the process of codification was also seen as more likely to restrain states than customary law, by virtue of the fact that it would be the product of conscious, scientific labor, as opposed to law ascertained in retrospect from the conduct of states.[321] The strict procedural rules of codification conferences would harness sovereign power into civilized debate, where equality of states would prevail over power disparity. Conferences would produce law, the story goes, that is crafted with the consent of all civilized states and with universal application. It would thus be law that is not produced abstractly, that is to say based on some prefabricated theories and explanations about law (such as the theories of positivism and naturalism), but law made to address the current needs of the international community.[322] As one commentator wrote characteristically, with codification

"[…] law is scientifically examined. It is rational, coherent, modern, obsolete law is removed, efficient rules substituted for inefficient."[323]

The codification rhetoric of the time paved the road for the development of a second generation of doctrines that allowed the new treaties to operate effectively. In order to ensure that treaties would not become obsolete,

---

[319] Scott (Progress), *supra* note 257, at 10.

[320] Brierly (Law of Nations), *supra* note 297, at 54.

[321] Oppenheim (Future), *supra* note 257, at 23 and 33, writes that "international law must no longer be left to mere chance" and what is needed is "conscious creation of law in contrast to the growth of law out of custom"; Root (Codification), *supra* note 310, at 681.

[322] Álvarez sees codification as a practical (and thus not theoretical) exercise; Álvarez (New International Law), *supra* note 27, at 45.

[323] Gahan (Codification), *supra* note 310, at 112.

mechanisms for the revision and secondary doctrines (e.g., on reservations or interpretation) would have to accompany codification.[324] Clarity on the topic of the sources was an imperative condition for progress. Corbett writes:

> "The movement towards general codification is gathering force, and it is not quite inconceivable that the widespread confusion in relation to the various ideas connoted by the word 'source' may manifest itself in an equal uncertainty as to what are the rules to be codified?"[325]

This is the promise of codification:

> "If only we succeeded in the clear enunciation of legal rules for all international relations; if only we could succeed in finding independent and unbiased men to whose judgment a state could confidently submit its cause; if only we could succeed in bringing such men together in an independent international court – there would be no reason why the great majority of states should not follow the example of the very small minority which has already agreed to settle all possible disputes by means of arbitration."[326]

If only ... Enthusiasm with codification was proven to be short-lived. By the mid-1930s the codification projects of the League of Nations and the Pan-American Union were proclaimed unsuccessful and the literature adopted a more pensive and ruminating tone.[327] The turn to caution did not dislodge the initial commitment in the core idea that 'international legislation' by means of codification was an essential step for the development of international law.

It was in this context that the possibility of a doctrine of sources started getting traction in international law argument: the idea of a closed list of law-making methods that can operate on a level or register that is indepen-

---

[324] Some authors were worried that codification would bring rigidity to the law, Baker (Codification), *supra* note 310, at 46 et seq.; de Visscher (Codification), *supra* note 310, at 386 et seq.

[325] P.E. Corbett, 'The Consent of States and the Sources of the Law of Nations', 6 *British Yearbook of International Law* (1925) 20, at 21.

[326] Oppenheim (Future), *supra* note 257, at 14.

[327] Álvarez (Impressions), *supra* note 310; Brierly (Future of Codification), *supra* note 310; Smith (International Law-Making), *supra* note 283; Gihl (International Legislation), *supra* note 296, at 64-73.

dent from theoretical rumination about the basis of obligation in public international law. This would help create the new common code of humanity on a manner based both on the consent of states and scientific observation, but without the pitfalls of high theory. To this we will return in a second.

*The new spirit*
There is finally *a fifth* trope, characteristic of interwar writing, which relates to the 'spirit' with which the project of the reconstruction of international law should be undertaken. Some authors understand this spirit as a state of mind, others as an ethical posture, or a method or approach to international law. Either way, for the interwar authors under review, it seems that it is not enough to get the principles of the new international law right – it also matters how you do it. The theme common to the literature is that the end of the Great War became a catalyst for the creation of such a new spirit whose guidance would be indispensable in order to achieve its objectives. Alejandro Álvarez, one of the champions of the psychological transformation of international law, wrote:

> "Furthermore, almost overnight there came into being a new psychology, a new mentality, a new ideology, the fruit of new circumstances and environment, as well as of new political, philosophic and social concepts; they repudiate many ideas and doctrines which were until then accepted without question."[328]

The psychological dimension of the new spirit involved a turn to optimism, modesty, and courage in the discharge of one's professional activities. The ethical dimension involved assuming personal responsibility for change, becoming personally and consciously engaged in the task of reconstruction, without complacency or dependency on prefabricated ideas. One should not only modernize and innovate, but also take the lead and invent.[329] On the methodological level, it involved the use of 'scientific' method in international law. Oppenheim suggests that this new approach to law involves four distinct aspects.[330] First, a positive approach, in the sense of giving up on the deductive methods of the natural sciences and adopting an inductive

---

[328] Álvarez (New International Law), *supra* note 27, at 37.
[329] Álvarez (New International Law), *supra* note 7, at 42.
[330] Oppenheim (Future), *supra* note 257, at 56 et seq.

approach based on close observation of the facts, as well as the identification of sociological, psychological, or other factors that are necessary in
order to make accurate inductions.[331] Second, the approach would have to
be 'impartial', in the sense of being free from the bias and animosity of
national politics. Third, it would have to be free from the 'domination of
phrases'. Here interwar scholars refer to their perception of the 'old' international law maxims and concepts which were portrayed as derived directly from the grand theories of naturalism and positivism instead of the
positive practice of states – "fanciful doctrines instead of rules of law", as
Oppenheim adds. Finally, the approach would have to be international in
terms of research and analysis, in the sense of taking aboard literature, practice and concepts that are not derived solely from one's intellectual tradition but from the ones of other states as well. A new spirit craving for reform,
re-conceptualization, transition to a "new" world order.

*A narrative of progress*
The five tropes of the interwar scholarship create a narrative of progress
that constructs a privileged ground for a new doctrine of the sources to
thrive.

*First*, a rejection of the foundationalism and formalism of what they perceived as the legal tradition of the previous centuries.[332] David Kennedy
explains how, in rejecting the traditions of naturalism and positivism, the
interwar project rejected in fact an "illusion" of the 'old' international law
of the 19th century. For Kennedy the inter-war project is a modern, rationalist project of "renewal through recollection" to explain how international
law was possible in a world of sovereign states. This was a project that
understood itself in philosophical battle with doubt, in argument against
legal order denial. How was law possible in a world of politics? Kennedy
argues that the Austinian challenge was actually "backdated" to the 19th
century. For Kennedy, it is only in the first half of the 20th century that the
Austinian question really perplexed the profession, and not at the end of the
19th century, as it was being argued at the time. Connecting interwar inter-

---

[331] E.C. Stowell, *International Law: A Restatement of Principles in Conformity with
Actual Practice* (1931); D. Schindler, 'Contribution à l'étude des facteurs sociologiques et
psychologiques du droit international', 46 *RCADI* (1933-IV) 229.
[332] Kennedy (History of an Illusion), *supra* note 280.

national law with the arrival of modernity, Kennedy claims that the anxiety about international law's possibility in a world of politics was much more a product of the 20th century. It is then that a "responsive theoretical tradition of positivism is elaborated, that naturalism can be seen as its natural, if unsatisfactory antagonist". After 1918 international lawyers felt the urgent need to develop a new polemic for international cosmopolitanism and they did so in part by re-interpreting the traditions of 19th century international law "as alter egos to their newly pragmatic sensibility". Only in the modern era would international law be anxious enough about its status and existence to reject philosophy, sovereignty and formalism so soundly, or to create them. For Kennedy, the 19th century we remember is largely "an aftershock of modernity's own violent arrival": "it is in this sense that international lawyers leave the 20th century clutching the memory of an illusion". It seems that the modernism, pragmatism, and progressivism of today's international law is more rhetorical effect and political claim than historical achievement, and more part of the field's internal dynamic than an artifact of a distant era: "Only by shooting its rapids can international lawyers become successful polemicists for the new. In this century international law has become a discipline of persuasion, its doctrines and institutions harnessed to narratives of progress toward the international, a place figured both as practical and as humane".

In international law, the 'critical' moment of the reconstruction project, i.e., the rejection of the grand theories of positivism and naturalism, created the necessary space for international jurists to imagine the possibility disconnecting the registers of practical application of a doctrine of the sources from 'high theory'. This double rejection tries to decouple sources theory from the question of the basis of obligation in international law. The foundational questions of the discipline (how can international law be 'law-proper' in the absence of a superior authority; what is the basic norm? etc.) were set aside or thrusted beyond the realm of necessary/relevant enquiry for everyday life. The practicing lawyer could now work with international law without having to reckon with such questions or, worse, having to take sides. The profession became liberated from the tyranny of explaining its own existence and could thus turn its attention to other matters.

The question of law-creation and law-ascertainment, the dual mission of the sources doctrine, was now to be determined not by recourse to theory but by some other new test, which would appear determinate, pragmatist, scientific, all at the same time. It is suggested here that the doctrine of the sources offered such a style of argument that claimed to be determinate, pragmatist, and scientific, able resolve the important question of law-creation/ascertainment while steering clear of the reefs of 'high theory'.

*Second*, the rejection of the extreme versions of positivism and naturalism permitted the new international law of the interwar period an uncanny eclecticism:[333] on the one hand, the right to keep the 'useful' components of positivism and naturalism, while on the other, not having to worry about how to connect them into a model that would necessarily stand the test of internal or external critique. The 'useful' component of positivism was the central role of the sovereign *voluntas* in lawmaking. New international rules would be irrelevant unless they remained grounded in sovereignty – anyway the point was not to reduce the role of the state in law making. The target was the caricatured extreme conception of sovereignty and theoretical discourse about the basis of obligation, not the role of the state in the development of rules. Thus, codification projects performed by professional lawyers and/or conferences with wide participation by all nations of the world would allow for the creation of treaty norms representing common, as opposed to individual or sovereign, interests, while being the product of sovereign will. Naturalism, on the other hand, pointed out the need to embed the law in morality and values that would prevent atrocities such as the ones committed during the Great War. International law should not only be a 'self-sufficient' body of consensually created rules. The addition of "General Principles of Law Recognized by Civilized Nations" in the list of sources of Article 38, as explained later in this chapter, would be able to at least partly cater for this need.

Any incompatibility between the positivist and naturalist elements in the doctrine would be resolved, one imagines, by some kind of benevolent coexistence or complementarity, managed by the skill of the international lawyer. The coexistence is justified by pragmatism (one needs both) and supported by faith in the capacity of the international law professional to manage this co-existence, with one eye fixed on the practice of states and

---

[333] The effort of successive generations of international lawyers to construct a model of international law simultaneously based on sovereign consent (concreteness) and normatively derived standards (normativity) has been explained beautifully in Koskenniemi (From Apology to Utopia), *supra* note 65.

the other on the future. Consequently one could accept different sources of international law derived either from consensual or non-consensual processes, without being troubled by the theoretical impurity of such an endeavor, and as long as the sources would serve the purposes of the new project of the reconstruction of international law. The doctrine of the sources, in this context, appears to offer a language, a style of legal argument able to accommodate both intellectual traditions, held together by the authority of Article 38 PCIJ Statute. Positivists would be pleased with the central role of consent-based sources, such as international treaties and, to a lesser extent, custom. Those leaning towards naturalism or the sociological approach would rejoice in the inclusion of general principles. Custom served both to deny the anarchy of extreme positivism and, at the same time, guarantee a process based on sovereign will. Custom thus presented a category onto which interwar scholars could project their fantasies of a naturally harmonious society capable of progress and growth but saved from the tyranny of the sovereign state.

*Third*, the 'constructive' moment of the new international law project, with its emphasis on new forms of law-making, brought new attention to the question of clarifying the forms and law-making processes of international law as such. Although much of the debate revolved around codification and the enhanced role of international treaties, interwar international law forged a strong link between legal determinacy and progress. Clearer norms and law-making methods would bring legal certainty, improve the binding force of rules and allow their better application by the Permanent Court of International Justice. The emphasis on international treaties was accompanied by the rise of a new body of specialized literature, devoted to technical aspects of treaties, for the first time in international law.[334]

Before we turn to the 'vocabulary of progress" of the sources doctrine, a brief digression to the drafting of Article 38 PCIJ Statute and its impact on the scholarship of the time is necessary.

---

[334] See, e.g., A. McNair, 'The Function and Differing Legal Character of Treaties', 11 *British Yearbook of International Law* (1930) 99; C.J.B. Hurst, 'The Effect of War on Treaties', 2 *British Yearbook of International Law* (1921-22) 37.

## 3.4    ARTICLE 38 AS PROGRESS

The story of the adoption of the Statute of the PCIJ and Article 38 in particular is often told and well documented.[335] In a few words, the chronicle of events could be recounted as follows. Article 14 of the Covenant of the League of Nations directed the Council of the League to formulate and submit to the members of the League plans for the establishment of a Permanent Court of International Justice. On February 12, 1920 the Council of the League adopted the suggestion of appointing an Advisory Committee of Jurists to prepare a plan for the establishment of the Court. The Committee was eventually composed by ten members, supplemented by James Brown Scott, who acted as legal adviser of Elihu Root. The Committee met in the Hague on June 16, 1920 and elected Baron Descamps (Belgium) as President, Bernard Loder (The Netherlands) as Vice-President, and Dionisio Anzilotti (Italy) as Secretary General. The mandate of the Advisory Committee of Jurists included the entire range of topics related to the organization, structure, and functioning of the Court, including the number and manner of appointment of the Judges, the seat of the Court, its rules of procedure and applicable law, the nature of its jurisdiction, and so on. Léon Bourgeois, delegated by the Council of the League to inaugurate the work of the Committee, summoned the Committee to its task with the following words:

> "Gentlemen, you are about to give life to the judicial power of humanity. Philosophers and historians have told us the laws of the growth and decadence of Empires. We look to you, gentlemen, for the laws that will assure the perpetuity of the only empire that never can decay, the empire of justice, which is the expression of eternal truth."[336]

This Herculean task had to be completed in no more than six weeks, between June 16 and July 24, 1920. In 35 sessions the Committee managed to draft, revise, and submit to the Council a preliminary text that eventually became, with only minor modifications, the final text of the Statute. On

---

[335]  Procès-verbaux of the Proceedings of the Committee, 16 June – 24 July 1920, with Annexes (1920).

[336]  Speech of Léon Bourgeois before the Advisory Committee of Jurists, 16 June 1920, as cited in A. Sanchez de Bustamante, *The World Court* (1925) at 97.

December 13, 1920, the Assembly of the League of Nations approved the Statute[337] and three days later, on December 16, the Protocol containing the Statute was opened for signature.[338] Within a year 46 states signed the Protocol, 26 of which deposited their ratifications within the same period. The election of the Judges took place in September 1921 and the Court was able to have its official inauguration on February 15, 1922. The League embarked on the project of a Court with the conviction that this was an unprecedented legal and political achievement that signified a new era for international relations, a place where nobody else has been before. In that ceremony, Sir Eric Drummond, the first Secretary General of the League, pronounced:

> "At last an international judicial organ has been established which is entirely free of political influences and absolutely independent of any political assembly in its deliberations."[339]

Even a cursory look at the *Procès-verbaux* of the Advisory Committee gives the impression of a group of jurists that worked under tremendous time-pressure but in a collegial spirit. The question of what are the rules that the Court must apply entered the debate during the 13th Session of the Committee and was discussed in only three sessions, between July 1st and 3rd 1920.[340] The President, Baron Descamps, presented an initial proposal that formed the basis of the debate.[341] It became immediately evident that the question of the rules to be applied by the Court was intricately connected to questions about the basis of obligation, the nature of international law, and the role of judicial institutions – questions that, not surprisingly, could not be answered unanimously by the members of the Committee. The range of views corresponded roughly to the broad disciplinary alignments of the

---

[337] Resolution concerning the Establishment of a Permanent Court of International Justice, Assembly of the League of Nations (13 December 1920).

[338] Protocol of Signature of the Statute of the Permanent Court of International Justice provided for by Art. 14 of the Covenant of the League of Nations with a text of this Statute, signed at Geneva, 16 December 1920 (in force 20 August 1921); 6 *League of Nations Treaty Series* 379.

[339] As cited in Sanchez de Bustamante (The World Court), *supra* note 336, at 111.

[340] Procès-verbaux, *supra* note 335, at 293-338.

[341] Annex 3 of the Procès-verbaux, *supra* note 335, at 306.

time on both sides of the Atlantic.[342] 'Positivists', 'naturalists' and those of the 'sociological school' re-stage in the *Procès-verbaux* some of the standard disagreements of the time about the nature of international law and the function of an international tribunal. For some, the rules to be applied became a question of whether the list should limit itself to 'positive law' or whether other rules should be included as well. Others wondered whether the Court should only apply existing law or develop or "ripen" new rules with its decisions. Others raised the question of *non liquet*, of whether the Court should decline to decide if no positive rule of law exists on the matter or whether it should rely on non-positive law for its judgment.

The Committee was divided on these 'hard' questions. The additional parameter was of course the role and the function of the first permanent international court in history and speculations about how its Statute should be drafted in order to achieve maximum endorsement by as many states as possible. Phillimore and Root, for example, expressed strong reservations about the proposal to extend the list of the rules that the Court should apply beyond "positive law", by which they referred primarily to international treaties and "statutes".[343] It was feared that states would hesitate to accept the jurisdiction of a Court that may apply rules to which states have not explicitly expressed their consent to and that for that reason the Court should be limited to applying law already in force. Others suggested that the Court has the duty to "develop" or "ripen" new law,[344] that equity and justice need to become part of the decision making process[345] and that the Court must have the freedom to apply principles to fill the gaps in existing law.[346] Descamps refuted concerns that the idea of justice varied from country to country by suggesting that this is not true "when it concerns the fundamental law of justice and injustice deeply engraved on the heart of every human being and which is given its highest and most authoritative expression in the legal conscience of civilized nations".[347]

---

[342] Members of the Committee acknowledged this in their statements. See, e.g., statement of Phillimore, Procès-verbaux, *supra* note 335, at 315.

[343] Statement by Root, Procès-verbaux, *supra* note 335, at 293-294; Statement by Phillimore, Procès-verbaux, *supra* note 335, at 295.

[344] Statement by Loder, Procès-verbaux, *supra* note 335, at 294.

[345] Statement by de Lapradelle, Procès-verbaux, *supra* note 335, at 295.

[346] Statement by Hagerup, Procès-verbaux, *supra* note 335, at 296.

[347] Procès-verbaux, *supra* note 335, at 310-311.

The division culminated with the question of whether to include General Principles of law in the list of rules, as the President Descamps suggested in his initial proposal. The deadlock persisted until the third day, when the solution proposed by the President managed to receive the support of all sides.[348] With the exception of Root and Phillimore, all other members of the Committee seemed willing at the end to accept a formulation that would include a reference to general principles of law, albeit as applicable only when no international convention or customary law could be found.[349] Root and Phillimore eventually consented out of "conciliatory spirit".[350] The role of the President seems to have been catalytic in achieving this outcome, as evidenced in his speech to the members:

> "Let us therefore no longer hesitate – I would put in this appeal all the ardour and all the foresight that my mind as a jurisconsult gives me – to insert, amongst the principles to be followed by the judge in the solution of the dispute submitted to him, the law of objective justice, at any rate in so far as it has a twofold confirmation of the concurrent teachings of jurisconsults of authority and the public conscience of civilized nations.
>
> On the threshold of the Palace of Peace where we meet daily there is a mosaic bearing the inscription *Sol Justitiæ Illustra Nos*. Let us draw inspiration and encouragement from this, and let us recognize that the conception of justice and injustice as indelibly written on the hearts of civilized peoples, and with the two additional guarantees I would give it, is not only the element *par excellence* making for progress in international law, but an indispensable complement to the application of the law, and as such essential to the judge for the performance of the great task entrusted to him."[351]

Consensus was reached on July 3, 1920. Article 38 survived the dissolution of the PCIJ to become Article 38(1) of the Statute of the ICJ the way we know it today with only minor modifications.[352] The adoption of Article 38 was welcomed as a moment of progress by international lawyers of the time. It was received with relief and hope that it will signify a new era in international law by virtue of three main reasons. First, because it ended

---

[348] Procès-verbaux, *supra* note 335, at 334 et seq.
[349] Statement by Ricci-Busatti, Procès-verbaux, *supra* note 335, at 318.
[350] Statement by de Lapradelle, Procès-verbaux, *supra* note 335, at 334.
[351] Speech by Baron Descamps, Procès-verbaux, *supra* note 335, at 324-325.
[352] *Supra* note 251.

what was perceived as an 'embarrassing uncertainty' about the sources of international law. Article 38, the story goes, brought important clarity and determinacy in the question of the law-making processes of international law. Second, because it would contribute to the quality of the judgments of the PCIJ and increase the legitimacy of the institution. Third, because it acknowledged the important role of general principles of law, which symbolized the corrective normative standards of justice, reason, equity and so on, which would prevent formalism in the application of the law. Hersch Lauterpacht writes in his classic monograph on *Private Law Sources and Analogies*:

"Concluding, as it does, a chapter of embarrassing uncertainty as to the sources of the law to be applied by international tribunals, it [Article 38] is most instructive from many points of view. It signifies the final and authoritative abandonment of the misleading doctrine that international law is a self-sufficient body of rules. The discussions conducted in this subject by the members of the Committee of Jurists charged with the drafting of the Statute show clearly that the authors of the draft were conscious of the importance of the rule adopted ultimately by the Committee. What, until now, was done spontaneously by individual arbitrators and in individual arbitration conventions, received here the sanction of practically the whole family of nations. What was, until now, exposing international arbitration to the reproach that it was not judicial, has here been included as a source of decision of the international judicial tribunal par excellence."[353]

Fischer Williams writes in another passage:

"[Before 1920] There was no established permanent court of international law; the lawyer advising a client, perhaps the government of his own country in the guise of a client, was often quite uncertain whether the matter in question would ever be referred to a tribunal at all; if it was to be referred to a tribunal, he had no knowledge of how that tribunal was likely to be constituted, and he might not even be sure what were the sources to which that tribunal was likely to appeal of the determination of the legal points at issue. The Institution of the Permanent Court of International Justice *has changed all this. We now have it laid down, by the authority of all states which have*

---

[353] Lauterpacht (Private Law Sources), *supra* note 254, at 67-68.

*become parties to the Statute of that Court, what are the sources of interna-
tional law.* [...]
Many international lawyers of outstanding eminence and authority might
have drafted this article differently had they been called on to do so in 1920,
but nevertheless it stands as the text of capital importance, *the solid basis of
rock on which the fabric of international law has to be built.*"[354]

The adoption of Article 38 is the founding moment of sources discourse as
we know it today. It signalled a gradual albeit profound transformation in
the way the entire concept of law-making was in the literature and practice
thereafter. This transformation, part and parcel with the general transformation of international law during the interwar period, did not take place
overnight but progressively and in steady pace. By the mid-1930s the majority of textbooks of public international law in most countries adopted
Article 38 as the standard starting point of a description of lawmaking in
international law.

## 3.5    THE VOCABULARY OF PROGRESS OF THE SOURCES

The emergence of the doctrine of the sources is best explained by pointing
to its 'vocabulary of progress', a set of narrative moves that are common to
the literature of the time. These moves are not only symptomatic of sources
discourse. They are also enabling moves since they actively create the discursive space for the doctrine to be accepted as an element of progress by
the mainstream view. They are grounded in the five tropes of the interwar
reconstruction project recounted above but, much more concretely, they
carve out the specific traits of a new style of argument about law-creation
and law-ascertainment. The narrative moves tell a before/after story, about
how international law was before and how it needs to become in order to
achieve progress: a story about how the 'old' international law was plagued
by an anarchic system of norm-making, pinned on an archaic idea of sovereignty and further weakened by sterile theoretical squabble. The narrative
moves try to purge these deficiencies and re-frame sources discourse along
the lines of a new doctrine. Two crucial narrative moves are identified here
and termed *standardization* and *formalization*.

---

[354]  Williams (Aspects), *supra* note 11, at 37-38 [emphasis added].

*Standardization*

The first narrative move is termed standardization. Standardization is a conscious process by which reality, in all its diversity, is re-organized on the basis of categories that carry the promise of universal legitimacy and application. In sources, standardization affects the structure and organization of the argumentative forms permitted within sources discourse, rather than the relationship of the doctrine of the sources to politics or the basis of obligation of international law, which was the role of the narrative move of formalization (see formalization, *infra*). Standardization is a narrative move that declares the doctrine of the sources as 'closed' (as comprising a determinate and finite list of sources) and 'universal' (as applicable to all areas of international practice and by all states) system of norm-types. The before/after story is the following: while under the 'old' international law one was never sure "what were the sources to which that tribunal was likely to appeal for the determination of the legal points at issue",[355] the new model of the sources 'changed all that'. Under standardization, the question of what are the sources of international law and what is the relationship between them can be answered determinately in the affirmative.

A 'standardized' doctrine based on Article 38 is a crucial before/after move. It tells a story of evolution by explaining a newly found possibility of a universal one-size-fits-all solution, despite not being able to reflect the diversity of all law-making methods that occurred in the actual practice of states. Standardization carries a political message as well, namely that closure and universality is better than a previously fragmented system where everything goes. Difference is toned down or set aside for the purpose of reaching a generally acceptable formulation that reflects as many views and practices as possible. For standardization to be acceptable, it must apply (or at least invoke) scientific method in order to discern common denominators, mostly at the cost of reducing reality into an artificially uniform texture. The amount of information about the object is reduced, with the result of fore-grounding specific properties only.

In sources theory, the process of standardization occurs by dissecting substance from form, that is to say by regarding the list of sources as forms that exist independently of the content of the primary rules that they embody. Standardization sustains the claim that the doctrine of the sources can

---

[355]  Ibid.

be immune to the critique that different fields of legal practice have different forms of lawmaking, practices and professional cultures. The doctrine determines the validity of norms regardless of their substantive content, e.g., regardless of whether they regulate the law of the sea, treaty law, diplomatic law, jurisdiction, and so on. The Report of the Advisory Committee of Jurists states:

> "Doubtless, on certain matters, for instance in Naval Prize Law, two systems of European jurisprudence exist, or at any rate did exist before the War; perhaps, on some points, differences still exist between the respective methods used by Europeans, Americans or Asiatics, in dealing with questions of International Law; but no matter what the main national tendencies in International Law may be, the meaning of the expression adopted by the Committee is not and cannot be to maintain existing distinctions between different conceptions of International Law, for such an intention would be opposed to the guiding principle upon which the establishment of a single Court of Justice for all nations is based: that is to say, the principle of the unity and universality of international law."[356]

Under standardization, the new 'doctrine of the sources of international law' begins to connote to a set of abstract criteria (tests, conditions, standards) that need to be met by any norm of international law, in whatever field and whatever its content, for it to qualify as a norm of public international law. Similarly, as a field of scholarly study the topic 'sources of international law' refers to an enquiry aimed at defining or refining such criteria and their modes of application without reference to a specific area of the application of the law. The doctrine of the sources is, in this sense, an exercise in abstraction. The abstraction, however, is not only descriptive: it is also prescriptive. Sources are not only a tool for telling how legal norms 'are' but also how they need to be in order to acquire binding effect. It is an endeavor to demarcate, in the best possible way, a set of ideal-type forms that, when applied to an infinite range of situations by an infinite number of users, would lead to reliable determinations of whether a particular norm is legal or not.

Standardization is precisely what Article 38 PCIJ Statute brings to sources debate. Prior to 1920, sources were not a settled domain of scientific or

---

[356] Procès-verbaux, *supra* note 335, at 709-710.

professional knowledge. This can be explained by reference to the preceding debate about positivism and naturalism – the fact that ideas about law making were directly linked to one's ideas about the basis of obligation in international law, positivist, naturalist, or other.[357] Consequently, each author appeared to have his own view about the number and properties of the sources. The terminology used, the list of sources, and the importance of the topic varied substantially from text to text. Most authors agreed that international custom and international treaties were part of the list[358] but this is where agreement ended. Some included in their list of sources divine law,[359] natural law,[360] ancient law,[361] general history,[362] Roman law,[363] principles of justice and reason,[364] the opinion of eminent jurists,[365] the universal consent of nations, international usage,[366] decisions of tribu-

---

[357] Koskenniemi (From Apology to Utopia), *supra* note 65, at 264.

[358] See, e.g., H. Wheaton, *Elements of International Law* (1866) at 23-24; S. Amos, *Lectures on International Law* (1874) 8-12; T.J. Lawrence, *The Principles of International Law* (1913) 98-114; R. Phillimore, *Commentaries upon International Law* (1879, Vol. 1) 68; H.S. Maine, *International Law – The Whewell Lectures* (1894) 1, at 20; T.D. Woolsey, *Introduction to the Study of International Law: Designed as an Aid to Teaching and in Historical Studies* (1899) 28; H.W. Halleck, *International Law or Rules Regulating the Intercourse of States in Peace and War* (1893, Vol. 1) 51-52, 62; B.B. Davis, *The Elements of International Law, With an Account of its Origin Sources and Development* (1908) 20-28; W.E. Hall, *A Treatise on International Law* (1909) 6-7; L. Oppenheim, *International Law: A Treatise* (1912, Vol. 1) 22-23; P. Heilborn, 'Les sources du droit international', 11 *RCADI* (1926-I) 1.

[359] Phillimore (Commentaries), *supra* note 358, at 68; Halleck (International Law), *supra* note 358, at 48.

[360] See, e.g., Maine (International Law), *supra* note 258, at 14; Davis (Elements), *supra* note 358, at 20 et seq.; Phillimore (Commentaries), *supra* note 358, at 68, equates natural law with the "will of god" as a source; W.O. Manning, *Commentaries on the Law of Nations* (1875) 67; L. Twiss, *The Law of Nations Considered as Independent Political Communities: On the Rights and Duties of Nations in Times of Peace* (1884) 146-147.

[361] Amos (Lectures), *supra* note 358.

[362] Wheaton (Elements), *supra* note 358, at 27; Davis (Elements), *supra* note 358, at 26; Halleck (International Law), *supra* note 358, at 57.

[363] Maine (International Law), *supra* note 358, at 20; Phillimore (Commentaries), *supra* note 358, at 30 et seq.; Halleck (International Law), *supra* note 358, at 57-58; Davis (Elements), *supra* note 358, at 20; J. Westlake, *International Law* (1910) at 15.

[364] Phillimore (Commentaries), *supra* note 358, at 68; Westlake (International Law), *supra* note 363, at 14-15.

[365] Halleck (International Law), *supra* note 358, at 60-61; Lawrence (Principles), *supra* note 358; Wheaton (Elements), *supra* note 358, at 26.

[366] Davis (Elements), *supra* note 358, at 23.

nals[367] (prize courts,[368] mixed tribunals,[369] local courts[370]), ordinances, commercial law and municipal law,[371] international state papers other than treaties and diplomatic correspondence and documents,[372] international conferences,[373] instructions issued by states for the guidance of their own affairs and tribunals,[374] the sea laws of various ports,[375] international public opinion,[376] and so on. Some understood the term source as referring only to the basis of obligation in international law;[377] others to the law making-processes as well as the places where one needs to look in order to find evidence of the existence of the rule of law.[378]

Article 38 has indeed 'changed all that', albeit gradually. By the mid-thirties, a decisive majority of textbooks of public international law adopted Article 38 as the standard starting point when describing lawmaking. In addition, specialized literature on the sources of international law appeared for the first time and sources became a recognized field of academic study.[379] Take, for example, the two successive editions of Brierly's popular text-

---

[367] Wheaton (Elements), *supra* note 358, at 26; Amos (Lectures), *supra* note 358; Woolsey (Introduction), *supra* note 358, at 28-29; Davis (Elements), *supra* note 358, at 24-25; Lawrence (Principles), *supra* note 358.

[368] Halleck (International Law), *supra* note 358, at 58-59; Lawrence (Principles), *supra* note 358.

[369] Halleck (International Law), *supra* note 358, at 59.

[370] Ibid.

[371] Davis (Elements), *supra* note 358, at 60; Halleck (International Law), *supra* note 358.

[372] Woolsey (Introduction), *supra* note 358, at 29; Amos (Lectures), *supra* note 358; Davis (Elements), *supra* note 358, at 25-26; Halleck (International Law), *supra* note 358, at 63-64; Lawrence (Principles), *supra* note 358.

[373] Lawrence (Principles), *supra* note 358.

[374] Lawrence (Principles), *supra* note 358; Wheaton (Elements), *supra* note 358, at 24-26.

[375] Woolsey (Introduction), *supra* note 358, at 28.

[376] Davis (Elements), *supra* note 358, at 27.

[377] Oppenheim (International Law), *supra* note 358, at 21-22; Phillimore (Commentaries), *supra* note 358, at 68.

[378] Woolsey (Introduction), *supra* note 358, at 28; Wheaton (Elements), *supra* note 358, at 23 et seq.

[379] The term sources appears in international law literature only in the mid-1920s: Heilborn (Sources), *supra* note 358, at 5 et seq.; Finch (Sources), *supra* note 285; M. Koppelmanas, 'Essai d'un théorie des sources formelles du droit international', 1 *Revue de Droit International* (1938) 101.

book. The 1928 Edition makes no reference whatsoever to Article 38 PCIJ when speaking of the sources. Instead, Brierly declares that the sources of international law are just custom and reason. Brierly adds that one is "probably justified" to add treaties as a third source.[380] Brierly is defensive in the passage on treaties, explaining to the reader the nature of treaties, their authority in the practice of states, and their necessity for international law. Custom comes first, reason follows, and treaties complete the set. Eight years later, the book's 2nd edition (1936) begins its section of the sources with the text of Article 38.[381] No explanation for the reference to Article 38 is given other than that this is a text of "highest authority", and one may "fairly assume" that it expresses the duty of every tribunal which is called upon to apply international law. The remaining of the section is structured on the basis of Article 38, following the order of the sources as listed there. Reason is no longer listed as a source of law but it is ousted to a separate section.[382] Brierly hastens to explain that reason needs to retain its place in the system of international law in the form of judicial corrective reason that, in case of need, would entail the discovery of legal principles by applying methods of legal reasoning. It is however no longer a primary source, as in the 1st Edition of the book, thus giving way to the list of Article 38.

Quite ironically, Judgments and Advisory Opinions of the PCIJ refrain from making explicit references to Article 38, to the term 'sources', or to a doctrine of the sources of international law.[383] Needless to say, most of these disputes did concern the existence or applicability of a certain legal norm, confirming the hypothesis that bringing clarity to legal obligations was a primary interwar concern. In most cases, and when determining the applicable law, the Court turns to specific rules of conventional or customary law without further a-do and sidestepping the phraseology, definitions, and structure of Article 38. Thus in the *Lotus* case, and when explaining the nature of public international law, the PCIJ defines international treaties

---

[380] Brierly (Law of Nations), *supra* note 297, at 39.

[381] Brierly (Law of Nations), *supra* note 297, at 46.

[382] Brierly (Law of Nations), *supra* note 297, at 55.

[383] This has also been noted in S. Rosenne, The Law and Practice of the International Court of Justice 1920-1996 (1997, Vol. III) 1595; Sørensen (Sources), *supra* note 252, at 38; and, more recently in A. Pellet's 'Commentary to Art. 38 ICJ Statute', in A. Zimmermann, C. Tomuschat and K. Oellers-Frahm, eds., *The Statute of the International Court of Justice. A Commentary* (2006) 695.

and custom by using different terminology than the phrasing of Article 38.[384]
When examining the process of formation of customary law, the Court refers to the role of publicists in the formation of customary law in a way that
would probably contradict Article 38's requirements of state practice and
opinio iuris.[385] Another decade needed to pass before the Court explicitly
relied on Article 38 as a means for determining the applicable law in the
*Serbian and Brazilian Loans* case.[386] But even there, Article 38 is used to
emphasize the applicability of international, and as opposed to national,
law by the Court, and not in order to enumerate or define the sources of
international law.[387] In the *Mavrommatis Case*, the Court states that "a principle taken from general international law cannot be regarded as constituting an obligation" for Britain unless it was reflected in an international
agreement.[388] The first Advisory Opinion that uses the term "source of international law" is the one on the *Danube Commission* in 1927.[389]

This discrepancy between the literature and the practice of the Court
appears a little peculiar in context. The jurisprudence of the PCIJ on the
sources of international law is a matter that has been covered extensively
by the literature.[390] Such studies acknowledge that PCIJ jurisprudence was
mostly concerned with the interpretation of rules rather than the determina-

---

[384] The PCIJ states: "International law governs relations between independent States.
The rules of law binding upon States therefore emanate from their own free will as expressed in conventions or by usages generally accepted as expressing principles of law and
established in order to regulate the relations between these co-existing independent communities or with a view to the achievement of common aims. Restrictions upon the independence of States cannot therefore be presumed"; The *Lotus* case, *supra* note 303, at 18.

[385] The *Lotus* case, *supra* note 303, at 26.

[386] Case Concerning the Payment of Various Loans Issued in France, PCIJ Series A –
No. 20/21 (12 July 1929) at 19.

[387] The Judgment reads: "Article 38 of the Statute cannot be regarded as excluding the
possibility of the Court's dealing with disputes which do not require the application of international law, seeing that the Statute itself expressly provides for this possibility. All that can
be said is that cases in which the Court must apply international law will, no doubt, be the
more frequent, for it is international law which governs relations between those who may be
subject to the Court's jurisdiction"; ibid., at 20.

[388] The Mavrommatis Jerusalem Concessions Case, PCIJ Series 1 – No. 5 (26 March
1925) at 27.

[389] Jurisdiction of the European Commission of the Danube Between Galatz and Braila,
PCIJ Series B – No. 14 (8 December 1927) at 22.

[390] H. Lauterpacht, *The Development of International Law by the Permanent Court of
International Justice* (1934); Sørensen (Sources), *supra* note 252.

tion of the applicable law, with some exceptions. In a recent study, Ole Spiermann argues that the decisions of the Court cannot be explained in "a unitary structure" and that "Article 38 of the Statute does not provide a language in which the Permanent Court's work and the several differences between various decisions can be expressed".[391] Regular and explicit references to Article 38 in fact seem to be a post-World War II phenomenon, although recent accounts often backdate it to the interwar period.[392]

*Formalization*

A *second* narrative move, closely related to the previous one, is termed *formalization*. Similarly to standardization, formalization is also a crucial move in the before/after narrative of progress. Formalization proclaims the existence of a (new) transcendental object (a new doctrine of the sources) whose properties are unaffected by the analyzing subject (the user or interpreter of the law). Unlike standardization, formalization does not determine the range of abstract categories that may constitute a valid source but rather the process by which the doctrine remains unaffected by ideology, politics or philosophical views about the nature of international law. Formalization is a narrative move that claims the possibility for a doctrine of the sources to operate autonomously and on a different 'register' than theoretical contemplation or political contest. The "I" of the subject applying the law is merely the executor of the doctrine or is even entirely removed from the picture. Formalization is essential for the new doctrine of the sources. Without it, the practical application of the doctrine would depend on external, non-objective points of reference and, as a consequence, disagreement could continue interminably without a possibility of closure. Formalization claims that the new doctrine enables one to decide whether norm x is "law" or not without reference to the question of the basis of obligation of international law. Sources would not have to be derived from either state consent or natural justice. Martti Koskenniemi writes:

> "A distinct, normative doctrine of sources can emerge only after these two views have been rejected. Something should not be law simply because its

---

[391] Spiermann (Argument in the Permanent Court), *supra* note 316, at 396.

[392] For the extensive list of references of the ICJ to Art. 38, see Pellet (Commentary), *supra* note 383, at 695. For references to Art. 38 by a large number of Arbitral Tribunals see Pellet (Commentary), *supra* note 383, at 691.

content corresponds to some *a priori* normative standards or state consent. To carry out its task, sources doctrine must become formal. That is, it must assume that something is not norm merely by virtue of its content reflecting natural justice or state consent. If sources doctrine did not contain such assumption, then it could not maintain law's distance from States' subjective, political views – the task for which it was created. Only if the criterion for law is formal, a decision applying it does not involve the implication that one sovereign's political views are preferred to those of another's."[393]

If not state consent or natural justice, then what? Standardization has already constructed a 'closed' and 'universal' list of sources, thus calling to end speculations about the range of permissible argumentative forms. One may only claim that a certain norm "is" conventional, customary, or a general principle. With formalization, Article 38 the doctrine and its application acquire an objective, technical, mechanical property. Thus when we speak of criteria or 'tests of validity' of international law, we think precisely of criteria that could be applied by an infinite number of people in an infinite number of circumstances and yield similar results. This way the process of law-identification seems like a technical exercise, removed from the realm of politics or philosophy, situated in the realm of technical-professional expertise. Thus a norm of customary law is ascertained categorically when the conditions of state practice and *opinio iuris* are met, period. A formal model would allow this conclusion to be reached by a trained professional, regardless of whether she thinks that the specific norm should be binding, fair, just, good, and so on.

In interwar literature, the narrative move of formalization is manifested in different ways, all of which are concerned precisely with creating space for the doctrine of sources to operate without reference to an external point. Typically, two different ways were identified. The first is to separate the practical application of the doctrine from the question of the basis of obligation of international law. The two 'registers', of high theory and practical application, were postulated as two separate levels or planes of contemplation, which could operate autonomously. Trying to bring 'terminological clarity' did this and a separation between the two registers that were as-

---

[393] Koskenniemi (From Apology to Utopia), *supra* note 65, at 265-266 [footnotes omitted].

cribed different names and role.[394] This literature has strived to explain the differences between terms such as 'source', 'cause', 'basis', 'evidence', 'material source', 'historical source', and so on. This approach did not require one to be agnostic about the basis of obligation. The important thing, however, is not to allow the level of high theory to affect one's practical application. Another way of solving the problem would be to melt the two registers into one another thus removing the need to reconcile the two. This way the doctrine of the sources can capture both the processes by which law is created and the places where law can be found. As Koskenniemi writes, this way sources doctrine "includes a concrete and a normative perspective within itself".[395]

Manning, for example, writes:

> "the word 'source' [...] as applied to law has, at the least, two distinct meanings which, however, are clearly connected. The one is that of the quarter to which recourse must be had to know what a rule of law is. The other is the immediate fact or group of facts which originally called a rule of law into existence. It is a peculiarity of the Law of Nations that, in reference to it, the two meanings are scarcely distinguishable."[396]

*The pursuit of correctness as progress*

The narrative moves of standardization (the reduction of the number of sources and different fields of practice into an exhaustive list) and formalization (the separation of the two 'registers' of practical application and high theory) frame a discourse that seems insulated from the experience of the everyday practice of the law (standardization) and the question of the basis of obligation (formalization). Thus the doctrine of the sources can create a formal language whose rules seem objectively ascertainable by the professional user. This creates a way of practicing international law that seems new, stable, determinate, and superior to the one of the 'old' international law. The 'new' doctrine of the sources is not framed as a project

---

[394] For some classic attempts to separate the various meanings of the term source along these lines see Corbett (Consent of States and Sources), *supra* note 325; T. Gihl, 'The Legal Character and Sources of International Law', 1 *Scandinavian Studies in Law* (1957) 53.

[395] Koskenniemi (From Apology to Utopia), *supra* note 65, at 267.

[396] Manning (Commentaries), *supra* note 360, at 66. For this approach see also R.R. Foulke, *A Treatise on International Law, With an Introductory Essay on the Definition and Nature of the Laws of Human Conduct* (1920, Vol. I) at 160.

directed at revealing justice or truth. By divorcing itself from the subjective standards of personal experience or theory, sources discourse becomes agnostic about justice, truth, or the ability of the discipline of international law to know them. Because these objects seem out of reach or, in any case, excluded from the tasks of sources theory, theoretical contemplation turns to decisions and judgments of practical thinking, what Panu Minkkinen calls 'correctness'.[397] If one cannot really determine what is just or true, the decision could as well be correct according to the rules of the game.

Along these lines, sources writing has turned its attention for nearly a century towards determinations of observable and verifiable juridical phenomena: whether or not, for example, norm $x$ 'is' a norm of law according to the doctrine of the sources; or whether interpretation $y$ of norm $z$ is 'correct', according to the same doctrine. The quest is for a technique, tool, or standard that would enable correctness to be determined with finality. By regarding itself not as an enterprise of high theory but as an exercise in practical thinking, the jouissance of the new field turns to inventing and sharpening abstract criteria (boundary conditions, tests of validity, definitions), the tools of the trade of making correct professional statements about the law. Article 38, initially concocted as a procedural guideline for the PCIJ, became the first generally accepted list of such professional criteria. For nearly nine decades thereafter, sources theory has 'progressed' in pursuit of formal correctness in the form of a newer, sharper, more potent doctrine with more determinate application. The pursuit of correctness has been the primary concern of the doctrine of the sources in the literature, mostly along two directions. The first will be termed here as the quest for determinacy; the second as the quest for social relevance.

*First*, the quest for determinacy. The idea here is that the doctrine of the sources as a whole, or each and every one of the individual sources listed, must be formulated as clearly and determinately as possible, in order it to be able to produce the desired effects of legal certainty and predictability when applied in an infinite number of cases by an infinite number of actors. If the formulation is proven not to be clear enough, then recourse needs to be found to a higher, superior, final, meta-criterion that will produce such a determination with finality. The quest for determinacy is couched in terms

---

[397] P. Minkkinen, *Thinking Without Desire: A First Philosophy of Law* (1999) at 3 and 9-47.

of the quality of the legal machinery. The idea here is that, if only we were able to create sharper criteria (categories, boundary-conditions, etc) for law-creation and law-identification, we would be able to remove indeterminacy and produce certainty and predictability in the application of the doctrine. The critique of indeterminacy has many guises. Sometimes it concerns the quality of our legal definitions of the different sources. Thus, if our understanding of what is a treaty, custom, general principles, or the nature and properties of their constituent elements are too crude or imprecise, we can replace or supplement this old understanding with a new one which is finer, more precise. If custom as a source of international law is criticized for being indeterminate due to the fact, for example, that the extent of state practice needed for its ascertainment remains unclear, the profession would then need to conduct studies to ascertain the extent of necessary practice. If Article 38 does not sufficiently define the concept of a treaty or the means for its interpretation, then perhaps an additional convention on the law of treaties may be needed; and so on. Other times, the problem can be traced to the conflict between sources or the lack of clear hierarchy between them. In this case scholarship must turn to creating conflict resolution doctrines in the form of hierarchical systems that privileges in a decisive way one component over the other. Thus, the story goes, we need to develop the necessary tools for the regulation of the relationship between different sources, or between norms belonging to the same formal source (e.g. between treaties), or between regimes or systems of norms. The last century has witnessed the creation of an intricate web of additional conditions, practices, and second-generation criteria to that effect, which came in waves to guarantee the sharpness of the way each period understands the sources.

*Second*, there is the quest for relevance. The problem here is not that the doctrine of the sources may have lost its logical or definitional sharpness but rather that it may have failed to contain or reflect recent developments in the practice of international lawmaking. The classical examples here are debates about "new" sources, relative normativity, or new lawmaking practices in emerging areas of international practice, such as international economic law, international environmental law, and so on, in recent years. This problem can be resolved by modernizing, to the extent possible, our understanding of the existing sources so as they can include, to the extent possible, such recent developments. This is the type of writing which tries to assimilate and regularize change in international law by passing it through the grind-mill of the classical understanding of the doctrine of the sources. Is development x a "new" source of international law? Or, is it the evolution/permutation of an existing source? The idea is to flex our understanding of each source in order to include developments in practice but put a firm stop before the imaginary breaking point of this understanding. It is a question of moving the invisible Rubicon to a different location, while allowing sources to maintain their on/off quality. To use a contemporary example: although, the story goes, General Assembly Resolutions, Codes of Conducts, and other 'soft-law' instruments cannot be considered as sources of international law proper, these new forms of law-making can nevertheless be brought within the ambit of Article 38 by means of upgrading their relevance in the determination of existing sources of law, such as international customary law. Our understanding of what is a treaty can change by including Memoranda of Understanding in this definition – or not.

## 3.6    DIGRESSION: SOURCES IN CONTEMPORARY TEXTBOOKS

The present chapter does not wish to bring within its purview contemporary sources discourse, the volume and complexity of which demands a separate study. A telling illustration of the narrative moves of standardization and formalization can be found in present-day textbooks. This illustration only serves to exemplify the function of the moves of standardization and formalization and does not aim to characterize an otherwise extremely complex discursive terrain.

*Between ambivalence and faith*
When reading passages on the sources of international law in popular present-day textbooks,[398] the reader is confronted with two contrasting feelings.

---

[398] For some classic post-1989 textbooks, see J. Dugard, *International Law – A South African Perspective* (2006) 27-46; M. Dixon, *Textbook on International Law* (2005) 21-48; I. Brownlie, *Principles of International Law* (2003) 3-31; Shaw (International Law), *supra* note 53, at 65-120; H. Thirlway, 'The Sources of International Law', in M. Evans, ed., *International Law* (2003) 117-143; P. Malanczuk, *Akehurst's Modern Introduction to International Law* (1997) 35-62; R. Jennings and A. Watts, eds., *Oppenheim's International Law* (1996) 22-52; R. Higgins, *Problems and Process: International Law and How We Use It* (1994) 17-38. Occasional references are made to other texts, such as P. Dailler and A. Pellet, *Droit International Public* (1999) 177-297; P.-M. Dupuy, *Droit International Public* (1993).

On the one hand, there is a reassuring feeling of certainty and order. A significant amount of uniformity is displayed in the tone, style, and substance of the texts. Accounts of the doctrine of the sources are normally brief and succinct. Authors agree on what are the sources of international law (mostly by reference to Art. 38 Statute ICJ) and on the role and importance of the doctrine at large (e.g., it determines the twin processes of law-creation and law-ascertainment). When discussing each source in detail, the impression is one of legal certainty, created by consistent references to the same classical cases and scholars. In this reading, sources appear to be a settled, traditional field of scientific knowledge, where brevity can be explained by the fact that the authors transmit information so basic that over-elaboration would be redundant. The consistency between the different accounts may even lead one to think that by reading one chapter on the sources of international law one 'has read them all', in the crass sense of having been exposed to an uncontroversial and sufficient threshold of knowledge. For one thing, repetition of a similar argument in a broad gamut of texts dramatically enhances the feeling of certainty about the nature of the knowledge that is being transmitted. This reading of the literature on the sources is optimistic about the potency of the doctrine to adequately regulate the processes of law-creation and law-ascertainment and, consequently, international law's capacity to regulate international affairs at large. Sources bring to mind 'grand days' of international law: moments in the history of the discipline (is it not also the reason why most of us joined the field?) when professionals feel confident that law is an effective tool for the regulation of conflict and dissonance.[399]

Yet there is another feeling, one of unease and disharmony, generated by the reading of the same texts. When reading the fine print one senses that the hand of the authors is less steady than originally assumed. One begins to think that, instead of a stylistic choice guarding against over-elaboration, brevity and uniformity are by-products of discomfort. In fact, most authors

---

[399] The phrase 'grand days' is borrowed from the homonymous novel on the League of Nations in F. Moorhouse, *Grand Days* (1994). Moorhouse recounts the story of the League of Nations through the eyes of Edith Berry, a young officer in the League Secretariat in Geneva. In her first encounter with internationalism, our heroine experiences the dream of the 'grand days' by imagining internationalism as a place where no one has ever been before: a brand new plane of contemplation and action which is above and beyond national politics, a sui generis location, a way of life, and a personal/professional identity that is autonomous from, and escapes and eludes, the shortcomings of national politics.

admit that the doctrine of the sources is fraught with terminological discrepancy, scholarly disagreement, logical or epistemological incoherence, inability to capture the diversity of modern law-making practices, inability to stand the test of 'high theory', and so on. Some authors wonder whether it is even sensible at all to identify or equate the diversity of law-making forms in international law with the list of sources to be applied by the World Court. This closer reading reveals that the list of sources is more controversial that initially assumed (what about General Assembly Resolutions, soft-law, or unilateral acts of states?) and that law-making practice has moved into directions often incompatible with Article 38. The process of the formation of some of the sources (such as custom or general principles) turns out to be less determinate than promised; and the distinction between the basis of obligation in international law and its law-making processes less stable than one would wish. Instead of providing concise answers, elaboration on the sources would probably open Pandora's Box, generating more questions to non-initiates than can be answered within the confines of a textbook. In this reading, sources are not a field of settled scientific knowledge but rather one plagued by recurring questions that continue to baffle even the best of scholars. This reading is also much less optimistic. It casts a shadow over the possibility of the 'grand days' of international law and over our power as professionals to live them. Sir Robert Jennings wrote in his seminal article not too long ago:

> "I doubt whether anybody is going to dissent from the proposition that there has never been a time when there has been so much confusion and doubt about the tests of validity – or sources – of international law, than the present."[400]

Yet this shadow is a fleeting one. In most textbooks, quick deliverance from the discomfort of these ruminations comes in the form of pragmatist faith. Difficulties associated with sources theory are not engaged with but rather set aside, bracketed, deferred to other enquiries, suspended. Scholars acknowledge that the doctrine of the sources as we know it today is problematic in a number of ways. Nonetheless this admission is accompanied by the conviction that, despite such shortcomings, the doctrine of the sources

---

[400]  R.Y. Jennings, 'What Is International Law and How Do We Tell It When We See It', 37 *Annuaire Suisse de Droit International* (1981) 59, at 60.

of Article 38 remains, will remain, and should remain central in international legal argument. Thirlway writes:

"The doctrine of the sources has attracted enormous amounts of discussion and criticism among international lawyers, and various proposals have been made for re-thinking the subject, or for getting rid of the idea of 'sources' altogether. While the traditional view presents some anomalies and difficulties, it has so far proved the most workable method of analyzing the way in which rules and principles develop that States in practice accept as governing their actions. The reasoning in the decisions of the International Court of Justice has consistently used the traditional terminology and structure of source-based law, and it seems unlikely that any other system will be able to replace it."[401]

At the beginning of the 21$^{st}$ century, the doctrine of the sources of international law is the profession's workhorse: reliable yet imperfect, concrete yet indeterminate, it stands for international law's foundation and defense. Sources sustain a memory and a promise of order, predictability, good administration of justice, rule of law, and other systemic goals that international law strives to achieve. Yet, and ever since the first articulation of the doctrine in Article 38 PCIJ Statute in the early 1920s, lawyers have been doubtful about its ability to *really* determine the twin processes of law-creation and law-ascertainment. The doctrine remains an apparatus that falls short and requires reinvention. In nearly a century of professional engagement with sources, debate has grown into a field of study of great sophistication, yet the even the term 'source' still evades a generally accepted definition. Despite its shortcomings, we routinely rely on the doctrine of the sources in our everyday work as international lawyers, in arguments before international courts, everyday policy debates or academic work. We still live international law in times when the idea that legal normativity possesses an objective on/off quality permeates much of the way we think. In the beginning of the 21$^{st}$ century, Article 38(1) is both an artifact of a bygone era of international law and our "melancholy second-best"[402] companion.

---

[401] Thirlway (Sources), *supra* note 398, at 120.

[402] This expression belongs to Martti Koskenniemi (Editor's Introduction, Sources of International Law), *supra* note 255, at xiii.

The ambivalent intellectual posture that acknowledges (some of the) limitations of the doctrine of the sources while defending and reinventing it
again and again on pragmatic grounds characterizes mainstream modern-
day literature. Caught between ambivalence and faith, sources debates continue in our times. Viewed from this angle, the doctrine seems to embody
paradigmatically the modernist experience with science. Each time that "all
that is solid melts into air",[403] each time we are confronted with the wonder
and dread of a doctrine dislodged in the quick-sands of everyday practice,
each time we find the strength and faith to salvage it and reinvent it. There
is still a sense that despite failed attempts to capture the multiplicity and
complexity of sources discourse in a single doctrine, we will eventually
manage to get it right. Either by refinement, renewal and modernization of
our perception; by a new perception more grounded in sociological or empirical observation; or perhaps by the invention of some meta-theory, meta-
criterion, meta-hierarchy, meta-standard, or other "decisive discourse", we
shall be able to make progress in our conception of the sources. Its present
failures, in some way or another, appear remediable. Each time, however,
we try to re-conceive the doctrine along these lines, we are confronted again
and again with the same shortcomings we wanted to avoid in the first place.
This cycle of critique and renewalism, ambivalence and faith, characterizes
present day sources discourse.

The two narrative moves of standardization and formalization discussed
are symptomatic of contemporary sources argument as well. The moves
remain crucial in creating a narrative site for a debate in which the language
of sources can be used and remain safe from the critiques of realism or high
theory.

*Standardization*

Standardization is a very familiar move in today's discourse, manifested in
textbooks by heavy reliance on Article 38(1) ICJ Statute. Most modern accounts on the sources begin by reference to Article 38(1). This otherwise
surprising use of an Article taken from the Statute of the International Court,
receives a standard explanation. First, authors begin with the caveat that it
is ultimately the will and the practice of states that determines what are the

---

[403]  M. Berman, *All That Is Solid Melts into Air: The Experience of Modernity* (1982).

sources of international law.[404] It is however useful not to "underestimate"[405] the importance of Article 38 but instead to "consult"[406] it as an indication or a "starting point"[407] of how state practice stands. The reader is told that the provisions of Article 38(1) were initially expressed in terms of the function of the Court: they were not meant to be a codification of the state of the law at the time. Article 38(1) remains nonetheless 'authoritative' because it is part of the UN Charter, which has been signed by virtually all states.[408] In addition, it continues to largely reflect the general practice of states and international tribunals.[409] For lack of any other formulation, it should be regarded as valid statement of the sources of international law today.[410] Caution, however, is also habitually advised: Article 38 is badly drafted, does not make a direct reference to the term sources, does not explain the hierarchy between norms, and confuses formal and material sources.[411] In addition, Article 38 does not truly reflect the variety of modern practices in law making.[412] During recent years, some authors warn that modern practice of law-making forces one to acknowledge the existence of new methods.[413] Even such authors, however, admit the need to assimilate such new law-making methods to the extent possible within the existing system of Article 38. John Dugard writes:

> "Article 38 was first drafted in 1920 for the Statute of the Permanent Court of International Justice. It no longer accurately reflects all the materials and

---

[404] Jennings and Watts (Oppenheim's International Law), *supra* note 398, at 24. See also A. Cassese, *International Law* (2005) at 153-155.

[405] Dixon (Textbook), *supra* note 398, at 22.

[406] Jennings and Watts (Oppenheim's International Law), *supra* note 398, at 24.

[407] Malanczuk (Akehurst's International Law), *supra* note 398, at 36.

[408] Shaw (International Law), *supra* note 53, at 67.

[409] Jennings and Watts (Oppenheim's International Law), *supra* note 398 at 24; Dixon (Textbook), *supra* note 398, at 22; Brownlie (Principles), *supra* note 398, at 5; Shaw (International Law), *supra* note 53, at 66-67; Thirlway (Sources), *supra* note 398, at 120-121.

[410] Brownlie (Principles), *supra* note 398 at 5; Shaw (International Law), *supra* note 53, at 66; Thirlway (Sources), *supra* note 398, at 120-121.

[411] Brownlie (Principles), *supra* note 398, at 5.

[412] Dixon (Textbook), *supra* note 398, at 22; Dugard (International Law), *supra* note 398, at 27.

[413] A. Aust, Handbook of International Law (2005) 5-12; Pellet (Droit International), *supra* note 398, at 265-297; Dugard (International Law), *supra* note 398, at 27-46; Degan (Sources), *supra* note 255, at 5-6 (1997); Danilenko (Law-Making), *supra* note 255, at 30-43.

forms of state practice that comprise today's sources of international law. Despite this, every effort is made to bring new developments in respect of sources of law within the categories of sources recognized in article 38. Inevitably, this, at times, leads to the expansion of these sources beyond those originally contemplated in 1920."[414]

At the end of these accounts, the reader is left suspended. Is Article 38(1) a description of the state of affairs? Or is it a prescription to be safeguarded in order to guarantee the integrity of the system? Is it both – or none? Textbooks write that Article 38(1) should not be treated as panacea but as a formula with normative authority. What does this mean in terms of our intellectual travail as professionals? Should one strive to re-conceive reality in a way compatible with Article 38(1) or move beyond it? Standardization, to begin with, is not unproblematic in its merits.[415]

Another illustrative example can be found in the debates about the unity of international law and the distinction between 'primary' and 'secondary' rules. The question of the unity of international law is not a new concern. Since the mid-nineties the question has received a new wave of attention,[416]

---

[414] Dugard (International Law), *supra* note 398, at 27.

[415] Many authors have realized the difficulties associated with the list of sources in Art. 38 ICJ Statute: R. Jennings, 'The Identification of International Law', in B. Cheng, ed., *International Law* (1982) 9; R.A. Falk, 'On the Quasi-Legislative Competence of the General Assembly', 60 *American Journal of International Law* (1966) 782; Y. Onuma, 'The ICJ: An Emperor Without Clothes? International Conflict Resolution, Article 38 of the ICJ Statute and the Sources of International Law', in N. Ando et al., eds., *Liber Amicorum Judge Shigeru Oda* (2002) 191.

[416] For some representative work, see R. Huesa Vinaixa and K. Wellens, eds., *L'influence des sources sur l'unité et la fragmentation du droit international* (2006); 'Diversity or Cacophony? New Sources of Norms in International Law: Symposium', 25 *Michigan Journal of International Law* (2004) 845; P.M. Dupuy, 'L'unité de l'ordre juridique international, Cours général de droit international public', 297 *RCADI* (2002) at 15-489; L.A.N.M. Barnhoorn and K. Wellens, eds., *Diversity in Secondary Rules and the Unity of International Law* (1995) and, in particular, the essay in this volume by K. Wellens, 'Diversity in Secondary Rules and the Unity of International Law: Some Reflections on Current Trends', at 3-39; I. Brownlie, *Problems Concerning the Unity of International Law, in International Law at the Time of its Codification: Essays in Honor of Roberto Ago* (1987) 153-162. See also the discussion on fragmentation in Chapter 3, *supra*. See also B. Simma, 'Self-Contained Regimes', 16 *Netherlands Yearbook of International Law* (1985) 112; and B. Simma and D. Pulkowski, 'Of Planets and the Universe: Self-Contained Regimes in International Law', 17 *European Journal of International Law* (2006) 483. Cf. A. Fischer-Lescano and G. Teubner, 'Regime-Collisions: The Vain Search for Legal Unity in the Fragmentation of Global Law', 25 *Michigan Journal of International Law* (2004) 999.

which eventually culminated with the recent work of the International Law Commission.[417] One of the main theses about the unity of international law suggests that international law has a 'general part', namely a set of doctrines common to all fields of specialized practice. Doctrines such as the one on the sources, state responsibility, reparation for injuries, and so on, are said to enjoy a relatively uniform application in all areas of international law. The uniform application of these doctrines, the story goes, is crucial for the maintenance of the unity of the system of international law. As Dupuy writes, formal unity of the system is essentially linked to the use of the same "secondary rules of recognition".[418] The doctrine of the sources is one example among many doctrines with the same effect.

"Prenons en quelques exemples: l'expression « responsabilité internationale » doit avoir le même objet et la même signification, quels que soient les types d'obligation à la violation desquels elle s'applique ; ceci, même si elle reçoit, dans son régime d'application. [...] *Leitmotiv* omniprésent, quelles que soient les originalités de son champ d'application, cet adage du *Lotus* sure le devoir de réparation marque ainsi d'unité de sens apporté à un terme comme à l'institution juridique à laquelle il se réfère, la responsabilité."[419]

Textbooks habitually represent international law this way. Introductory chapters initiate the reader to the 'general part' of international law, consisting of themes deemed common to all specialized fields.[420] The sources are *par excellence* a doctrine that is described as one which applies uniformly. In the same vein some authors employ the distinction between "primary" and "secondary" rules within a legal system, usually citing H.L.A. Hart and Roberto Ago's well-known analyses.[421] Primary are rules containing the

---

[417] Fragmentation of International Law: Difficulties Arising from the Diversification and Expansion of International Law, Report of the Study Group of the International Law Commission, finalized by Martti Koskenniemi, UN Doc. A/CN.4/L.682 (13 April 2006).

[418] Dupuy writes that formal unity is « essentiellement liée à l'utilisation des mêmes règles secondaires, de reconnaissance, de production et de jugement»; Dupuy (L'unité), *supra* note 416, at 39.

[419] P.M. Dupuy, 'Préface: Fragmentation du droit international ou des perceptions qu'on a?', in Huesa Vinaixa and Wellens (L'influence des sources), *supra* note 416, at xv-xvi.

[420] Dupuy (L'unité), *supra* note 416, at 428-432.

[421] The intellectual origins of the primary/secondary rules distinction can be traced to the work of different authors. See, e.g., H.L.A. Hart, *The Concept of Law* (1961) at 77-96. Roberto Ago's ILC Reports on State Responsibility also elaborate on the distinction: see R. Ago, *Fifth Report on State Responsibility, Yearbook of the International Law Commis-*

substantive rights and obligations of the subjects of the law, while secondary are those directed at managing, from a systemic point of view, the creation, application and functioning of the system's primary rules. According
to this model, the doctrine of the sources belongs to international law's
secondary rules, in the sense that it comprises a set of criteria that help
determine the creation of primary rules that lay down the rights and obligation of the subjects of the law.[422] The idea of "international custom, as
evidence of a general practice accepted as law", to use the classical definition of custom in Article 38(1)(b), is about an abstraction that is potentially
applicable to any international norm that claims such a status regardless of
its content and area of application, as long as it concerns behavior of states.

*Formalization*
In today's literature, and similarly to the interwar period, the narrative move
of formalization is manifested in different ways, all of which are concerned
precisely with separating the two 'registers' of high theory and practical
application and eliminating any confusion in that regard.[423] Sometimes these
debates concern the "quasi-constitutional" function of the doctrine of the
sources; often times the dual nature of the doctrine of the sources as defining the dual processes of law-creation and law-ascertainment; and other
times the distinction between "formal" and "material" sources. Let us briefly
see these in turn.

In the textbooks under review, many authors try to establish a clear distinction between domestic legal systems governed by a constitution, on the

---

sion (1976, Vol. II) at 6 et seq. For a review of this debate, see J. Crawford, *The International Law Commission's Articles on State Responsibility: Introduction, Text, and Commentaries* (2002) at 14-16. Crawford points to Alf Ross' usage of the terms in A. Ross, *On Law
and Justice* (1958) at 209-210. See also the debate in Koskenniemi (Fragmentation of International Law), *supra* note 417, at para. 138 et seq.

[422] Thirlway (Sources), *supra* note 398, at 117-120.

[423] For post-War debates, see G.G. Fitzmaurice, 'Some Problems Regarding the Formal
Sources of International Law', in Symbolae Verzijl: *présentées au professeur J.H.W. Verzijl
à l'occasion de son LXX-ième anniversaire* (1958) 153-176; C. Parry, *The Sources and
Evidences of International Law* (1965) at 1; G.J.H. van Hoof, *Rethinking the Sources of
International Law* (1983) at 13-17, 57-60 and 71-82. See also Thirlway (Sources), *supra*
note 398, at 119; Jennings and Watts (Oppenheim's International Law), *supra* note 398,
at 23.

one hand, and international law on the other.[424] Constitutionalism proper implies, amongst other things, a legislature capable of producing legal rules of general application and a coercive power of enforcement. The same norms that govern the conduct of the actors of the system are the same norms that are applied by the Courts of the same domestic system, thus allowing a direct correspondence between law-making and law-application, between law-creation and law-ascertainment, and so on. The characteristics obviously do not exist in international law, the story goes. Any system of law, however, needs a method of identifying the processes by which legal norms are created or ascertained. In the absence of a world constitution that would stipulate the processes by which international law norms come to existence; and in the absence of a world legislature that would produce norms of universal application, states have devised a set of accepted methods by which rules come into existence and by which the content of norms can be identified, called the doctrine of the sources.[425] This often means that there is some times no direct correspondence between how law is made and what law can be applied, or between law-creation and law-ascertainment. The doctrine of the sources cannot perform its constitutional function as well as national constitutions do because of its birth defects. Sources are therefore a second-best constitutional apparatus ('quasi-constitutional') that is nevertheless able to perform its function despite its handicaps.

"Ascertainment of the law on any given point in domestic legal orders is not usually too difficult a process. [...] The contrast is very striking when one considers the situation in international law. [...] There is no single body able to create laws internationally binding upon everyone, nor a proper system of courts with comprehensive and compulsory jurisdiction to interpret and extend the law. One is therefore faced with the problem of discovering where the law is to be found and how can one tell whether a particular proposition amounts to a legal rule. This perplexity is reinforced because of the anarchic nature of world affairs and the clash of competing sovereignties. Nevertheless, international law does exist and it is ascertainable. There are 'sources' available from which the rules may be extracted and analyzed.

---

[424] Brownlie (Principles), *supra* note 398, at 3; Shaw (International Law), *supra* note 53, at 65; Thirlway (Sources), *supra* note 398, at 118; Malanczuk (Akehurst's International Law), *supra* note 398, at 35.

[425] Dixon (Textbook), *supra* note 398, at 21; Shaw (International Law), *supra* note 53, at 66.

By 'sources' one means those provisions operating within the legal system on a technical level, and such ultimate sources as reason or morality are excluded, as are more functional sources such as libraries and journals. What is intended is a survey of the process whereby rules of international law emerge."[426] (Footnotes omitted)

Another way of separating the two registers (of high theory and practical application) is by asserting that the doctrine of the sources simultaneously regulates two different aspects of normativity: law-creation (the processes by which legal norms come to being in international law); and law-ascertainment (how can we tell law when we see it or what are the forms of legal and non-legal norms).[427] Most authors recognize that fusing law-creation and law-ascertainment in the same doctrine constitutes some form of intellectual compromise. They therefore find the distinction to be a "complication" of the functioning of the doctrine, a distinction "difficult to maintain"[428] and as a paradox, but one that nevertheless should not be seen as deeply problematic or disturbing. Some suggest that it is the nature of international relations that requires this kind of compromise and the reader is assured that this does not affect the functionality of the doctrine.[429] Law-creation and law-ascertainment, however, are two logically distinct aspects of normativity as they describe the processes for achieving two different ends. The first one (law-creation) is a descriptive notion, as it explains the ways in which states create law. The second is prescriptive, as it tells us how norms need to look like from the formal point of view in order to be considered as law, without reference to the process that created them. When fused into one doctrine, these two different ways of approaching normativity render the doctrine of the sources circular, faltering between a descriptive and a prescriptive function. Sir Robert Jennings writes, once more:

"It should be remembered at the outset that in considering the sources of international law, we are looking not only at the tests of validity of the law – the touchstone of what is law and what is not – but also at the ways in which law is made and changed. This is a complication not found, at least not to the

---

[426] Shaw (International Law), *supra* note 53, at 65-66.
[427] Dixon (Textbook), *supra* note 398, at 21 and 23.
[428] Brownlie (Principles), *supra* note 398, at 3.
[429] Ibid., at 3-4.

same degree, in domestic systems of law. [...] But in international law the questions of whether a rule of customary law exists, and how customary law is made, tend in practice to coalesce."[430]

Often scholars use the distinction between "formal" and "material" sources to underline the difference between the two.[431] Brownlie explains that "formal" are those legal procedures and methods for the creation of rules of general application which are legally binding on the addresses. "Material" sources, on the other hand, provide evidence of the existence of rules that have the status of legally binding rules of general application.[432] In international law it is said that, in the absence of a world constitution and a world legislature that would provide clear answers to these questions, law-creation and law-ascertainment may be legitimately fused.[433] The questions of 'high theory' are seen as somehow belonging to a different 'register' than the one of the sources, one in which enquiries may take place but without affecting the functioning of the doctrine of the sources in its everyday application. Although of course the two registers are inter-related, in the sense that answering the question of what is the basis of obligation in international law could have serious ramifications on the law-creation and law-ascertainment processes, international lawyers try to segregate the two registers to protect the 'everyday' practice of the law from the uncertainties of the ruminations of high theory. Hence sources, in the sense of tests of the validity of rules, are seen in today's literature as a rather technical exercise of applying an abstract, formal model to facts. By offering an acceptable (and sometimes even convincing) description of the processes by which international law is made or ascertained, the doctrine of the sources seems to allow the functioning of 'everyday practice' of the law in a way that it is unaffected by questions of 'high theory'. Foundational questions are set aside, suspended, or even rendered irrelevant: if all states of the interna-

---

[430] Jennings (What is International Law), *supra* note 400, at 60.

[431] See Brownlie (Principles), *supra* note 398 at 3; Shaw (International Law), *supra* note 53, at 67; Malanczuk (Akehurst's International Law), *supra* note 398, at 35; Dixon (Textbook), *supra* note 398, at 23; Thirlway (Sources), *supra* note 398, at 118-119; Dailler and Pellet (Droit International), *supra* note 398, at 111-112; Jennings and Watts (Oppenheim's International Law), *supra* note 398, at 23; Dupuy (Droit International), *supra* note 398, at 179; Van Hoof (Rethinking), *supra* note 423, at 46-56.

[432] Brownlie (Principles), *supra* note 398, at 3.

[433] Danilenko (Law-Making), *supra* note 255.

tional community seem to agree that treaties, custom, and general principles are the primary forms that international law may take, international
law may continue existing in the relations between these states, despite the
fact that the edifice in its totality could be found incoherent or unfair by
theoretical critiques which are external to the sources debate. Thirlway writes
of the separation of the two "registers":

> "None of the theories advanced commands universal assent; but nor are any
> of the actually essential to international legal relations in practice. The issue
> is fortunately one of purely academic interest. The realistic answer to the co-
> nundrum can probably only be that this is the way international society oper-
> ates, and has operated for centuries, and probably the only way in which
> anything that can claim to be a society or community could possibly oper-
> ate."[434]

## 3.7    An (Un)Stable Vocabulary

If only, however, it was that easy. The vocabulary of progress of the sources
doctrine (the moves of standardization and formalization) breaks under the
weight of its claims. The narrative move of standardization can only defend
its bid for progress as long as the list of sources of Article 38 remains 'closed'
and 'stable' when applied by an infinite number of users in an infinite number of circumstances. Standardization claims to bring determinacy by replacing a previously anarchic field with a closed and finite list that can be
used with certainty and predictability before international courts. A theoretically infinite range of sources is now reduced to a closed list of three
'primary' sources that can constitute permissible autonomous bases of legality; and two 'subsidiary' sources. According to this logic, comity, reason, or non-binding 'international engagements'[435] could no longer be
invoked as autonomous sources of legal obligation. Should such instru-

---

[434] Thirlway (Sources), *supra* note 398, at 119.

[435] The term "international engagement" which was used in Art. 18 of the Covenant of
the League of Nations was abandoned in Art. 102 of the UN Charter that only speaks of
international agreements, partly because the term was considered too wide and imprecise,
allowing instruments that were not 'hard' treaties to enter the definition. For a discussion
and relevant sources see the Commentary to Art. 102 in B. Simma et al., eds., *The Charter of
the United Nations: A Commentary* (2002, Vol. II), 1277-1282.

ments provide evidence for the existence of a rule of customary international law, they could be relevant on that basis only. Even if one were to accept the eventual addition of a new source to the list (e.g., unilateral acts of states), this addition would have to be permanent and simply extend the list of sources but not alter the closed nature of the system. The study of potential new additions to the doctrine can be done separately and without affecting its application. Until that re-thinking takes place, and in a way reflective of general consent, the practitioner should continue taking cues from the generally accepted list of Article 38. Sources discourse thus allows one to contest another's view on what is binding on the basis of a limited set of arguments, regardless of whether these arguments are *truly* representative of law-making practices in a world out there. Sources discourse this way claims a language of communication based on certain and predictable rules, not on a true representation of reality of law-making processes. The list of sources is also postulated as 'stable', in the sense of each source being distinguishable from the one next to it. Each source is determined by different boundary conditions that circumscribe its abstract form. One can only argue whether something "is" law only if it "is" has the normative form of a treaty, custom, or general principle. Standardization can only work if it can remain closed and stable each and every time that it is used.

Similarly, the narrative move of formalization can only be successful if the conditions for the creation/ascertainment of each source of law can maintain their autonomy from politics or 'high theory' at all times. They must remain technical, transcendental, apolitical, and neutral. By doing so, formalization presents itself as a progressive, anti-foundationalist move, which escapes the conceptualism of the 'old' international law and liberates the practice from the tyranny of non-objective parameters. Formalization can defend its claim to progress only as long as it can successfully (and permanently) disconnect sources doctrine from politics and high theory. Its bid would fail the moment one can demonstrate that sources discourse fails to maintain this autonomy.

Recent work has demonstrated that sources discourse fails to meet the standards set out by standardization and formalization. When it comes to the claims of standardization (the doctrine being 'closed' and 'stable'), David Kennedy writes that, aside from a set of abstract categories, sources discourse is a set of well worked out argumentative practices about the bind-

ing nature of international legal instruments.[436] For Kennedy, sources discourse allows two rhetorical styles, which he respectively calls "hard" and
"soft".[437] "Hard" are arguments based on the consent of states while "soft"
rely on some extra-consensual binding authority. The literature embraces
this distinction but presents a stable opposition between "hard" and "soft"
sources, with treaties belonging to the former category while general principles, and sometimes custom, belong to the latter. As Kennedy demonstrates, however, the various sources evade stable classification as either
exclusively "hard" or "soft", as you can always present a "soft" version of
'hard' sources and the other way round. One may switch continuously from
a "hard" to a "soft" rhetorical style of argument but neither argument can be
convincing by itself. The debate thus could go on interminably without
resolution. The continuous peregrination defeats any effort to protect the
closed nature of the doctrine or the stability and autonomy of the separate
sources from each other. As Kennedy writes, "the two opposed themes
present rhetorical possibilities and strategies more than decisive identifica-
tions and differentiations".[438]

Speaking of the claim of sources as a technical language disconnected
from politics or high theory, Kennedy also explains that closure cannot be
brought without a meta-discourse that validates one's decisions and renders
an external point of reference part and parcel of the final outcome. Although
justice or truth is too elusive to serve as the declared object of sources
discourse, positive law cannot be studied scientifically without encounter-
ing them again and again. Despite grand theories and a sophisticated doctrinal web, which at least appears to provide a solid technical professional
language, determinations about the law encounter in each instance the same
high theory they wished to avoid by turning to practical thinking. In the
end, the two registers cannot be kept apart. As Kennedy writes characteristically:

"Discourse about sources searches abstractly to delimit the norms which bind
sovereigns in a way that relies neither on the interests of sovereigns nor on

---

[436] Kennedy (Sources), *supra* note 256.

[437] Ibid., at 20 et seq. Koskenniemi describes a similar dynamic in international legal
argument in his metaphor of "ascending" and "descending" patterns of justification. See
Koskenniemi (From Apology to Utopia), *supra* note 65, esp. at 40-51 and 264-341.

[438] Koskenniemi (From Apology to Utopia), *supra* note 65, at 88.

some vision of the good which is independent of state interests. The search is for a decisive discourse – not for a persuasive justification – which can continually distinguish binding from nonbinding norms while remaining open to expressions of sovereign will. The argumentative moves made by those engaged in sources discourse reflect this central goal. The result is a discourse of evasion which constantly combines that which it cannot differentiate and emphasizes that which it can express only by hyperbolic exclusion. Pursued in this fashion, sources doctrine moves us forward from theory towards other doctrines which it supplements, remaining both authoritatively independent and parasitic. This paradoxical position between theoretical discourse and the doctrines of substance and process in maintained by endlessly embracing and managing a set of ephemeral rhetorical differences. The turn to sources doctrine thus seems to provide an escape from fruitless theoretical argument, moving us towards legal order, precisely by opening up an endlessly proliferating field of legal argumentation."[439]

The paradox of formalization is its claim to be both the product of social observation (sociological move) and a defense against the indeterminacy of 'external' theory. In trying to be anti-foundationalist, in its move away from high theory, formalization falls into the trap of essentializing the science of social observation. Things seem to appear in a world out there, passing before the eyes of the scholar who merely reports them. The problem is, however, as Koskenniemi remarks, that "'social facts' do not come before our eyes 'an sich'".[440] To understand what takes place in the social world we need to interpret, and this process involves both external elements as well as a subjective understanding. Thinking about the sources in terms of correctness is about what Kennedy calls a quest for a "decisive discourse",[441] namely a way of continually distinguishing binding from non-binding norms, while remaining open to expressions of sovereign will. Whenever confronted with interminable disagreement about whether a norm x is customary or not, the discipline translates this problem as one of correctness, as a technical lapse, without accepting that no end may be brought to the debate unless a choice is made by reference to an external point of view. Deliverance is

---

[439] Kennedy (Sources), *supra* note 256, at 95-96.

[440] The same point is made by Koskenniemi (From Apology to Utopia), *supra* note 65, at 340.

[441] Kennedy (Sources), *supra* note 256, at 95.

found in more technical solutions, which simply relocate the problem into a different doctrine, technique or criterion.

One needs not go far to illustrate the point: standardization and formalization claim determinacy by reducing the list of possible legal instruments that qualify as sources to a closed list of abstract categories of norms. Before the arrival of Article 38, the story goes, a Court would debate indefinitely whether reason, comity, or Roman law are sources of international law – an admittedly uncomfortable situation for any judicial institution to be in. Now such debates become redundant and indeed transformed into legal-technical questions of whether a certain instrument fulfills the conditions of any of the sources of Article 38, e.g., whether it 'is' an international treaty, custom, general principle. This however does not bring closure. Each time someone makes a 'hard' argument (e.g., the obligation is binding because it is contained in a treaty), another could respond using a 'soft' argument.

> "In a schematic and preliminary way, we can imagine the arguments that might be made on behalf of hard and soft sources in a world of autonomous states. Suppose that one sovereign state (State 1) when invoking a norm against another (State 2) argues that the norm invoked is authoritative and binding because it is 'hard'. A hard source is binding because the state to be bound has agreed that it is binding, so that its autonomy will not be threatened by compliance. State 2 may […] attack the source directly. It may argue that if its consent is the basis for its being bound, it has changed its mind, or did not intend to consent in the first place.
> These classic responses force State 1 to argue that such change is not permissible […] because if everyone did it would be a mess; because State 1 would not want its treaty partners to do so; because you just have to keep your word; etc. One may invoke a doctrinal expression of these conclusions such as pacta sunt servanda. State 2, against whom the norm is invoked, might respond that these norms or considerations have nothing to do with consent. It they do, State 2 might simply reinvoke its initial objection that it does not *now* consent to this application or interpretation. Perhaps State 2 is willing in similar circumstances to let its treaty partners off as well, or finds the state of the system less important than its own release from the particular norm. In responding, State 1 has forced State 2 to shift gears and argue from some non-consensual perspective. To State 2, all hard sources have become soft sources in disguise."[442]

---

[442]   Ibid., at 39.

Take the example of a treaty. Disagreement as to whether a legal instrument is a treaty in the sense of Article 38 would require a definition of what a treaty is. Such a definition is provided in Article 2 of the 1969 Vienna Convention on the Law of Treaties. This Article would only be helpful if it was not amenable to "hard" and "soft" arguments, which appear equally legitimate or which would transmute into each other. The ICJ has on many occasions battled with the question with contradictory results.[443] Is a given agreement a treaty because the parties intended it to be a treaty ("hard") or because it 'objectively' meets the definition of Article 2, or for maintaining the legal certainty of the system, and aside from the intention of the parties ("soft")? Who decides what was the initial intention of the parties? Is it the parties themselves, or some objective evidence of their intentions? Since Article 38 ICJ Statute and Article 2 VCLT do not in themselves bring determinacy, one needs to resort to yet another doctrine of interpreting the evidence of that would help one apply these definitions. A doctrine of interpretation, say Articles 31 and 32 of the Vienna Convention on the Law of Treaties, would however also be open to "hard" and "soft" forms of argument. In order to interpret a treaty provision should one look at the intention of the drafters ("hard"), the objective meaning of the terms ("soft") or the object and purpose ("hard"/"soft")? The search for a 'decisive discourse' can continue indefinitely and without closure.

## 3.8    CONCLUSION

The present case study tried to seek out the discursive structures that produced meaning about progress in the case of the doctrine of the sources of

---

[443] See for example, the findings in the Aegean Sea Continental Shelf Case (*Greece* v. *Turkey*) (Judgment of 19 December 1978), *ICJ Rep.* (1978) at 3; South West Africa Cases (*Ethiopia* v. *South Africa*; *Liberia* v. *South Africa*) (Judgment of 21 December 1962), *ICJ Rep.* (1962) at 319; Case Concerning Maritime Delimitation and Territorial Questions Between Qatar and Bahrain (*Qatar* v. *Bahrain*) (Jurisdiction and Admissibility) (Judgment of 5 February 1995), *ICJ Rep.* (1995) at 6. In each one of these cases, the Court has resorted to a different criterion to determine whether a certain instrument was an international treaty, ranging from the intentions of the parties (SWA Cases) to subsequent reliance (Aegean Sea) to a 'reasonable man's' criterion (*Qatar* v. *Bahrain*). For a discussion, see C. Chinkin, 'A Mirage in the Sand? Distinguishing between Binding and Non-Binding Relations Between States', 10 *Leiden Journal of International Law* (1997) 223.

international law. The rhetoric about the reconstruction of international law, which dominated international law debates in the wake of the Great War; and the narrative moves of 'standardization' and 'formalization' in literature that followed the adoption of the Statute of the Permanent Court of International Justice, weave a historical narrative of progress. This narrative presents pre-1920 doctrine of the sources as unable to fulfill its role as a tool for separating law from non-law. The reason given is that the doctrine was indeterminate: it was too open-ended (nobody knew the exact number and nature of the sources) and too dependent on theoretical/political opinion (pinned on partial philosophical theories). On the antipodes, the post-1920 doctrine of the sources under Article 38 Statute PCIJ is presented as hugely superior on account of its alleged determinacy. The problem of open-endedness was resolved with the move to standardization (a new 'closed' and 'universal' list of sources). The problem of dependence on philosophical opinion was resolved with the move to formalization, the creation of a set of secondary rules belonging to a different register than 'high theory' or politics. The transition from fragmentation to standardization, from philosophy/politics to technique, from academic formalism to pragmatism, is the totalizing narrative that 'speaks itself' and produces meaning about progress in sources discourse. The narrative moves of standardization and formalization capitalize on a background story that privileges determinacy, scientific technique, and pragmatism, to leave no choice as to the meaning of progressiveness in doctrinal debates.

Like Chapter 2, the case study of Chapter 3 goes, however, a step further to demonstrate that the projected virtue of determinacy of the new doctrine is based on notions that are themselves neither stable nor determinate. Closure and universality are subverted each time they were put to application. The 'new' doctrine of the sources, despite its claim to limit the range of sources that could be invoked, allows two opposing patterns of argument ('hard' and 'soft') to operate simultaneously within each of the sources of the list of Article 38 PCIJ. Instead of bringing closure, the possibility of both 'soft' and 'hard' patterns of argument enables the debate to continue interminably. The only way to bring closure is to invoke yet another and new decisive discourse, this time external to Article 38. The same holds for the narrative move of formalization. Formalization aspired to disconnect the 'registers' of high theory and practical application in order to allow a technical (non-political, non-theoretical) application of the doctrine. It was however demonstrated that the two registers collapsed into each other each time one would seek their autonomous application.

Like the vocabulary of absolutism and democracy, the vocabulary of standardization and formalization, far from having a stable content, can be better understood as a style of argument that helped vest with legitimacy a project for the reconstruction of public international law. 'Talking sources' is not 'more' determinate than 'talking theory'. At the same time, the language of the sources is able to capture anew the fantasy of the international lawyer as a discourse that is able to jump over the ruptures of everyday experience. Legitimacy in sources discourse is thus produced not because pragmatism or Article 38 PCIJ Statute had the capacity to decisively tell whether a certain norm 'is' one of public international law. Legitimacy is produced via the *invocation* of the vocabulary of pragmatism and Article 38. In that sense, progress in sources discourse does not have an essence: it is the product of a narrative whose essence is floating, allowing a multiplicity of meanings according to the occasion. Like in the case of Seferiades, one could argue that the iteration of meanings is what enables the success of the language of the sources doctrine. As explained in the digression to the contemporary literature, literature on the sources has found peace in bracketing (setting aside) all the hard questions that would bring out the indeterminacy of the doctrine. The feeling of certainty in the literature is forged by standard references to classical cases and materials. In such references the iteration of the vocabulary is either silenced or under-played. The success of the vocabulary of the sources rests in its capacity to legitimize itself as progressive, regardless of whether it is determinate or stable. The authors of the new doctrine are not the authors of determinate/rational set of technical tools, but the controllers of a set of discursive structures that legitimize legal-social outcomes.

## Chapter 4
## INTERNATIONAL LAW AS PROGRESS/PROGRESS WITHIN INTERNATIONAL LAW – THE NEW TRIBUNALISM

### 4.1    INTRODUCTION

The third and final case study turns to yet another plane of international legal argument and a third style of progress narratives. It turns to international institutions and looks at the way in which the establishment of new international institutions can be considered simultaneously *as* social progress *and* progress *within* international law. Specifically, Chapter 4 takes issue with international law's recent fascination with international courts and tribunals – or what is called here, for argument's sake, 'the new tribunalism'. In the course of the past two decades international judicial dispute settlement has stridently re-entered the stage of international law argument to claim a central role. Even if one sets aside the most enthusiastic advocates of the phenomenon of "proliferation" or "multiplication" of tribunals, as the trend is usually captioned in international law talk,[444] international law-

---

[444] On the topic of proliferation/multiplication, see generally C. Brown, *A Common Law of International Adjudication* (2007); T. Treves, 'Judicial Lawmaking in an Era of "Proliferation" of International Courts and Tribunals: Development or Fragmentation of International Law?', in Wolfrum and Röben (Developments), *supra* note 255, at 587-620; P.S. Rao, 'Multiple International Judicial Forums: A Reflection of the Growing Strength of International Law or Its Fragmentation?', 25 *Michigan Journal of International Law* (2004) 929; F. Pocar, 'The Proliferation of International Criminal Courts and Tribunals: A Necessity in the Current International Community', 2 *JICJ* (2004) 304; L. Reed, 'Great Expectations: Where Does the Proliferation of International Dispute Resolution Tribunals Leave International Law?', 96 *American Society of International Law Proceedings* (2002) 219; T. Buergenthal, 'Proliferation of International Courts and Tribunals: Is It Good or Is It Bad?', 14 *Leiden Journal of International Law* (2001) 267; H. Thirlway (Proliferation), *supra* note 30; D. Praeger, 'The Proliferation of International Judicial Organs: The Role of the International Court of Justice', in Blokker and Schermers (Proliferation of International Organizations), *supra* note 30, at 279-95; P.C. Szasz, 'The Proliferation of Administrative Tribunals', in Blokker and Schermers (Proliferation of International Organizations), *supra* note 30, at 241-249; B. Kingsbury, 'Is the Proliferation of International Courts and Tribunals a Systemic Problem?', 31 *New York University Journal of International Law and Politics* (1999) 679; J. Charney, 'The Impact on the International Legal System of the Growth of Interna-

yers in all quarters of the discipline are becoming increasingly comfortable in dealing in their everyday work with international, internationalized and hybrid judicial techniques, bodies, and processes. Not only as an important new parameter broadening the range of available situational or long-term policy choices (e.g., choices between different dispute settlement solutions, post-conflict management strategies, or even architectures of multilateral treaties or organizations), but also as a trendy and lucrative domain of professional expertise for academics, practitioners, functionaries. Although the most visible manifestation of the new tribunalism can be found in debates about international criminal justice, the discipline in its entirety witnesses a rejuvenated faith in the potential of international judicial institutions to further its objectives.

Tribunals-related literature is obviously not a coherent body of texts. It is work produced in different parts of the world, notably on both sides of the Atlantic. Most of this work seems to be concerned with specific cases and procedural issues rather than with articulating an analytical framework for the study of the international judiciary. In its heterogeneity, this scholarship reflects the variety of personal-professional projects that constitute the discipline of public international law. Nonetheless a sense of cohesion can be traced in the various texts. This cohesion is forged by a certainty, sometimes stated overtly, other times assumed, that the turn to adjudication constitutes a moment of disciplinary progress: an institutional-professional development with benevolent systemic consequences.[445] The term "new

---

tional Courts and Tribunals', 31 *New York University Journal of International Law and Politics* (1999) 697; J. Charney, 'Is International Law Threatened by Multiple International Tribunals?', 271 *Recueil des Cours* (1998) 101; G. Hafner, 'Should One Fear the Proliferation Mechanisms for the Peaceful Settlement of Disputes?', in L. Caflisch, *Règlement Pacifique des différences entre états* (1998) 25-41; L. Boisson de Chazournes, *Multiplication des instances de règlement des différences: vers la promotion de la règle de droit (Zero Issue) Forum* (1998) 14-16; R. Jennings, 'The Proliferation of Adjudicatory Bodies: Dangers and Possible Answers', in L. Boisson des Chazournes, ed., *Implications of the Proliferation of International Adjudicatory Bodies for Dispute Resolution: Proceedings of a Forum Co-Sponsored by the ASIL and the HEI* (1995) 2-7.

[445] In recent years several authors have tried to perform comprehensive and elaborate cost/benefit analyses of whether proliferation is a "good thing" or not. Typically such analyses conclude that the benefits greatly outweigh the costs. For some notable ones, see Buergenthal (Good or Bad?), *supra* note 444; Charney (Impact), *supra* note 444; Charney (Is International Law Threatened), *supra* note 444; R. Higgins, 'The ICJ, the ECJ and the Integrity of International Law', 52 *International and Comparative Law Quarterly* (2003) 1;

tribunalism" is used in this chapter in order to caption the different expressions of this narrative of progress in international law literature. Post-1980 literature relating to international courts and tribunals this way forms the horizon of the field of enquiry of this case study.

Proliferation of courts and tribunals is typically seen as progress in two different ways. First, as a process of internal maturation, marking the completion of international law's institutional structure (the missing 'third pillar' of the international division of powers),[446] thus leading to more cases resolved before courts, more case law, more determinate rules, more certainty and predictability, more precedent, more thickening of the texture of the legal fabric (progress *within* international law). Second, as the hallmark of a new rule-oriented approach, widely regarded as an absolute and necessary condition for social progress (international law *as* progress).[447] Along these lines, the mere phenomenon of proliferation, the mere creation of more international judicial institutions, is said to have an immanent positive value.[448]

The understanding of creating new courts 'in itself' as a moment of progress is already a radical shift compared to the past, when skepticism prevailed (see Section 4.2.1, *infra*). But the new literature on tribunals raises the stakes much more. It makes bold statements about a new paradigm of international lawyering that revolves around the development of judicial institutions. This new paradigm, the story goes, initiates a new rule-oriented approach to international governance, whose beneficiaries are the entire community of states and their citizens, as opposed to narrow sovereign, bi-lateral or other partial interests. For some, proliferation is accompanied by an attitude shift: allegedly, and more than any other actor, courts are today willing to assume responsibility for social progress and apply international law in a manner beneficial for international community as a

---

Societé Française pour le Droit International, *La Juridictionnalisation du droit international: Colloque de Lille* (2003); and the Editorial comments, 2 *JICJ* (2004) at 300 et seq.

[446] Rosenne explains the necessity of the International Court of Justice on the grounds that "[since] the world organization already possessed executive, deliberative, and administrative organs, [it] would be incomplete unless it possessed a fully integrated judicial system of its own"; S. Rosenne, *The World Court: What It Is and How It Works* (1962) 36.

[447] This idea dates back to the Kantian claim about the importance of international dispute settlement. See I. Kant, 'Perpetual Peace', in I. Kant, *Political Writings* (1991) 93, at 102-105.

[448] Thirlway (Proliferation), *supra* note 30, at 255 (footnotes omitted).

whole.[449] For others, the new professional community of 'dispute settlers' can forge a new culture of cooperation based on the respect of democratic values of pluralism, persuasive authority, positive conflict, comity, and so on.[450] Tribunals, along these lines, are able to serve justice in specific disputes (this is the so-called 'private' function of international dispute settlement) without sacrificing, and while nurturing, the universality of international law ('public' function).

These are mighty claims. In this light, the new tribunalism is an appealing story of disciplinary progress that a jurist can intuitively recognize: a story about how institutional development (e.g., courts), a new professional culture (e.g., rule oriented approach), and a substantive social goal (rule of law, more justice, less war) can bear fruit if pursued with persistence and commitment. It is a compelling story about how international law may finally be able to travel the coveted distance from a power-oriented to a rule-oriented approach, from indeterminacy to determinacy, from impunity to accountability, from justice without peace (and peace without justice) to peace with justice. Tribunals, in this vein, are not only the latest addition to the repertoire of international legal action. They are also the catalyst for coping with the realist challenges of the 21st century.

Like the two previous case studies, the present one does not address the ontological/policy question of whether proliferation of tribunals *is* progress for or within international law. The purpose is rather to expose the structures within tribunals' discourse that generate the feeling of progress associated with the phenomenon of proliferation. It explores the proposition that, although progress may be a convenient label to caption a certain international law development, it is ultimately a term devoid of meaning unless placed within the context of a narrative – a story about how things were, how things are, and how things need to be. Such narratives of progress, it is argued, do not 'speak themselves': their plot is not merely recorded by the author. Instead, their plot is created by the author, based on concrete (epistemic, ideological, or other) choices and is expressed through a 'vocabulary' – a set of assumptions, images, metaphors and so on. As a conse-

---

[449] P. Sands, 'Turtles and Torturers: The Transformation of International Law', 33 *New York University Journal of International Law and Politics* (2001) 527, at 536.

[450] A.M. Slaughter, 'A Global Community of Courts', 44 *Harvard International Law Journal* (2003) 191, at 194.

quence, such narratives of progress compete with and exclude alternative ones; they also constitute the basis for policies and decisions with tangible effects on everyday life. In this context, progress narratives are no longer mere descriptive statements but powerful rhetorical strategies of (de)legitimation.

A 'progress kick', the zeal generated by the feeling part of a moment of disciplinary progress, yields tremendous energy and can be a compelling source of institutional, doctrinal, or social transformation, storming any resistance by force. Associating oneself with a global progressive movement can justify one's renewed commitment to a previously criticized profession. It can generate professional certainty that we are on the right track, thus reinforcing international law's position relative to other sciences of governance. The lawyers are back, primed by a persuasive story about how law can perform a catalytic role in fostering peace and justice. Indeed, proliferation of tribunals involves major policy decisions such as deciding UN strategy on post-conflict reconstruction, norm development, re-ranking of expenditure priorities, re-designing academic curricula – choosing few among many battles to fight when resources are scarce. What if, however, the narrative is not an objective representation of reality (does not 'speak itself') but based on partial epistemic choices? Then one will have taken for granted what yet needs to be proven. Instead of using tribunals as a means of promoting certain goals, the defense of the progress narrative itself will have become the self-referential goal of the intellectual pursuit. At that moment, initial exhilaration and confidence gives way to what Pierre Schlag calls *ennui*,[451] a feeling of weariness and discontent with the narrative and an eventual shift to new projects. There is good evidence that tribunals literature has started experiencing this feeling of *ennui*.[452]

Seen in this light, the event of the new tribunalism can help understand the pivotal role of progress narratives in international law work. Section 4.2

---

[451] P. Schlag, 'Normative and Nowhere to Go', 43 *Stanford Law Review* (1990) 167, at 184.

[452] Tribunal literature shows signs of reaching this moment of ennui after the initial exhilaration. Compare for example recent work by Romano and others that take a markedly more pragmatic assessment about the social impact of proliferation and contrast their previous writings. See, e.g., C. Romano, 'The Shift from the Consensual to the Compulsory Paradigm in International Adjudication: Elements for a Theory of Consent', 39 *New York University Journal of International Law and Politics* (2007) 791, at 834-837.

outlines the main thrust of the progress narrative of the 'new tribunalism' and explains what is new and noteworthy in today's engagement with international courts. Section 4.3 performs a discourse analysis of the relevant literature and describes the discursive structures (vocabularies) of the new tribunalism. Section 4.4 performs a critique of the vocabularies in order to demonstrate that, despite their claims, they do not reflect a 'world out there' but are unstable discursive structures. Section 4.5 closes the chapter with a re-assessment of the new tribunalism in the light of the above.

## 4.2    The New Tribunalism

### 4.2.1    Tribunals and pre-1980s international law

Professional interest in international courts and tribunals is hardly a novelty. International courts have always stood as important paragons of internationalism, even if sentiments towards them oscillated considerably. Since 1899 and the formal inauguration of the era of adjudication with the launching of the Permanent Court of Arbitration, the international judiciary has been a global constant of the profession, an emblematic sign of its rule-oriented culture and trade-mark of its liberal-democratic ideology. Tribunals belong, so to speak, to the universal language of public international law. Featured in every textbook or university course, they are entities to be reckoned with by students and policy-makers alike. Their pronouncements are classic sources of normative authority and the prospect of appearing before one is a major foreign policy consideration.

It is not hard to guess some of the reasons behind international law's traditional interest in courts. International adjudication seems to exemplify central credos of internationalism. Take, for example, the idea that before international arbitral or judicial institutions one considers problems from a truly 'international' standpoint, rather than considering them as problems that have to be worked out bilaterally between sovereign states: "[T]o apply to the Court, is to place oneself on the plane of international law" – this is the metaphor of the "international plane" employed by the International Court of Justice in the *Nottebohm* case,[453] capturing the imagination of

---

[453] The celebrated metaphor of the international plane descends from the Judgment of the International Court of Justice in the Nottebohm case (second phase) (*Lichtenstein* v.

generations of scholars about the existence of an international mind, standpoint, or sensibility, providing a space for conflict resolution which is above and beyond national politics.[454] The judiciary is also the place where public international lawyers are at their best, as judges or advocates, repositories of the knowledge for the management of the procedural and substantive norms that govern these institutions. The metaphor of the international plane assumes the existence of a class of professionals who imagine looking down from the international plane towards the problem, equipped with their internationalist professional expertise, which is resistant to partial political or ideological interests. Recent literature, and in some contrast to the more cautious approach of the past, has started portraying international judges as individuals exhibiting such rare professionalism, high moral character, independence and wisdom that escape conventional standards.[455] Tribunals and international judges are pictured as able to resolve disputes with one eye to the specific needs of each case and another to forging the legitimacy and universality of international law as a system, by means of *obiter dicta*, elucidation or corrective interpretation of existing norms.[456]

---

*Guatemala*), Judgment of 6 April 1955, *ICJ Rep.* 1955, 4, at 20-21. The Court stated: "But the issue which the Court must decide is not one which pertains to the legal system of Liechtenstein. It does not depend on the law or on the decision of Liechtenstein whether that State is entitled to exercise its protection, in the case under consideration. To exercise protection, to apply to the Court, is to place oneself on the plane of international law. It is international law which determines whether a State is entitled to exercise protection and to seise the Court." On the metaphor of the international plane, see A. Riles, 'The View from the International Plane: Perspective and Scale in the Architecture of Colonial International Law', 6 *Law and Critique* (1995) 39.

[454] N.M. Butler, *The International Mind: An Argument for the Judicial Settlement of International Disputes* (1912) at 102: "The international mind is nothing else than the habit of thinking of foreign relations and business, and the habit of dealing with them, which regard the several nations of the civilized world as friendly and cooperating equals in aiding the progress of civilization, in developing commerce and industry, and in spreading enlightenment and culture throughout the world."

[455] See, e.g., M. Reisman, 'Judge Shigeru Oda: A Tribute to an International Treasure', 16 *Leiden Journal of International Law* (2003) 57. See also D. Terris, C. Romano and L. Swigart, eds., *The International Judge: An Introduction to the Men and Women Who Decide the World's Cases* (2007).

[456] Karen Knop explains how the doctrine of the general principles of law has been used by international tribunals to reinforce their claims of being able "to do justice to diversity without sacrificing universality"; K. Knop, *Reflections on Thomas Franck, Race and Nationalism* (1960); K. Knop, 'General Principles of Law' and Situated Generality', 35 *New York Journal of International Law and Politics* (2003) 437, at 439 and 455-469.

In addition to its internationalist outlook, the international judiciary is often seen as the location *par excellence* where law may be carefully dissected from politics. It is the space where formal rules appear to be applied and enforced with an acceptable degree of certainty and predictability and where the parties expect to enjoy the protection of equitable procedural principles. Some of the most emblematic doctrines and secondary rules of international law (e.g., sources, state responsibility) and procedural principles (e.g., equality of arms, *audi altera partem*) operate at their best before tribunals, where the language of law is spoken with as few diversions as possible. All this seems to add up to relative fairness, equality, and predictability in the process, substituting coercive force with the language of law while relocating the initial international dispute to a symbolic adversarial battleground. Hence tribunals are traditionally believed to contribute positively to the aims of public international law, as mechanisms essential for maintaining international peace and as necessary components of any internationalist governance project. The starting assumption of this contention is that the creation of tribunals signifies the recognition from the side of states of the importance of the rule of law in their relations. It is to be presumed that more tribunals will lead to more justice and to more situations in which resort to forcible means of settling disputes is avoided; the proliferation of institutions and mechanisms will lead to a higher proportion of disputes being settled this way. This in turn will result to more pronouncements about international law, which will strengthen its materiel and increase its volume of pronouncements, leading to more certainty and predictability in dispute settlement in the future.

Despite various critiques that can be leveled against such a chain of reasoning, mainstream scholarship has always accepted it as axiomatic. Lasting or newly found mythologies have been created about some international courts, such as the ICJ, the International Criminal Court (ICC), or the European Court of Human Rights (ECHR). Fluency with their work is the benchmark of one's initiation into the deeper secrets of the discipline and the usual material for student examinations. The normative value of their judgments and *obiter dicta* is a standard way of validating one's legal argument. For nearly a century 'international dispute settlement' has already existed as a separate sub-field of the study of international law, associated with awe-inspiring figures of the discipline, such as Max Huber, James Brown Scott, Manley Hudson, Alejandro Álvarez, Steven Schwebel, Hersch

Lauterpacht, Robert Jennings, Shabtai Rosenne, Taslim Olawale Elias, and many others.

Now, despite the prominent role of courts in the dream of a peaceful international community, the opinion of international lawyers about courts has been ambivalent and, until very recently, skeptical. The judicialization of international law may have always been a declared goal of the discipline since 1899 or earlier but one was never sure whether this could ever be attained or how to precipitate the process. Creating more tribunals, although part of the overall plan, was never a real priority and came second to other institutional developments that were considered much more capable of ensuring systemic goals.

With the danger of over-simplification, mainstream skepticism about international courts and tribunals can be boiled down to two different concerns. The first has a typically positivist accent. It questions whether an international judicial system is at all feasible on the face of other structural pathologies in international law at large.[457] Authors here are worried that international courts will remain a distant dream as long as international law has bad quality (indeterminate/political/few) rules and norms, gaps in the body of its law, lack of enforcement mechanisms and compulsory jurisdiction,[458] and so on. The main priority was therefore the creation of better international law rather than more judicial institutions.[459] In 1949 the President of the ICJ himself advised against "extravagant faith" in the possibility of peace through judicial means and stated that "the International Judge alone cannot assure peace".[460]

The second set of concerns has a more realist accent. It worries that, due to the nature of international politics, courts give way to political pressure

---

[457] For a typical example of these concerns see P. Weil, 'Towards Relative Normativity in International Law', 77 *American Journal of International Law* (1983) 413.

[458] The small number of states having accepted the jurisdiction of the ICJ and the number of reservations were a constant concern. See, e.g., C.H.M. Waldock, 'Decline of the Optional Clause', 32 *British Yearbook of International Law* (1956) 269; this is one of the main arguments in Romano (Shift), *supra* note 452.

[459] The interwar period (1918-1939) identified the development of new law (codification) as the main priority. From the large body of literature on codification in the period, see Baker (Codification), *supra* note 310, at 40; de Visscher (Codification), *supra* note 310; Root (Codification), *supra* note 310; Cole (Codification), *supra* note 310; Scott (Codification), *supra* note 310; McNair (Present Position), *supra* note 310; Urrutia (Codification), *supra* note 310; Brierly (Future), *supra* note 310; Sibert (Quelques aspects), *supra* note 310.

[460] J. Basdevant, 'Peace through International Adjudication?' (Brochure, translated 1949).

and are powerless to handle sensitive disputes, even when the latter revolve around a strong legal component.[461] In its most extreme version, this concern repeats the credos of realism: judges can never apply the law impartially but will favor the interests of the states that appointed them; and courts are the victim of conflicting interests among the states that use and control it. In its milder form, this concern captures the disappointment of scholars in the handling of particular cases by international tribunals. Post-War II literature (1965-1989), liberal, realist, and post-colonial, was the most dramatic in its predilection,[462] although this style of argument has found strong support at all post-1918 times, including today. This is particularly the case with "neo-conservative", or "neo-con", or "nationalist international law" writings.[463] The term "neo-conservative" is a figurative term borrowed from US domestic politics and launched recently in international law debates to describe a style of scholarship that has become prominent in the United States during the last years and sees international law as the product of states pursuing their interests on the international stage which does not pull states towards compliance contrary to their interests, and therefore its possibilities for what it can achieve are limited. The specificity of the neo-conservative argument can be better understood when situated in the context of contemporary domestic political debates in the United States about the relevance of international law for the American legal order and its foreign

---

[461] M. Katz, *The Relevance of International Adjudication* (1968), esp. at 145 et seq.

[462] See, e.g., the '"General Debate" on the Role of International Tribunals in International Law', in H. Mosler and R. Bernhardt, eds., *Judicial Settlement of International Disputes*, (1974) at 165-187.

[463] For a brilliant review of neo-conservative work see A. Lorite Escorihuela, 'Cultural Relativism the American Way: The Nationalist School of International Law in the United States', 5 *Global Jurist Frontiers* (2005), <www.bepress.com/gj/frontiers/vol5 /iss1/art2>; I. De la Rasilla del Moral, 'All Roads Lead to Rome or the Liberal Cosmopolitan Agenda as a Blueprint for a Neoconservative Legal Order', 7 *Global Jurist* (2007) 2, at 1. For representative 'neo-con' literature, see J.R. Goldsmith and E.A. Posner, *The Limits of International Law* (2005); E.A. Posner, 'International Law and the Disaggregated State', 32 *Florida State University Law Review* (2005) 797; J.R. Bolton, 'Is There Really "Law" in International Law?', 10 *Transnational Law and Contemporary Problems* (2000) 1; E.A. Posner and J.C. Yoo, 'Judicial Interdependence in International Tribunals', 93 *California Law Review* (2005) 1; E.A. Posner and J.C. Yoo, 'A Theory of International Adjudication', John M. Olin Law and Economics Working Paper No. 206, <www.law.uchicago.edu/Lawecon/index.html>. Cf. L.R. Helfer and A.M. Slaughter, 'Why States Create International Tribunals: A Response to Professors Posner and Yoo', 93 *California Law Review* (2005) 899.

policy. The tenor of the neo-conservative argument on the instant question of proliferation of international courts is that the whole movement of proliferation needs to be met with caution since the only "effective" international tribunals are so-called "dependent" tribunals, by which they mean *ad hoc* tribunals staffed by judges closely controlled by governments or threats of retaliation. By contrast, "independent" tribunals meaning tribunals that resemble domestic courts, pose a danger to international cooperation. Independent judicial decision makers are suspect because they are more likely to allow moral ideals, ideological imperatives, or the interest of third parties to influence their judgments.

In previous decades critiques of international adjudication were most vocal in the capacity of courts to handle the so-called "hard" or "big" cases".[464] Such were the *South West Africa*[465] and the *Hostages*[466] cases before the ICJ, but this view was believed to hold for most instances where significant political interests intersected with the object of the dispute.[467]

---

[464] The term "big case" was prominently used by Falk and described as a "controversy of major significance among the actors in the political arena"; R. Falk, *Reviving the World Court* (1986) at xiii.

[465] South West Africa (Second Phase), 1966 *ICJ Rep.* 6. Friedman, for example, wrote in 1967: "The International Court of Justice, like its predecessor, represents an important but as yet weak attempt to detach international legal issues from national prejudices and passions"; W.G. Friedmann, 'The Jurisprudential Implications of the South West Africa Case', 6 *Columbia Journal of Transnational Law* (1967) 1, at 2 and 10-14. For surveys of the views condemning the South West Africa Judgment, see J. Dugard, *The South West Africa/Namibia Dispute* (1973), esp. at 332-374, 554-559; and R. Falk, 'The South West Africa Cases: An Appraisal', XXI *International Organization* (1967) 1, who acted as legal counsel for Ethiopia and Liberia in the case.

[466] See case concerning United States Diplomatic and Consular Staff in Tehran (*U.S.* v. *Iran*), Judgment, *ICJ Rep.* 3 (1980). See R.A. Falk, 'The Iran Hostage Crisis: Easy Answers and Hard Questions', 74 *American Journal of International Law* (1980) 411; R.A. Falk, 'Realistic Horizons for International Adjudication', 11 *Virginia Journal of International Law* (1971) 314.

[467] According to Friedmann, "[i]t is to be feared that the Judgment of the International Court in the South West Africa case has dealt a devastating blow to the hope that the International Court might be able to deal with explosive and delicate international issues"; Friedmann (Implications of SWA cases), *supra* note 465, at 16. The type of "expectations" that should be placed upon international courts and whether they should be expected to deal with "hard" political cases was at the heart of these debates. See, e.g., E. Gordon, 'Old Orthodoxies amid New Experiences: The South West Africa (Namibia) Litigation and the Uncertain Jurisprudence of the International Court of Justice', 1 *Denver Journal of International Law* (1971) 65.

The impartiality of the international judge and the fair composition of the bench were often put to question, especially in the context of Cold War or post-colonialism debates.[468] Scholars were asked to nuance their expectations about the potential of international courts in a world of sovereign states and some warned that a certain type of disputes should be altogether kept away from international courts.[469] In a profession prepared to give only "two cheers"[470] to adjudication the project of creating of new international tribunals (today's "proliferation") was considered a luxury problem,[471] even a potentially destabilizing and hazardous development. It is only during the mid-1980s and, notably, after 1989 that a new form of engagement with international courts and tribunals entered the stage of international law argument.

### 4.2.2   Facts and trends of proliferation

Attitudes have changed during the past two decades. Post-1980s tribunal-related debate has built its coherence around the terms "proliferation" and "multiplication" of international courts and tribunals, introduced to label the sudden increase in the numbers of new international judicial bodies with general or specialized competence applying international law.[472] When one speaks of proliferation of international courts and tribunals today, one usually refers to two complementary trends. First, a numerical increase in the institutions performing a judicial or semi-judicial function but also in their caseload. Literature has documented quite extensively the various pa-

---

[468] See, e.g., T.O. Elias, 'Does the International Court of Justice, as It Is Presently Shaped, Correspond to the Requirements Which Follow from its Functions as the Central Judicial Body of the International Community?', Report in Mosler and Bernhardt, *supra* note 462, at 19-31.

[469] Falk (Reviving), *supra* note 464, esp. Chapter 1; Katz suggested that "Cold War disputes" were unsuitable for adjudication; see Katz (Relevance of Adjudication), *supra* note 461, at 7-40.

[470] R.R. Baxter, 'Two Cheers for International Adjudication', 65 *American Bar Association Journal* (1979) 1185, at 1188-1189; Baxter feared that the world may be still far from being able to give a "third cheer" to adjudication, primarily on account of the fact that the system was not sufficiently used and supported by states.

[471] P. Jessup, 'Do New Problems Need New Courts?', 65 *Proceedings of the American Society of International Law* 261-268 (1971) at 266-267.

[472] For some examples of this tendency, see note 444, *supra*.

rameters of this demographic growth.[473] Although criminal justice, international economic law and the environment are the fastest growing components, numbers seem to have increased in most areas of international legal practice. Although a steady increase in the number of tribunals has been occurring ever since the end of World War II, the growth-rate has accelerated dramatically since 1989[474] and the system has evolved "beyond recognition".[475] The Project for International Courts and Tribunals (PICT) lists in its "matrix" some 25 permanent, formal, independent international courts.[476] Other authors count more than 50 international courts and tribunals in existence.[477] If one includes other institutions exercising judicial or quasi-judicial functions, the number easily climbs to seventy or more.[478] The widely told story is that whereas in 1946 the ICJ was the only standing international Court, the situation has changed dramatically today with more than 25 permanent international courts in operation. Among many new institutions, one must single out the International Tribunal for the Law of the Sea (ITLOS), several new or reinvigorated tribunals dealing with economic disputes or economic integration,[479] mass claim reparation tribunals or pro-

---

[473] See, e.g., C. Tomuschat, International Courts and Tribunals with Regionally restricted and/or Specialized Jurisdiction, in Judicial Settlement of International Disputes: ICJ, other Courts and Tribunals, Arbitration and Conciliation (1987) at 285-416; C. Romano, 'The Proliferation of International Judicial Bodies: The Pieces of the Puzzle', 31 *New York University Journal of International Law and Politics* (1999) 709; R. Alford, 'The Proliferation of International Courts and Tribunals: International Adjudication in Ascendance', 94 *American Society of International Law Proceedings* (2000) 160; S. Spellicsy, 'The Proliferation of International Tribunals: A Chink in the Armor', 40 *Columbia Journal of Transnational Law* (2001) 143; C. Brown, 'The Proliferation of International Courts and Tribunals: Finding Your Way through the Maze', 3 *Melbourne Journal of International Law* (2002) 453.

[474] Romano (Shift), *supra* note 452, at 803-834.

[475] Sands (Turtles and Torturers), *supra* note 449, at 553.

[476] See <www.pict-pcti.org/publications/synoptic_chart.html>.

[477] Alford (Proliferation), *supra* note 473, at 160.

[478] Spellicsy (Proliferation), *supra* note 473, at 146.

[479] World Trade Organization Dispute Settlement Mechanism; North American Free Trade Agreement Dispute Settlement Panels; European Court of Justice; Court of Justice of the European Free Trade Agreement (EFTA); Court of Justice of the Benelux Economic Union; Court of Justice of the Andean Community (Andean Community); Central American Court of Justice (Organization of Central American States); Court of Justice for the Common Market for Eastern and Southern Africa; Common Court of Justice and Arbitration of the Organization for the Harmonization of Corporate Law in Africa; Judicial Tribunal of the Organization of Arab Petroleum Exporting Countries (OAPEC, 1978); Court of Justice of the Arab Maghreb Union.

cesses,[480] human rights tribunals,[481] the ICC, several international or internationalized criminal tribunals under the auspices of or in agreement with the United Nations,[482] and many others that fit in none of the above categories.[483]

There has been a corresponding increase in the case law of existing institutions. The ICJ, the ECHR, or the World Trade Organization Dispute Settlement Mechanism (WTO DSM) have never been so busy before. In addition, the total number of international claims settled by courts has increased substantially as well, thanks to the establishment of new mass claims judicial procedures. It is reported that the Iran-US Claims Tribunal (IUSCT) has resolved more than 3,000 claims, the Claims Resolution Tribunal for Dormant Accounts in Switzerland (CRT) has rendered more than 7,500 decisions, the Commission for Real Property Claims of Displaced Persons and Refugees in Bosnia and Herzegovina (CRPC) has rendered more than 25,000 decisions,[484] and the United Nations Compensation Commission (UNCC) has resolved in excess of 125,000 claims.[485]

There is also a second trend, parallel and complementary to the first one. The quantitative increase is embellished with an unprecedented diversification of the structural characteristics (e.g., scope, jurisdiction, binding na-

---

[480] E.g., Iran-United States Claims Tribunal; United Nations Compensation Commission; Ethiopia-Eritrea Boundary Commission; Eritrea-Ethiopia Claims Commission; Commission for Real Property Claims of Displaced Persons and Refugees in Bosnia and Herzegovina; Claims Resolution Tribunal for Dormant Accounts in Switzerland; Marshall Islands Nuclear Claims Tribunals; Housing and Property Claims Commission in Kosovo; International Commission on Holocaust Era Insurance; German Forced Labor Compensation Program.

[481] European Court of Human Rights; Inter-American Court of Human Rights; African Court of Human and Peoples' Rights.

[482] International Criminal Tribunal for the Former Yugoslavia; International Criminal Tribunal for Rwanda; The Special Court for Sierra Leone; Special Tribunal to Try Suspects in Assassination of Rafiq Hariri.

[483] E.g., Permanent Court of Arbitration, International Center for the Settlement of Investment Disputes (ICSID), the World Bank Inspection Panel Procedure, the Extraordinary Chambers in the Court of Cambodia for the Prosecution of Crimes Committed During the Period of Democratic Kampuchea, and many more.

[484] For a recent analysis, see A. Buyse, *Post-Conflict Housing Restitution: The European Human Rights Perspective, with a Case Study on Bosnia and Herzegovina* (2007) at 275-311.

[485] Data as presented in Alford (Proliferation), *supra* note 473, at 160.

ture of findings, enforcement mechanisms, and so on) of the new institutions. In 1946 the ICJ was the stereotype of an inter-state, international judicial organ with general competence. The literature observes that the variety in formats today challenges traditional categories of the discipline. National and international, diplomatic and judicial, binding and non-binding, are some of the oppositions that traditional textbooks adhered to in order to classify international judicial dispute settlement methods. Even today, most texts of international dispute settlement exclude from their scope diplomatic, political, internationalized, or other alternative means of international dispute resolution, in order to devote their attention to inter-state permanent judicial institutions, such as the ICJ or the ITLOS.

Recent developments blur and transcend in their individuality these classical dividing lines, creating a great variety of formats. 'Judicialized institutions' such as the WTO DSM straddle the distinction between diplomatic and legal means; the creation of 'internationalized' or 'mixed' tribunals, such as the one in Cambodia seems to bridge the divide between national and international adjudication. A long list of hybrid solutions, such as the UNCC, the CRT, the Housing and Property Claims Commission in Kosovo (HPCC), compulsory or directed conciliation methods, Truth and Reconciliation commissions in lieu of judicial closure, explode classical categories into a polyphony of creativity and adaptability.

### 4.2.3    The new form of engagement

The traditional form of scholarly engagement with tribunals fades next to the spirited comeback of tribunal-related work in public international law during the past two decades, which has taken by surprise some observers.[486] Today's engagement seems to be permeated by a different sensibility, both in terms of its intensity and attitude. In contrast to previous decades, today's argument is upbeat and certain, casting away realist concerns about judicial independence and positivist concerns about the pathology of international law. The force of the new institutional development appears to be

---

[486] Kissinger writes in 2001: "In less than a decade, an unprecedented concept has emerged to submit international politics to judicial procedures. It has spread with extraordinary speed and has not been subjected to systematic debate, partly because of the intimidating passion of its advocates"; H. Kissinger, *Does America Need a Foreign Policy?* (2001) at 273.

beyond doubt or contestation. Proliferation seem to have an immanent value "in itself" to be considered an element of progress in international law.

> "An international judicial or arbitral body has in itself some claim to be re-garded as a good thing: opposition to the establishment of such a body has to be based on questioning whether it is actually needed rather than on any de-nial of its virtues. The creation of new tribunals may indeed be regarded as an encouraging sign, as amounting to the 'expression d'adhésion plus grande des acteurs de la vie internationale à la doctrine de la primauté de la règle de droit dans les rapports internationaux [...]'."[487]

This conviction has even become an "article of faith" among contemporary international lawyers:

> "The whole question of the empirical impact of international courts and tribu-nals on behavior and attitudes has not yet been sufficiently studied, although the work on compliance and on other effects of rules and decisions is growing steadily. Nevertheless, it is an article of faith among most international law-yers that the growing availability and use of international tribunals advances the rule of law in international relations. Within this professional cadre, most of the concern expressed with regard to the proliferation of international courts and tribunals is not about the intrinsic desirability of creating such in-stitutions but about the systemic problems may give rise."[488]

Proliferation is often regarded as the latest episode in a long process of maturation of the discipline and the transition to a rule-oriented model, what Jennings calls the "quiet revolution of international law".[489] Proliferation brings advancement and improved levels of effectiveness:

---

[487] Thirlway (Proliferation), *supra* note 30, at 255 (footnotes omitted).

[488] Kingsbury (Proliferation), *supra* note 444, at 20. See also Buergenthal (Good or Bad?), *supra* note 444; Charney (Is International Law Threatened), *supra* note 444, at 101; Romano writes: "When future international legal scholars look back at international law and organizations at the end of the twentieth century, they probably will refer to the enormous expansion and transformation of the international judiciary as the single most important development in the post Cold-War age"; Romano (Pieces of a Puzzle), *supra* note 474, at 709.

[489] Jennings (Implications), *supra* note 444, at 1.

"[...] the combined effect of these two recent developments [the increased density, volume, and complexity of international norms; and greater commitment to the rule of law in international relations], greater acceptance of the compulsory jurisdiction of international courts and tribunals and the institutionalization of international dispute settlement mechanisms, entails the advancement of international law in new and improved levels of effectiveness."[490]

It is also a sign of the growing strength of international law, reducing arbitrariness and power play in international relations.

"[I]t is a sign of maturity and growing importance of the rule of law in international affairs that international machinery and an appropriate judicial system also accompany the creation of any new and comprehensive international legal regime. The judicial enforcement of international rights and obligations reduces arbitrariness and power plays in international relations."[491]

For many, the 'new' judicial dispute settlement system performs a markedly different function than in the past. From one-among-many mechanisms available in international law for the peaceful resolution of disputes (Art. 33 UN Charter), international tribunals arguably serve today a much more important systemic cause. They are mechanisms for the application and interpretation of the rules of law, thus performing a unifying and stabilizing constitutional function for international law.[492] The importance of the development, for some, even justifies the creation of new field of study, "international judicial law and organization", which should be studied separately from the traditional subject of "international dispute settlement".

---

[490] Y. Shany, *The Competing Jurisdictions of International Courts and Tribunals* (2003) at 4-5.

[491] Rao (Multiple Judicial Forums), *supra* note 444, at 960 (footnote references in the original omitted).

[492] For the "constitutionalist" thesis and the significance of international tribunals in the process, see E.-U. Petersmann, 'Constitutionalism and International Adjudication: How to Constitutionalize the U.N. Dispute Settlement System?', 31 *New York University Journal of International Law and Politics* (1999) 753; P.M. Dupuy, 'The Danger of Fragmentation or Unification of the International Legal System and the International Court of Justice', 31 *New York University Journal of International Law and Politics* (1999) 791; J. Allain, 'The Continued Evolution of International Adjudication', in J. Levasseur, ed., *Looking Ahead: International Law in the 21st Century* (2002) 50-71, at 65 and 71.

"The intent is to show that 'international judicial law and organization' can and should be studied as a discipline in its own right, without the need to be subsumed under the general category of 'Peaceful Settlement of International Disputes'."[493]

The underlying logic here is that, although in the past judicial settlement was merely a means of seeking a peaceful solution to an international dispute, international courts are, much like domestic courts, third-parties applying and interpreting the law in an independent manner, performing a deeper systemic-constitutional function than the "political" or "diplomatic" means of dispute settlement listed in Article 33 of the UN Charter (the 'public' function of international dispute settlement). This is an important cultural shift compared to the past. From the interpretation of legal norms to the outbreak of violence, tribunals no longer simply resolve disputes between parties ('private' function of courts) but are said to foster the growth of a plethora of systemic goods. Looking down from the international plane, they deter international crimes, avert the displacement of populations,[494] save lives, become bulwarks against evil,[495] bring peace[496] and normalcy,[497] reduce arbitrariness,[498] and strengthen the fabric of international law with their pronouncements. International law appears, indeed, so much stronger and more potent with tribunals in its institutional machinery. And international lawyers emerge more vindicated, relevant, and definitely back in business. Even if tribunals do not always work precisely the way one would hope, they are at least a good 'second-best' response, and there is always

---

[493] Romano (Pieces of a Puzzle), *supra* note 474, at 711. See also Allain (Continued Evolution), *supra* note 492.

[494] See, e.g., N. Pillay, 'International Criminal Tribunals as a Deterrent to Displacement', in A. Bayefsky and J. Fitzpatrick, eds., *Human Rights and Forced Displacement* (2000) 262-266.

[495] Address by the UN Secretary General at the Rome Conference on 15 June 1998, as cited in I. Tallgren, 'We Did It? The Vertigo of Law and Everyday Life at the Diplomatic Conference on the Establishment of an International Criminal Court', 12 *Leiden Journal of International Law* (1999) 683, at 683.

[496] R.J. Goldstone, 'Justice as a Tool for Peace-Making: Truth Commissions and International Criminal Tribunals', 28 *New York University Journal of International Law and Politics* (1996) 485, esp. at 488-490.

[497] Yuval Shany, *The Competing Jurisdictions of International Courts and Tribunals* (2003) 7.

[498] Rao (Multiple Judicial Forums), *supra* note 444, at 960.

room for improvement. One needs to start somewhere and, after all, the ICJ, the ICTY, the ITLOS, despite all valid criticisms leveled against them, haven't they all had an overall positive effect on public international law? The story goes that although we may be still looking at the early stages of the process, and although we have to beware systemic hazards, international law may be finally experiencing the long-awaited historical moment of the evolution of the third pillar (next to legislature and the executive) of international governance, the coming of age of international adjudication.

Seen this way, the narrative of progress of the new tribunalism has irresistible allure for the international law professional. First, because it tells a compelling story about how international law may finally be able to travel the coveted distance from a power-oriented to a rule-oriented approach, from indeterminacy to determinacy, from impunity to accountability, from justice without peace (and peace without justice) to peace with justice. The path of progress passes through the development of yet another generation of improved legal doctrines and institutions – international adjudication. Second, in the narrative of proliferation international lawyers are given a central role, as builders and defenders of the integrity of the system. Third, with the new tribunalism international law can carve out a new sovereign ground for itself and maintain its autonomy on the face of the new post-Cold-War realist challenges. Fourth, the new tribunalism appears to be a 'real', tangible institutional development, as opposed to a mere theoretical possibility. Proliferation appears to be 'happening out there' with palpable examples and as an expression of deep social forces.

Have we not, after all, managed to establish the International Criminal Court, a dream-come-true of many generations? Is it also not true that the International Court of Justice was never so busy before? Has the relative success of the ICTY and ICTR not triggered a domino effect in the domestic orders of many states that now endorse universal jurisdiction? For the first time powerful states have found themselves on the losing side of important cases before international tribunals, rebutting the realist claim that international courts would bow to power. International judges have also become better professionals, voting on occasion even against the state of their nationality, and projects for the creation of new codes of professional ethics are under way. Finally, the story of progress appears to 'speak itself'. What can be wrong about international tribunals after all? One can 'intuitively' assume that more tribunals can only lead to more cases being dealt

with judicially, more precedent, more rule oriented culture, more accountability, more justice, more peace. A system of international tribunals will
hush the last remaining skeptics about international law's claim to being
'law proper'. The argument goes that proliferation, if managed correctly,
will bring systemic benefits whose beneficiaries are both the collectivity
and individual, such as justice, peace, rule of law, legal certainty and predictability, deterrence of crimes, end to impunity, etc.

The cultural shift is also reflected in developments in the sociology of
the profession, which has undergone a striking transformation. An astound-
ing amount of monographs, new journals, edited volumes, law review articles, even "manuals" of international tribunals are showcased in publishers'
lists during the last years.[499] Specialized LL.M. Programs, summer schools,
seminars, and new subjects in university curricula respond to market pressure and forge of a new field of scientific study. New professional associations, non-governmental organizations (NGOs) and academic institutes have
emerged,[500] dealing with tribunals, judicial processes, or the phenomenon
of proliferation.[501] Tribunals have also become a distinct niche of professional practice. Twenty years ago the idea of international advocacy as a
career choice sounded a little absurd. Not only because there were not enough
opportunity to practice such a profession; not only because advocacy, say,
before the ICJ was a privilege belonging to a small elite of QCs and professors from London or Paris; but also because international tribunals somehow appeared too marginal to the overall international law project to deserve
one's whole-hearted commitment. Tribunals were simply not seen as the

---

[499] P. Sands, *Manual on International Courts and Tribunals* (1999). The volume of
tribunal related work is reflected in the Selected Bibliography of International Dispute Settlement, published quarterly by the *Leiden Journal of International Law*, comprising hundreds
of titles each year. See also the forthcoming *Journal of International Dispute Settlement*
(Oxford University Press, 2010).

[500] Project for International Courts and Tribunals (<www.pict-pcti.org/>); The New York
University Transitional Justice Project (<www.nyuhr.org/transitional.html>); Transitional
Justice Project of the Notre Dame Law School Center for Civil and Human Rights (<www.nd.
edu/~cchr/programs/tjp.html>); Grotius Center for International Legal Studies of Leiden
University (<www.campusdenhaag.nl/pagina/16>).

[501] See, e.g., International Center for Transitional Justice (<www.ictj.org>); Coalition
for International Justice (<www.cij.org>); No Peace Without Justice (<www.npwj.org/>);
The International Justice Mission (<www.ijm.org>); Advocates International ().

place where catalytic new developments were taking place. Today, prosecuting international crimes, say, in Sierra Leone or working for the Registry of the ICC is considered hip, sexy, and potentially one's key career move to enter the inner circles of the profession and to climb academic hierarchies. Universities willing to seize the moment receive nowadays troops of post-graduate students wishing to enter the practice of international tribunals. Cities such as The Hague welcome the arrival of hundreds, nowadays thousands, legal or paralegal professionals, employed by or around international tribunals.

The sociology of this new professional community is worthy of a separate study. What is arresting at first sight is the shared feeling of belonging to a professional caste. A whole lot of professional associations,[502] newsletters,[503] and common social activities related to tribunals are created, forging alliances and the feeling of community across different judicial institutions. Professionals of the international judiciary in The Hague, from students and interns to registry and press officers, IT specialists, translators, prosecutors, defense attorneys, even Judges, recognize fellow professionals in each other, partaking in complementary projects of international justice. They socialize together in ex-pat circles in The Hague that span different tribunals but are, more or less, limited to them, attend and organize their own events, and so on. The Hague claims the title of "Legal Capital of the World" for precisely the same reason.[504]

---

[502] See, e.g., The International Criminal Bar (<www.icb-bpi.org/>); International Criminal Defense Attorneys Association (<www.aiad-icdaa.org>); the International Criminal Law Network (www.icln.net/).

[503] See, e.g., International Justice Tribune, self-described as "independent website providing information and documentation in international justice", <www.justicetribune.com> (as downloaded in March 2006); The International Courts and Tribunals Project (<www.worldlii.org/int/cases/>, as downloaded in March 2006), "a comprehensive search facility for final decisions of all international and multi-national courts and tribunals, whether global or regional".

[504] See the "Hague Legal Capital" coalition (<www.thehaguelegalcapital.nl/>) and the "Hague Justice Portal", <www.haguejusticeportal.net>, containing information about all different tribunals, international criminal law activities and seminars, etc. See also P.J. van Krieken and D. McKay, eds., *The Hague: Legal Capital of the World* (2005).

## 4.3    Two Vocabularies of Progress

The feeling of progress associated with the new tribunalism is intricately related with the argument of two distinct styles of argument that dominate international law debates today. These styles are called here mainstream, inasmuch as they constitute generally acceptable argumentative styles about international law. They enjoy the confidence of large segments of the profession and occupy dominant positions in the debate and often identify themselves by opposition to the other. As such, they are common reference points, symbolizing two distinct orthodoxies about the discipline of international law. It is argued here that the conglomerate of assumptions, metaphors, and other discursive structures that constitute each one of these styles of argument, what is called their 'vocabularies', are to be credited with the feeling of progress experienced in our encounter with international tribunals. The two vocabularies are named here, for argument's sake, "lawyer-as-architect" and "lawyer-as-social-engineer" and are described in turn.

### 4.3.1    The 'lawyer-as-architect'

The first vocabulary appears to be, on the face of it, politically agnostic, evolutionary,[505] and firmly rooted in the practices and insights of traditional European-style positivism.[506] The vocabulary, for the purposes of this study, is reduced into a narrative of progress, a before/after account of public international law's evolution, which is manifested in the literature with four narrative moves. *First*, an objective historical account: proliferation of tribunals is described as a natural and long-awaited historical development. *Second*, the existence of a system (albeit nascent or imperfect) of

---

[505] Romano begins his article with Ockham's principle of parsimony: "Entia non sunt multiplicanda praeter necessitatem" [Entities should not be multiplied unnecessarily]; Romano (Pieces of a Puzzle), *supra* note 474, at 709.

[506] For some representative writings in this approach, see Thirlway (Proliferation), *supra* note 30; Hafner (Should One Fear), *supra* note 444; Jennings (Dangers and Possible Answers), *supra* note 444; Treves (Judicial Lawmaking), *supra* note 444; Boisson des Chazournes (Multiplication des instances), *supra* note 444; Praeger (Proliferation of International Judicial Organs), *supra* note 444; Pocar (Proliferation of International Criminal Courts), *supra* note 444; Dupuy (Danger of Fragmentation), *supra* note 492; Shany (Competing Jurisdictions), *supra* note 497; Petersmann (Constitutionalism), *supra* note 492; Rao (Multiple Judicial Forums), *supra* note 444.

international justice. *Third*, judicialization seen as a moment of disciplinary progress. *Fourth*, the identification of an important role for the international lawyer as a defender of the coherence of the system.

*Historical account*

The first component of the vocabulary of the 'lawyer-as-architect' is an evolutionary account of the history of international law. The story goes that the advent of tribunals is a 'natural' stage in the evolution of the discipline. As Guillaume assures as, "in all human communities justice had to be done and judicial institutions were established as soon as such communities were organized".[507] Proliferation, in this sense, constitutes a decisive turning point in the long history of international law because it evidences its legalization and constitutionalization. It signifies an important paradigm shift in favor of law over politics and legal discourse over power-based diplomacy. Until recently international law was not ready or mature enough to sustain a developed system of international justice, due to structural deficiencies, pathologies or birth defects, these colleagues argue.[508] The absence of an obligation to settle disputes peacefully, the power of the sovereign state to flout the rules, the limited regulatory domain of international law, the anarchic or fragmented development of its norms and doctrines, the absence of enforcement mechanisms, the lack of compulsory jurisdiction, are all reasons that prevented a system of international courts to emerge and flourish. The proliferation of tribunals, according to this view, is "feature of a growing sophistication in the relationship of states",[509] the "expansion of international law"[510] or its "quiet revolution", as Sir Robert Jennings put it once, referring to a "radical change in character of the discipline".[511]

---

[507] G. Guillaume, 'The Future of International Law and Institutions', 44 *International and Comparative Law Quarterly* (1995) 848.

[508] Rao (Multiple Judicial Forums), *supra* note 444; Thirlway (Proliferation), *supra* note 30; Romano (Pieces of a Puzzle), *supra* note 474. See also Shany (Competing Jurisdictions), *supra* note 497, at 1-11, esp. 1-5; Hafner (Should One Fear), *supra* note 444.

[509] M.C.W. Pinto, Pre-eminence of the International Court of Justice, in C. Peck and R.S. Lee, eds., Increasing the Effectiveness of the International Court of Justice (1997) 281-309, at 282.

[510] Dupuy (Danger of Fragmentation), *supra* note 492, at 795.

[511] Jennings (Proliferation), *supra* note 444, at 2; Allain (Continued Evolution), *supra* note 492, at 57 et seq.

Why did this legalization take place today and not in the past? The answer is found for these authors in the enabling concurrence of a number of variables and factors. So, for example, the diversification of the ways in which states relate to each other and the regulation of previously unregulated domains have led to the codification of new law and the creation of regulatory frameworks and corresponding international organizations.[512] Such areas of practice fell once within the reserved domain of the sovereign states (such as criminal justice or human rights); were the object of bi- or pluri-lateral regulation only (trade in goods or services); or were simply unregulated (natural resources, the high seas, biotechnology, etc.). Other variables include the increased inter-dependence of states, technological advances, globalization, the positive record of existing tribunals, the greater acceptance of the compulsory jurisdiction of tribunals, the need for specialized expertise on the bench or tailor-made rules of procedure and evidence (e.g., intervention rules, publicity, language, time-lines), the progressive acceptance of compulsory jurisdiction clauses,[513] and so on. Dispute settlement mechanisms are said to have sprung into existence, in order to enforce the application of the new norms.[514]

Let us briefly observe, already at this stage, the style of this historical account. The creation of new courts and tribunals is presented, sometimes overtly, other times implicitly, as a natural development of a historical process, complying with an inevitable historical determinism: *ubi societas, ibi jus* – now perhaps *ibi curia*? History is linear and progress is evolutionary, with direct correlation between cause and effect: fact x brings systemic reaction y. One can speak of a process that started in Versailles and culminated in Rwanda.[515] Remarkably, all factors and variables are regarded as belonging to a world external to the public international lawyer herself. The regulatory domain of international law expands, states recognize the im-

---

[512] G. Guillaume, 'The Proliferation of International Judicial Bodies: The Outlook for the International Legal Order', 27 October 2000, Speech to the Sixth Committee of the General Assembly of the United Nations, <www.icj-cij.org>; Shany (Competing Jurisdictions), *supra* note 497, at 1-2; Romano (Pieces of a Puzzle), *supra* note 474; Spellicsy (Chink in the Armor), *supra* note 473.

[513] This is the main argument in Romano (Shift), *supra* note 452.

[514] Guillaume (Outlook), *supra* note 512, at 2; Romano (Pieces of a Puzzle), *supra* note 474, at 710; Thirlway (Proliferation), *supra* note 30, at 253.

[515] See, e.g., the historical narrative in Bassiouni (Versailles to Rwanda), *supra* note 12.

portance of law, diversify their ways of relating to each other. Tribunals emerge, sprout, spring out like mushrooms in a natural chain of cause and effect, but not as parts of ideological projects or historical conjunctures in which the discipline, the members of the professional community, play an organic role. Much like Seferiades, the scholar speaking of proliferation today adopts the posture of a dispassionate, neutral, objective chronicler that merely transcribes events as they unfold before her sight, from a seemingly external point of view. Her agency in the process of organization and representation of these developments or variables is underplayed. The language used to convey the observations is descriptive and technical. The reader is assured that this is how 'it happened'. In this account of progress, the "I" of the author is absent, and the story speaks itself.

### A system of international courts and tribunals

But let us move on a little. Complementary to the historical account is the system-building component of the argument. In the literature, the development of judicial institutions is generally seen as sporadic, fragmented, and anarchic.[516] New institutions are described as having paid little attention to compatibility issues with pre-existing ones. Because of the decentralized method of delineation, jurisdictional overlaps and conflicts were created.[517] At the same time, different developments in the world of the international judiciary can (and should be) seen as part of an inter-connected system[518] or as the pieces of a puzzle.[519]

This is puzzling imagery indeed. The argument goes like this. Typically, authors begin by defining what a tribunal is and, on that basis, distinguish between those institutions that qualify as such and the rest.[520] Such a typology is necessary because it can help one decide which tribunals should be

---

[516] See R. Jennings, 'The Judiciary, International and National, and the Development of International Law', 45 *International and Comparative Law Quarterly* (1996) 5; Hafner (Should One Fear), *supra* note 444; Rosenne (Law and Practice), *supra* note 383, at 529.

[517] Shany (Competing Jurisdictions), *supra* note 497, at 8.

[518] Shany (Competing Jurisdictions), *supra* note 497, at 105-108.

[519] Romano (Pieces of a Puzzle), *supra* note 474.

[520] Several authors think that it is necessary to begin with the definition question of what is a tribunal in order to assert the extent of the problem. See Thirlway (Proliferation), *supra* note 30, at 251; Hafner (Should One Fear), *supra* note 444, at 27; Shany (Competing Jurisdictions), *supra* note 497, at 12-15.

studied in order to determine their systemic effects, positive or negative.[521] For example, if the pronouncements of a given court do not formally qualify as a subsidiary source of international law in accordance with Article 38 of the Statute of the ICJ, then potential conflicts between this court and others are academic (thus not real). Hence such courts should not be taken into consideration in the enquiry.[522] Jennings suggests for this reason the need to compile "a comprehensive list of tribunals" to take stock of the existing range of institutions.[523] Along these lines several authors have pieced together detailed charts, typologies and taxonomies of international courts and tribunals, mapping out the complex morphological diversity in elaborate classification systems.[524] Institutions are ordered according to their constitutive instrument, jurisdiction, institutional autonomy, popularity, and so on. For some authors, this kind of demographic work is an object of study in itself. The systematic mapping of international courts and tribunals is precisely one of the declared objectives of the *Project for International Courts and Tribunals* (PICT). PICT explains the rationale of the exercise as follows:

> "The PICT Research Matrix is the first comprehensive, systematic, and holistic mapping of the international judicial system. [...] [T]his stupefying variety [of institutions] can itself be the object of research. To date, the international judicial process and organization has not been considered a field of study in itself. Scholars and practitioners of one forum are rarely familiar with the law and procedure of another. Moreover, international courts and tribunals are not only judicial bodies – and as such a worthwhile object of research only for legal scholars – but also international organizations. They have bureaucratic and administrative aspects that can be compared. Comparisons allow cross-

---

[521] Thirlway (Proliferation), *supra* note 30, at 251; Shany (Competing Jurisdictions), *supra* note 497, at 13.

[522] Thirlway (Proliferation), *supra* note 30, at 266; H. Thirlway, 'The Proliferation of International Judicial Organs and the Formation of International Law', in W. Heere, ed., *International Law and the Hague's 750th Anniversary* (1999) 433-441, at 433.

[523] Jennings (Proliferation), *supra* note 444.

[524] Tomuschat (International Courts and Tribunals), *supra* note 473. Tomuschat identifies four reference points namely 1) on the basis of international law; 2) a binding decision is handed down by 3) a permanent body of independent persons after 4) formalized proceedings have been conducted pursuant to a body of rules which are not at the disposal of the parties (at 397). See also Brown (Maze), *supra* note 473.

fertilization and sheds new light on the functioning of each body, contributing to a more efficient, equitable and effective delivery of justice."[525]

The literature describes the quantitative increase as being characterized by exponential growth of tribunals during the last two decades in almost all fields of international legal practice. Although criminal justice, international economic law and the environment are the fastest growing components, the numbers are up across the board, adding up to unmistakable growth everywhere. One should add here the increase in the workload of traditional dispute settlement institutions, such as the World Court, which were never so busy in the history. The quantitative increase is accompanied by diversification in scope (universal v. regional mechanisms), jurisdiction (*ratione materiae, personae, temporis, loci*), binding nature of findings, enforcement mechanisms, and so on.

The literature observes that the variety in formats seems to challenge classical classifications of the discipline. Textbook accounts of "international law dispute settlement mechanisms" habitually revolve round Article 33 of the UN Charter. Methods are divided into diplomatic (negotiation, enquiry, mediation, conciliation), legal (arbitration, judicial dispute settlement), and political (resort to regional agencies or arrangements). Legal means used to be contrasted to diplomatic-political ones on account of the standards applied (law and determination of rights as opposed to reconciling interests) and the binding (or not) nature of the outcome. In their individuality, the literature agrees, recent developments seem to blur or transcend these distinctions, creating an infinite variety of formats.[526] 'Judicialized institutions' such as the WTO DSM straddle the distinction between diplomatic v. legal means; the creation of 'internationalized' or 'mixed' tribunals, such as the ones in Cambodia or Sierra Leone seem to bridge the divide between national v international adjudication. A long list of hybrid solutions, such as the United National Compensation Commission, the Claims Resolution Tribunal for Dormant Accounts in Switzerland, The Housing and Property Claims Commission in Kosovo, compulsory or directed conciliation methods, explode classical categories into a polyphony

---

[525] PICT Research Matrix, <www.pict-pcti.org/matrix/matrixintro.html>.

[526] A. Peters, 'International Dispute Settlement: A Network of Cooperational Duties', 14 *European Journal of International Law* (2003) 1.

of creativity and adaptability. The literature is interested in impact of such demographic growth over the system, such as the fragmentation of its norms,[527] conflicting or overlapping jurisdictions,[528] forum-shopping, lack of hierarchy (role of ICJ and other tribunals), and so on. Most of the new debates take place under the rubrics of the "proliferation" or "multiplication" of tribunals and their consequences for the international system, as explained at the beginning. More recently, the related questions of post-conflict and transitional justice,[529] the emerging profession of the international judiciary and its independence,[530] 'international legal procedure', and so on, are becoming part of a new debate about the role of adjudication in international law. The literature, however, sees a pattern in all this diversity leading to a system of international justice. For Romano, the "Matrix" of judicial institutions

> "[…] depicts the beginning of a process towards the construction of a coherent international order based on justice, an order where all participants (sovereign states, individuals, multinational corporations, etc) can be held accountable for their actions or seek redress through an impartial, independent, objective, and law-based judicial institution."[531]

The 'system' of international justice extends to its professionals and the creation of a new category of international practice, the international judiciary,[532] referring to judges working in different international institutions. There are several reasons enabling (and, in some cases, demanding) one to see the existence of a common professional body spanning different institu-

---

[527] A. Boyle, 'Dispute Settlement and the Law of the Sea Convention: Problems of Fragmentation and Jurisdiction', 46 *ICLQ* (1997) 37.

[528] V. Lowe, 'Overlapping Jurisdiction of International Tribunals', 20 *Australian Yearbook of International Law* (1999) 191.

[529] R. Teitel, *Transitional Justice* (2004).

[530] R. Mackenzie and P. Sands, 'International Courts and Tribunals and the Independence of the International Judge', 44 *Harvard International Law Journal* (2003) 271; M. Kuijer, *The Blindfold of Lady Justice: Judicial Independence and Impartiality in Light of the Requirement of Art. 6 ECHR* (2004).

[531] Romano (Pieces of a Puzzle), *supra* note 474, at 751.

[532] See, e.g. Terris, Romano and Swigart (The International Judge), *supra* note 455. See also the special issue on 'The Independence and Accountability of The International Judge', in 2 *The Law and Practice of International Courts and Tribunals* (2003). See also Mackenzie and Sands (Independence), *supra* note 530.

tions. Some pragmatic reasons can be attributed to the common nature of the functions performed by professional international judges regardless of the institution in which they serve: "they share a common characteristic insofar as they all, at least potentially, play a central role in interpreting and applying international law".[533] Others reasons can be traced to the gradual but certain formation of a new sensibility amongst professionals of international judicial institutions, that acknowledges the common function and common identity. The new sensibility is committed to the promotion of the rule of law and is oriented towards meting out justice without deference to traditional interference of the sovereign state in the administration of justice.[534] Consequently, international judges have common problems and concerns and one could find comprehensive solutions, such as standards of impartiality for the international judiciary[535] and legal norms to promote the independence and accountability of international tribunals at large.[536] Sands goes as far as to identify a professional community of nearly 200 serving judges, encompassing all areas from traditional inter-state judicial institutions (such as the International Court of Justice or the European Court of Human Rights) to international (and internationalized) criminal tribunals and standing arbitration institutions (such as the International Center for the Settlement of Investment Disputes) or inspections panels (such as the World Bank Inspection Panel) at various multilateral development organizations.[537] The International Law Association has created a "Study Group on Practice and Procedure of International Tribunals", which has identified the issues of the independence of the international judiciary, professional ethics, and *litis pendens* as constituting its agenda for the years to come.[538]

---

[533] Mackenzie and Sands (Independence), *supra* note 530, at 271.

[534] Sands writes that "the powerful new international judiciary [...] has taken on a life of its own and has already, in many instances, shown itself unwilling to defer to traditional conceptions of sovereignty and state power"; Sands (Turtles and Torturers), *supra* note 449, at 553.

[535] Brown (Maze), *supra* note 473.

[536] D. Shelton, 'Legal Norms to Promote the Independence and Accountability of International Tribunals', 2 *The Law and Practice of International Courts and Tribunals* (2003) 27.

[537] Mackenzie and Sands (Independence), *supra* note 530, at 273-274.

[538] See the Study Group's 'Burgh House Principles on the Independence of the International Judiciary', <www.ila-hq.org/html/main_studygroup.asp>.

System building has recently been explored also on the level of a common procedural law of international tribunals.[539] Although the tenor of such analyses is to explore similarities and identify gaps rather than postulate a system, the ideal of a system of an international adjudication remains the standard against which such a research is conducted. Most authors will confirm, albeit carefully and conditionally, the proliferation of tribunals has led to what can be regarded as an international system of courts[540] or a community of courts comprising an 'informal system'.[541] Authors will typically go at lengths explaining the structural and morphological similarities between courts that justify such a conclusion, carefully underlining disparities and the limits of such an understanding.

*Judicialization as progress*
So, what is the grid on which the system of international tribunals is constructed? What unites a disparate array of judicial institutions into a system that signified progress or forward movement for public international law? Here comes as a wedge the third narrative move of the lawyer-as-architect vocabulary: tribunals are believed to provoke similar systemic effects to international law, positive or negative, albeit of varying intensity. In addition, the existence of a system of tribunals helps international law reinforce its sovereign ground as a discourse, science, discipline, practice that can operate autonomously from politics. Here are some of the effects tribunals are assumed to bring to public international law.

*Justice*: it is to be presumed that more tribunals will lead to more justice and to more situations in which resort to forcible means of settling disputes is avoided; the proliferation of institutions and mechanisms will lead to a higher proportion of disputes being settled this way;[542] It reduces the powers of the sovereign states to appreciate themselves the legality of their acts.[543]

*Peace*: Provided that certain conditions are met, tribunals can also bring peace.[544] The idea here is that tribunals, especially, criminal tribunals, can

---

[539]  See notably, Brown (Common Law of Adjudication), *supra* note 444.
[540]  Shany (Competing Jurisdictions), *supra* note 497, at 105-108.
[541]  Brown (Common Law of Adjudication), *supra* note 444, at 257-258.
[542]  Dupuy (Danger of Fragmentation), *supra* note 492, at 796.
[543]  Praeger (The Role of the International Court), *supra* note 444, at 279.
[544]  See S.C. Res. 827, U.N. SCOR, 48th Sess., Res. and Dec., U.N. Doc. S/INF/49 (1993), which states in its Preamble: "Convinced that in the particular circumstances of the

bring peace in a number of psychological ways: exposure of the truth can help individualize guilt and thus avoid the imposition of collective guilt on an ethnic, religious, or other group; a "healing process" is initiated through the public acknowledgment to the victims; by ensuring that truth is recorded more accurately and more faithfully than otherwise would have been the case; it is one of the best ways to curb criminal conduct (deterrence).

*Rule of law*: the creation of tribunals signifies the recognition from the side of states of the importance of the rule of law in their relations;[545] this in turn will result to more pronouncements about international law, which will strengthen the materiel of its norms.[546]

*Certainty and predictability*: The argument here is that gaps in the law will be sorted out by the accumulation of case law; and increase its volume of pronouncements, leading to more certainty and predictability in dispute settlement in the future.

*Efficiency:* by helping the implementation of obligations and by generating a more refined and precise system of interpretation of norms.[547]

*Normalcy*: the more adjudication, the more the international law system becomes similar to a domestic legal system, through a routine subjection of international disputes to settlement by independent third parties, as opposed to non-judicial solutions that used to be routine in the past.[548]

*Quality through specialization*: specialized tribunals will, arguably, possess expertise in particular areas of the law, which may render them more

former Yugoslavia the establishment as an ad hoc measure by the Council of an international tribunal and the prosecution of persons responsible for serious violations of international humanitarian law would enable this aim to be achieved and would contribute to the restoration and maintenance of peace,   Believing that the establishment of an international tribunal and the prosecution of persons responsible for the above-mentioned violations of international humanitarian law will contribute to ensuring that such violations are halted and effectively addressed [...]".

[545] R. Ranjeva, 'Quelques observations sur l'intérêt á avoir une juridiction internationale unique', (Zero Issue) *International Law Forum* (1998) 10; Goldstone (Justice), *supra* note 496, at 500.

[546] Goldstone (Justice), *supra* note 496, at 499.

[547] Dupuy (Danger of Fragmentation), *supra* note 492, at 796.

[548] "The result of this impressive proliferation of new judicial and quasi-judicial bodies [...] and the augmentation of pre-existing compulsory jurisdictions is that in many areas of international relations, and in regard to a significant number of international actors, interna-

appropriate for the resolution of particular kinds of disputes.[549] Additionally, their statutes and rules of procedure may also be geared to deal more
suitably with specific kinds of disputes (say the arrest of ships at ITLOS).

*Renewed interest in international law*: Tribunals give rise to an international resurgence of interest in international law.[550]

What is striking in the above statements, however, is how little they are
supported by empirical evidence or relevant sociological research.[551] The
benign effect of tribunals on international law is treated as a self-evident
fact. One will have to suppose that such statements are made in good faith
by the literature and that they implicitly allude to some valid previous professional experience in similar situations, which is either exclusively the
author's or common to the profession at large. One can also assume that the
unspoken backdrop of such analogies is the domestic system and the effects of civil, administrative, or criminal justice on the behavior of citizens
or the improvement of the quality of the system in domestic legal orders; or
even previous cases that international law had to deal with. But the literature reviewed here rarely resorts to comparisons or analogies with previous
cases, domestic or international. The language is normative and the authority of the scholar as such legitimizes the various statements. The effect is
further amplified by the standard professional practice of cross-citation and

---

tional law offers relatively sophisticated and effective dispute-settlement procedures, culminating in judicial or quasi judicial proceedings. Thus, despite the lingering problem of
enforcement, it is safe to assert that the recent strengthening of dispute-settlement facilities
has contributed to greater legal normalcy in the operation of international law, assimilating
to a considerable degree its dispute settlement procedures to those prevalent in domestic
legal systems"; Shany (Competing Jurisdictions), *supra* note 497, at 7. See also Allain (Continued Evolution), *supra* note 492, at 65 and 71. Dupuy writes that "[...] the growing number of international jurisdictions and international institutions of control should be seen,
from a technical point of view, as a decisive step in the evolution of the international legal
system as it develops a real judicial function"; Dupuy (Danger of Fragmentation), *supra*
note 492, at 796.

[549] Thirlway (Proliferation), *supra* note 30, at 257.

[550] Goldstone (Justice), *supra* note 496, at 500; Rao (Multiple Judicial Forums), *supra*
note 444.

[551] This has also been noticed in F. Mégret, 'Three Dangers for the International Criminal Court: A Critical Look at a Consensual Project', XII *Finnish Yearbook of International
Law* (2001) 193.

cross-referencing between influential authors. The self-referential nature of the discourse forges and solidifies the impression of the existence of a common professional knowledge or experience.

This self-referential practice has profound consequences over the discourse. First, it legitimizes the original statement and creates tacit consent to its authority. Contestation of such statements by a critic would both audaciously challenge the integrity of the author and doubt collective professional wisdom. Hence critical enquiries are automatically ousted to the margins of the debate. This reverses (and increases) the level of proof needed for the credibility of these critiques, as the person contesting would have to adduce empirical evidence contradicting what is believed to be common professional knowledge and experience, even if the original claim was not supported by empirical evidence. This practice of legitimation constitutes the "grid" on which the 'system' of international justice is built and adds enormous persuasive power to the argument.

*The international lawyer*
The circle is closed with the final narrative move, which regards the international law professional as a key actor for the new tribunalism. In this first vocabulary of the 'lawyer-as-architect', the jurist has an important role to play in establishing clearer hierarchies of norms, institutions, and powers on the international level, to enhance certainty, predictability and fairness. Her intellectual travail consists of designing and defending the coherence of the system in a way that would withstand both the test of high theory and the challenges of the practice. In this model, the international lawyer is the system's architect. She welcomes the arrival of the age of adjudication as an important new development but also a system-building challenge.

The system-building function of the jurist becomes apparent by looking at another debate common in tribunals literature, namely the possible systemic hazards of fragmentation.[552] Two types of fragmentation hazards are identified. *First*, the quality of international law norms or doctrines.[553] Differ-

---

[552] Literature in unison addresses the fear of fragmentation as the primary danger of the phenomenon of proliferation. Guillaume (Future), *supra* note 507; Thirlway (Proliferation), *supra* note 30; Boisson de Chazournes (Multiplication), *supra* note 444, at 14; Dupuy (Danger of Fragmentation), *supra* note 492.

[553] See also M. Shahabudeen, *Precedent at the World Court* (1996) 67; Guillaume (Future), *supra* note 507, at 862; Dupuy (Danger of Fragmentation), *supra* note 492, at 797-798.

ent courts may take different views on specific problems, leading to a multiplicity of interpretations (at best), or a "cacophony of views", as Judge
Oda put it.[554] If one allows multiple interpretations of the same norm or
doctrine without, at the same time, devising ways of resolving conflicts, the
story goes, we are undermining the determinacy of an already fragile system. *Second*, the fear of fragmentation through competing, conflicting, or
overlapping jurisdictions.[555] Some even see a "battle" of tribunals raging
out there.[556] The availability of many dispute settlement mechanisms may
lead to situations in which more than one tribunal may assert jurisdiction
over one dispute. A whole set of questions then emerge. What happens when
more than one institution becomes seized of the same case? What is the
value of the pronouncements on fact and law of the one court over the next
one? And how does one resolve conflicting judgments? What if each one of
the parties submits the dispute to different competent forums? What are the
consequences of two rival decisions on the same dispute, especially mutually contradictory ones? Further, tribunals may differ in terms of their conditions of operation or the means of enforcement, which may encourage
parties to indulge in forum-shopping, in other words to seize the instance
the most favorable to its interests.[557] The lack of clear hierarchies between
institutions and the existing normative framework render it very difficult to
resolve such conflicts. The spin-off effect could be the undermining of the
position of existing institutions, such as the ICJ, since other courts may
start competing with it. As Kingsbury puts it, "issues that could previously

---

[554] S. Oda, 'The International Court of Justice from the Bench', 244 *RCADI* (1993) 9,
at 139.

[555] See generally Shany (Competing Jurisdictions), *supra* note 497. See also Dupuy
(Danger of Fragmentation), *supra* note 492, at 797; Thirlway (Proliferation), *supra* note 30.
For concerns about proliferation diminishing the salience of the ICJ in particular, see H.
Lauterpacht, *The Development of International Law by the International Court* (1982) 4-5;
Guillaume (Future), *supra* note 507; S. Oda, 'Dispute Settlement Prospects in the Law of
the Sea', 44 *International and Comparative Law Quarterly* (1995) 863.

[556] N. Lavranos, 'Concurrence of Jurisdictions between the ECJ and Other International Courts and Tribunals', 14 *European Environmental Law Review* (2005) 213; see also
'The Battle Between International Courts and Tribunals', Seminar of the Amsterdam Center
for International Law, 21 October 2005 (<www.jur.uva.nl/aciluk/events.cfm>, last visited
March 2006).

[557] Thirlway (Proliferation), *supra* note 30, at 259.

be delicately finessed in one body are abruptly forced in another", forcing adverse comparisons to be drawn between institutions.[558]

The fear or fragmentation is not new in international law. Similar debates have taken place in different times and contexts.[559] In the seventies the profession asked itself whether international economic law is a part of public international law or whether it is a different discipline with its own specificity which threatens the overall unity of the discipline.[560] Same with the debate on self-contained regimes and their relationship to general international law.[561] How do scholars deal with the fear of fragmentation in international tribunals? The general call is for more thorough research into the systemic effects of the different types of fragmentation, in order to assert the extent to which they the overall coherence of the system is *really* threatened. As one author remarks, "until that work is done, the complacent and the critic alike will be at a disadvantage".[562] In these debates, unity and fragmentation acquire a boundary, on/off quality: there is a critical point where the system gets fragmented. Until we reach that point unity and coherence are preserved. Authors are quick to admit that the idea of fragmentation presupposes the idea of unity that could be fictional in some respects.

---

[558] Kingsbury (Is Proliferation a Systemic Problem), *supra* note 444, at 684.

[559] During the last decade, fragmentation has become an extremely popular research field. See Report of the Study Group on Fragmentation of International Law, *supra* note 417. Some interesting recent work on fragmentation includes M. Craven, 'Unity, Diversity, and the Fragmentation of International Law', 14 *Finnish Yearbook of International Law* (2005) 3; G. Hafner, 'Pros and Cons Ensuing from Fragmentation of International Law', 25 *Michigan Journal of International Law* (2004) 849; J. Pauwelyn, 'Bridging Fragmentation and Unity: International Law as a Universe of Inter-Connected Islands', 25 *Michigan Journal of International Law* (2004) 903.

[560] The question of whether international economic law should be seen as a "chapter" of public international law or as a separate discipline of its own specificity dominated the early days of international economic law debates. Public international law scholars argued against the autonomy of international economic law and used arguments in favor of the unity of the discipline and expressed fears of fragmentation. See P. Weil, 'Le Droit International Économique: Mythe ou Réalité?', in *Colloque D'Orléans, Aspects du Droit International Économique: Élaboration, Contrôle, Sanction* (1972) 1. For an opposite view, see Trachtman (The International Economic Law Revolution), *supra* note 19.

[561] Simma (Self-Contained Regimes), *supra* note 416.

[562] N. Miller, 'An International Jurisprudence? The Operation of "Precedent" across International Tribunals', 15 *Leiden Journal of International Law* (2003) 483, at 526.

Unity "is to some extent a fiction – a valuable fiction, and one to be cherished, but [still] a fiction".[563]

Despite this warning, scholars paradoxically believe that there exists a real critical moment when the system loses its unity or coherence and that this should be avoided. The question is thus not only whether we can live with a fragmented international law *in abstracto*, but whether "the proliferation of tribunals [is] such as to lead to a greater or more marked fragmentation than that which has always existed".[564] The struggle therefore is about deciding where the critical line should be drawn, and how to define that boundary in legal terms. This is primarily "conceptual", system building work, and not an invitation for situational solutions.[565] It poses a "theoretical challenge" of whether international law is "one coordinated system" or "an accumulation of independent self-contained regimes".[566] Solutions need to be found along the lines of first, avoiding the conflict between norms and institutions. If this cannot be avoided and genuine conflict arises, then international law needs to operationalize doctrinal solutions that could be applied to an infinite number of conflict situations and resolve such conflicts.

This is a solution reminiscent of the sources of international law doctrine, which constitutes the foundation of our hierarchical system of norms. Article 38 lists abstract categories, boundary conditions, for the creation or ascertainment of norms, which can theoretically be applied to an infinite number of circumstances and irrespective of the content of the norm. Thus, secondary doctrines of conflict resolution (or jurisdiction-regulating norms), should be devised along these lines in order to help determine with relative certainty, without reference to the content of each specific case, and when applied in an infinite number of circumstances, which norm will prevail.

Much in the same vein, authors try to resolve the problem of proliferation of international tribunals by first, establishing whether the system has

---

[563] Thirlway (Proliferation), *supra* note 30, at 266; Dupuy (Danger of Fragmentation), *supra* note 492.

[564] Thirlway (Proliferation), *supra* note 30, at 267.

[565] This is the approach chosen by Joost Pauwelyn: "This book does not go into specific cases of interplay or conflict between WTO rules and other rules of international law. Rather, it attempts to provide a conceptual framework within which the interplay between norms can be examined"; J. Pauwelyn, *Conflict of Norms in Public International Law: How WTO Relates to Other Rules of International Law* (2003) at 3.

[566] Shany (Competing Jurisdictions), *supra* note 497, at 10-11.

reached the critical fragmentation point; and then by suggesting the creation of conflict resolution doctrines (or jurisdiction-regulating norms) to
explain away or resolve the conflict. When it comes to the quality of norms
and doctrines, a number of important areas are identified where the impact
of the practice of tribunals needs to be studied carefully, such as sources of
international law, the law of treaties, state responsibility, rules of procedure, and so on. Another way is to examine whether courts refer to each
other's pronouncements 'sufficiently' to create unity in the system.[567] Authors have generally identified a list of problem cases, but their views as to
whether they lead to conflict of norms have varied. Jennings, for example,
finds a conflict between the *Loizidou* v. *Turkey* case[568] pronouncement on
the admissibility of territorial limitations on a state's acceptance of the jurisdiction of the court and the jurisprudence of the ICJ with regard to its
own Statute;[569] whereas Thirlway concludes that the two pronouncements
were in fact compatible.[570] The ICTY and the ICJ both had to deal with the
question of whether there has been genocide in the former Yugoslavia or
whether the conflict was an international one.[571] The Tadić/Nicaragua Cases
question on the attribution of acts to a state of acts of individuals; the Pinochet
and Belgium/Congo Cases; the teleological interpretation of treaty provisions common in human rights debates (especially after Comment 24 of
HRC); the question of binding nature of provisional measures. When it
comes to conflicting/overlapping jurisdictions of tribunals, one would have
to look, once more, into the practice, and see whether there is a danger of
reaching the critical threshold of fragmentation. Authors look at the MOX
Plant/OSPAR cases between Ireland and the UK to determine whether such
cases exemplify conflict between tribunals that is systemically troubling
and whether more instances are likely to occur in the future.

---

[567] Miller describes his project as a survey of the case law of important judicial institutions looking "not for commonalities of result but for instances of one body referring to the
decision of another". Miller concludes that there are patterns discernible in the interaction of
tribunals at this stage but the parameters influencing these patterns remain unclear; Miller
(An International Jurisprudence), *supra* note 562.

[568] ECHR, 23 March 1995, Judgment No. 40/1993/435/514.

[569] Jennings (Proliferation), *supra* note 444, at 5-6.

[570] Thirlway (Formation of International Law), *supra* note 522.

[571] Guillaume (Future), *supra* note 507, at 862.

How would one protect the system from fragmentation? In response to the two types of fragmentation hazards mentioned (conflict of norms and conflict of jurisdictions), one could devise conflict resolution doctrines for each. When it comes to conflict of norms Pauwelyn, for example, creates an analytical framework by first deciding which norms should be included of his classification scheme ("hard", "soft", "super-norms", "obligations", "processes"), and then determines the difference between different kinds of conflicts and interpretative differences ("inherent normative conflicts" and "conflicts in the applicable law"), and builds his framework on such abstract categories without looking at the content of any norm in particular.[572] In the end he comes up with an elaborate set of eight conflict resolution steps to be applied.[573] When it comes to conflicts of jurisdictions, once more a repertoire of doctrinal solutions could be deployed. One obvious albeit radical way is to establish a formal hierarchy of institutions. States could nominate a Court that will perform a supervisory or appellate role to resolve conflicts of norms or jurisdictions. The ICJ, some authors propose, could potentially perform this role, since it is the official organ of the UN, one of the most prestigious of these tribunals, and thus the one best suited for the job.[574] But there could be other hierarchical solutions as well, such as Art. 177 of the Treaty of Rome;[575] or Article 287 of the United Nations Convention on the Law of the Sea (UNCLOS), which are designed to ensure a single identifiable tribunal for any given dispute; or even the *Chorzow Factory case* principle, according to which Courts would have to yield jurisdiction to other tribunals if those claim exclusive jurisdiction according to their statutes, and one can then imagine or devise a whole new set of secondary doctrines defining what is "exclusive jurisdiction". Alternatively, one could "identify and study rules of international law which might gov-

---

[572] Pauwelyn (Conflict of Norms), *supra* note 565, at 5-11.

[573] Ibid., at 436-438.

[574] A typical statement of this claim can be found at F. Orrego Vicuña and C. Pinto, *The Peaceful Settlement of Disputes: Prospects for the 21st Century*, Preliminary Report Prepared for the 1999 Centennial of the First International Peace Conference, C.E. Doc. CAHDI (98) 15. See also Pinto (Pre-Eminence of The International Court of Justice), *supra* note 509. This is endorsed by a number of other scholars, such as Guillaume (Future), *supra* note 507; Thirlway (Proliferation), *supra* note 30 at 270-278; Dupuy (Danger of Fragmentation), *supra* note 492, at 798-807.

[575] Guillaume (Future), *supra* note 507, at 862; Jennings (Proliferation), *supra* note 444, at 7.

ern competition between different jurisdictions, and to consider introduc-ing additional norms and arrangements".[576] Forum selection principles, the role of the *res iudicata* principle, abuse of rights, judicial comity, conflict-ing treaty obligations are some of the potentially useful norms, but one could consider several ways of calibrating or reforming the system as well, by introducing stay of proceedings or doctrines borrowed from private in-ternational law.

## 4.3.2   The 'lawyer-as-social-engineer'

The second vocabulary of progress of the new tribunalism is more politi-cally conscious and presents itself as the pragmatist alternative to the 'law-yer-as-architect' vocabulary.[577] The 'lawyer-as-social-engineer' also tells a before/after story of progress. This time it concerns the self-constitution of international society and it has its own idea about progress. At the same time, the role and function of law and tribunals in the picture are very dif-ferent. The liberal view fashions itself as a sophisticated correction of the positivist one, which is described as inadequate, formalist, and obsolete. The narrative moves of this second vocabulary are very similar to the first one, and go as follows:

*Historical account*
Historical account performs a crucial role in this second vocabulary as well. For the 'lawyer-as-social-engineer' proliferation is not the inevitable cul-mination of a long historical process of evolution from a power- to a rule-oriented approach to law, but evidence of a more mature way of dealing with dissonance. Both law and politics were always part of the interna-

---

[576]  Shany (Competing Jurisdictions), *supra* note 497, at 11.

[577]  For classical expressions of this view see generally A.M. Slaughter, *A New World Order* (2004), esp. 65-103; A.M. Slaughter, 'Toward A Theory of Effective Supranational Adjudication', 107 *Yale Law Journal* (1997) 273; Charney (Is International Law Threat-ened), *supra* note 444; Charney (Impact), *supra* note 444; A. Chayes and A. Chayes, *The New Sovereignty – Compliance with International Regulatory Agreements* (1998), esp. at 197-229; D. Sullivan, 'Effective International Dispute Settlement Mechanisms and the Necessary Condition of Liberal Democracy', 81 *Georgetown Law Journal* (1993) 2369; W.J. Aceves, 'Liberalism and International Legal Scholarship: The Pinochet Case and the Move Toward a Universal System of Transnational Law Litigation', 41 *Harvard Interna-tional Law Journal* (2000) 129.

tional system according to this view: international law always had multiple options in its dispute settlement system and, despite appearances, the ICJ never stood alone.[578] The difference is that, for a variety of reasons, tribunals could not be used in the past as extensively as they do today. The distance traveled in our understanding of international society during the last decades is not measured in a paradigm shift from 'politics' to 'law' but in a move from 'less' to 'more' mature ways of exercising international governance. In this scheme tribunals do not perform the constitutional function of the ultimate enforcer of rules of law, but are yet another instrument of managing conflict in international relations. Tribunals are part of a multiplicity of "international information, enforcement, and harmonization networks"[579] and an "instrument of active management"[580] of compliance with international norms in a world of liberal states. Now, if one looks for reasons why proliferation became possible today as opposed to the past, a number of factors could be identified, ranging from pure practicality, to globalization, the de-centralization of international governance and pivotal political developments, such as the gradual 'democratization' of the world and the emergence of liberalism as the dominant socio-political paradigm.[581] So tribunals could be no more than

> "a case of international lawyers doing what comes naturally, but in a world increasingly dependent on the reliable performance of international regimes, states and their citizens may also be less willing to rest content with either negotiation or the hope that some ad hoc arrangement of umpire a dispute will be set up in the event of an impasse".[582]

Alternatively, there are other "legitimate reasons" that help explain why states and other members of the international community could prefer to have available a variety of international tribunals to solve their disputes.

> "They include, but are not limited to, the desire of secrecy, control over the membership of the forum, panels with special expertise or perceived regional

---

[578] Charney (Impact), *supra* note 444, at 698.
[579] Slaughter (New World Order), *supra* note 577, at 100.
[580] Chayes and Chayes (The New Sovereignty), *supra* note 577, at 200-225.
[581] Charney (Is International Law Threatened), *supra* note 444, at 117-135.
[582] Chayes and Chayes (New Sovereignty), *supra* note 577, at 216.

sensibilities, preclusion of third state intervention, and forums that can re-solve disputes in which non-state entities may appear as parties."[583]

But, most importantly, the end of the Cold War is the event that unlocked the process of the progressive move of international law to the rule of law and adjudication. The Cold War and its antagonistic nature did not allow the application of international law[584] or encouraged "discretionary behav-ior associated with the doctrine of national sovereignty".[585] The competing hegemonies of the East and the West were so focused in securing strategic advantages and negotiating power that the application of laid law was not within their list of top priorities. In such an environment judicial institu-tions could not succeed due to the absence of a common understanding of norms, procedures, institutions, principles, politics – the cultural coherence needed for their flourishing.[586] The end of bi-polar international law and the advent to multilateralism, on the one hand, the abandonment of Marx-ist-Leninist interpretations of international law, on the other, the fact that capitalist, market-based economies and free-trade doctrines have remained the only plausible way to viable economic development.

*Democracy, peace and international courts*
This is a variant of the "how nations behave" thesis.[587] There is a direct correlation to be drawn between liberal democracy and compliance with

---

[583] Charney (Impact), *supra* note 444, at 698. See also Charney (Is International Law Threatened), *supra* note 444, at 132.

[584] M. Reisman, 'International Law after the Cold War', 84 *American Journal of Inter-national Law* (1990) 859.

[585] Falk (Realistic Horizons), *supra* note 465, at 325.

[586] Milton Katz wrote in 1968: "It will be useful to enquire how far the apparent irrel-evance of international law adjudication or arbitration to the settlement of Cold War dis-putes may result from the absence of tribunals to determine and apply the law; or, if tribunals exist, from their lack of adequate means to assert their authority; of, if the means exist, from the tribunal's lack of a will to use the means available. How far may the apparent irrelevance result in some inadequacy in the content of international law as the law then stands? How far may the irrelevance derive from limitations inherent in the nature of adjudication, as exhib-ited by older and more highly evolved legal systems than international law?"; Katz (Rel-evance of International Adjudication), *supra* note 461, at 10-11.

[587] See L. Henkin, *How Nations Behave – Law and Foreign Policy* (1979); B. Russett, *Grasping the Democratic Peace: Principles for a post-Cold War World* (1993); For expres-sions of the rational actor view in liberal political and international relations theory see, e.g.,

rules of law. In its internationalist version this thesis claims by and large that although there are serious differences from a religious, linguistic and cultural standpoint between liberal states, such states share certain basic traits, and in particular a fundamental commitment to individual civil rights and liberties. Liberal states are more prepared than other states to accept the rule of law and the possibility of limitation of their rights for the general good. The task of the scholar is to provide a systematic study of international affairs by analyzing the behavioral patterns of 'democratic' and 'non-democratic' states and to identify the principal variables that influence state behavior.

The liberal view is not based on hard statistical evidence either, but rather on assumptions about behavioral propensities of states (how states behave). These assumptions have been crafted on a pragmatic assessment of state behavior. Thus, according to Slaughter, there are several attributes that describe with reasonable accuracy liberal states and provide a basis for a more generalized distinction between liberal and non-liberal states: peace (liberal states tend to have peaceful albeit not always harmonious relations between themselves); liberal democratic government; a dense network of transnational transactions by social and economic actors; multiple channels of communication and action that are both transnational and trans-governmental rather than formally inter-state; and a blurring of the distinction between domestic and foreign issues.[588] In this model, the propensity to comply with international law is the general rule whereas not observing the law is an aberration.[589] Non-compliance can be explained on the basis of factors that pull states in that direction, because it is easier or more efficient for them do so (such as ambiguity of norms. The same way one could make lists of factors pulling towards compliance, one could understand – or even justify – noncompliance as a rational choice: noncompliance is a "premeditated and deliberate violation of a treaty obligation".[590]

What is more 'sophisticated' about this way of looking at the world? To begin with, law here is not seen as a set of prohibitions with on-off quality

---

J. Elster, *The Cement of Society: A Study of Social Order* (1989); R.C. Ellickson, *Order Without Law: How Neighbors Settle Disputes* (1991); F. Schauer, *Playing by the Rules: A Philosophical Examination of Rule-Based Decision-Making in Law and Life* (1991).

[588] Slaughter (International Law), *supra* note 100, at 510 et seq.

[589] Chayes and Chayes (New Sovereignty), *supra* note 577, at 10.

[590] Ibid., at 9.

but as one among many institutions necessary in order to manage an issue-area over time. Traditional scholars with their emphasis on classifications, hierarchies, and rule-fetishism have over-rated the power of the law to contain international relations. There are clearly things that law cannot do and other solutions need to be found. In that sense, legal argument has different characteristics (and thus, different advantages, disadvantages, and uses) compared to other discourses, such as politics. Although traditionalists regard conflict as something that needs to be avoided, liberals see conflicts of views within the system as a routine manifestation of individual actors seeking customized ways to maximize their interest. Actually conflict can be a productive source of progress if managed well. The liberal view claims to be more pragmatic and sophisticated because it appears to embrace conflict instead as something good that could potentially enrich international law. Maturity in international law here comes by means of developing expert ways of managing difference to the service of 'good politics' – meaning a liberal political agenda. Embracing conflict and a continuum of dispute settlement mechanisms means for the liberals that one is no longer obsessed with devising an economy of normativity or a doctrine of sources. Relative normativity and interpretative ambiguity are embraced as a routine manifestation of conflict, and as a tool for its resolution. In this sense, it would make sense to see questions of treaty interpretation less like a matter of applying in the best way Articles 31 and 32 of the Vienna Convention and more as questions about "the requirements and functioning of a regime".[591]

In this scheme tribunals are not the ultimate enforcers of rules of law but yet another instrument of managing international relations or, as some authors put it, a component of a variety of "international information, enforcement, and harmonization networks"[592] or an "instrument of active management"[593] of compliance with international norms in a world of liberal states. Where traditional international law saw a hierarchical system of tribunals, with a world supreme court (or doctrines exercising the same function) at the center, resolving disputes between states and pronouncing on rules of law, liberals see "a system composed of both horizontal and vertical networks of national and international judges, usually arising from

---

[591] Ibid., at 206.
[592] Slaughter (New World Order), *supra* note 577, at 100.
[593] Chayes and Chayes (The New Sovereignty), *supra* note 577, at 200-225.

jurisdiction over a common area of the law or a particular region of the world".[594] Binding judicial resolution of international disputes (international tribunals) is not *necessarily* the best way of resolving international disputes. They would see no hierarchy either between the dispute settlement means mentioned in Article 33 of the Charter and would be in favor of hybrid forms of dispute settlement, provided they do the job. They would reject the obsession of some public international lawyers with legally binding means, as these are formalistic and thus not efficient. They recognize advantages to all different means and regard them as expressions against of the propensity of rational actors to find solutions more suited to their own needs without being hung-up on formal categories. Even within judicial resolution, different institutions may have comparative advantages but common interests, so it may be fruitful to see them not as fighting for supremacy but as fellow professionals who participate in a common judicial enterprise.

Liberals see also the creation of a international system of international justice and a corresponding profession. One can speak of an "international judiciary" because judges sitting in different tribunals share a common characteristic insofar as they all, at least potentially, play a central role in interpreting and applying international law. Another reason for the creation of the profession can be traced to the gradual but certain formation of a new sensibility amongst professionals of international judicial institutions, that acknowledges the common function and common identity. This "self-awareness"[595] has been groomed by frequent personal and institutional contacts among the community and have led to the realization that each of them represents (and serves) not only a particular polity, but they are also "fellow professionals in an endeavor that transcends national borders".[596]

*Tribunals as progress*
But, is the proliferation of tribunals a good or a bad thing? The response is savvy, dispassionate, and managerial: tribunals are good only as long as they 'work'[597] but the conviction is that they normally do.[598] The liberal

---

[594] Slaughter (New World Order), *supra* note 577, at 67.

[595] Ibid., at 192.

[596] Ibid.

[597] See A.M. Slaughter and A. Stone, 'Assessing the Effectiveness of International Adjudication', 89 *Proceedings of the American Society of International Law* (1995) 91; Chayes and Chayes (New Sovereignty), *supra* note 577, at 200-225.

[598] Helfer and Slaughter (Response to Posner and Yoo), *supra* note 463.

agenda towards tribunals could be described as an effort to neither "over-estimate" nor "under-estimate" their role in a world of liberal states. In other words, to avoid both the mystification of legal architects and the dismissal of the realists. The search of a reasonable standard, or a balance between these two extremes, is a standard trope of liberal scholarship since the early post-war period.[599] The four corners of the search of the third way are cir-cumscribed, on the one hand, and similarly to the legal architects, by the assumption that more law and more tribunals are a good thing.

> "Tribunals evidence the understanding that the effectiveness of international law can be increased by equipping legal obligations with means of their deter-mination and enforcement."[600]

Apart from the immanent link between democracy and rule of law, a strong link is being drawn between justice and peace. Judicial, as opposed to dip-lomatic, settlement of international disputes performs a special symbolic role for such authors who go as far as to say that there can be "no peace without justice". As Inis Claude writes, "peaceful settlement of disputes is perhaps the oldest and most ubiquitous of the approaches to peace which have been formulated by thinkers about international relations".[601] They offer an ever-grown diversity of dispute settlement means, with the added advantage of finality and binding-ness, which is sometimes a good thing. What liberal scholars fear is not fragmentation, but rather avoiding extremes of all sorts, from fragmentation to over-formalization of the system. What we need is not unity but not disrupting a reasonable level of coherence in the system. Not absolute conformity with the law, but how to contain devi-ance within acceptable levels.[602] No rigid hierarchies, but a continuum of diverse forums with different comparative advantages;[603] and so on. How

---

[599] The effort to avoid extreme swings of the pendulum towards either formalism or cynical realism is a standard concern of liberal scholarship since the post-war period. See, e.g., J. Kunz, 'The Swing of the Pendulum: From Over-estimation to Under-estimation of International Law', 44 *American Journal of International Law* (1950) 135.

[600] S. Schwebel, Address by the President of the International Court of Justice to the General Assembly of the United Nations, 28 October 1998, <www.icj-cij.org>.

[601] Claude (Swords), *supra* note 8, at 199.

[602] Chayes and Chayes (New Sovereignty), *supra* note 577, at 17.

[603] Charney (Impact), *supra* note 444, at 698.

do liberal scholars deal with their fear of extremity? The answer is through sociological observation and piecemeal social engineering. Already in 1945 Karl Popper outlined this approach. The "piecemeal engineer"

> "may or may not have a blueprint of society before his mind, he may or may not hope that mankind will one day realize an ideal state, and achieve happiness and perfection on earth.. But he will be aware that perfection, if at all attainable, is far distant, and that every generation of men, and therefore also the living, have a claim; [...] The piecemeal engineer will, accordingly, adopt a method of searching for, and fighting against, the greatest and most urgent evils of society, rather than searching for, and fighting for, its greatest ultimate good. This difference is far from being merely verbal. In fact, it is most important. It is the difference between a reasonable method of improving the lot of man, and a method which, if really tried, may easily lead to an intolerable increase in human suffering."[604]

*The international lawyer*
In unison, liberal internationalist scholars will be quick to confirm that the task of the jurist is to identify factors that lead states towards either compliance with or towards disregard for the law and develop techniques of social engineering based on this knowledge. This is not a theoretical enquiry *in abstracto*, as the 'legal architects' sought to do with their quest for normative hierarchies and conflict resolution doctrines. Piecemeal social engineers claim to reject narratives of historical necessity ('historicism') and they believe that the task of the science is rather to suggest situational solutions. Each problem could and should have its own solution in a world of liberal states and any enquiry into the nature of the system or of international law is not with a view to producing a theoretically coherent answer to reply to the skeptics but a functional exercise that improves the system by lending it coherence and legitimacy through a more meaningful explanation. The explanation does not need to stand the test of high theory but the one of persuasion. In a celebrated passage of *How Nations Behave* Louis Henkin explains the task ahead in such terms.

> "The undertaking is ambitious and, I believe, important. Answers to some of the questions raised here would, at least, help us to appreciate the place of

---

[604] K.R. Popper, 'The Open Society and Its Enemies', Vol. 1, *The Spell of Plato* (1962) 158.

law in international life and understand the 'pathology' of international behavior with respect to law. Answers might even help us find ways to extend
the domain of the law and improve law observance, for greater order and stability in international relations. Unfortunately, what may properly be called
'answers' are not possible to come by. The processes by which decisions
policy are made are mysterious altogether. [...] The motivations of governmental behavior are complex and often unclear to the actors themselves. If we
can sometimes identify actors that contribute to national policy, and find law
among them, there are no scales to determine the weight of each of them. If in
an occasional decision the influence of law can be shown and measured, any
generalizations would still be deficient, given the inevitable inadequacy of
sampling. [...] In substantial measure, then, the exploration must be *a priori*
and speculative, less scientific than impressionistic. I shall assert propositions
about how nations behave, based on what appears reasonable, on what international actors have done and said, on the opinions of observers, on impressions gained from some experience in a foreign office. These suggestions
may perhaps be only 'education in the obvious'. [...] Still, at the least, one
may learn whether the behavior of nations in regard to international law is
susceptible of meaningful study, and what additional knowledge might make
such a study more fruitful."[605]

This is precisely what Jon Charney sets out to do in his is his Hague Academy courses.[606] In this important text Charney asks whether tribunalism
pulls more towards relative coherence in the system or against it. Relative
coherence means for him that the system continues to work and being legitimate. The decision of whether to invest further or not in tribunals is a
political decision taken on precisely these grounds, namely the effect of the
"pull" of tribunals towards the one or the other extreme. Others claim, in a
similar vein, that classical cost and benefit analysis can be used in order to
determine whether a specific tribunal is needed or not. The idea here is that
one invests resources in a particular solution "up to the point where the
value of the incremental benefit from an additional unit equals the cost of
the last unit of additional enforcement".[607] What is acceptable in terms of
compliance will reflect the perspectives and interests of the participants in
an ongoing political process, rather than some external, scientifically of

---

[605] Henkin (How Nations Behave), *supra* note 587, at 6-7.
[606] Charney (Is International Law Threatened), *supra* note 444.
[607] Chayes and Chayes (New Sovereignty), *supra* note 577, at 20.

market-validated standard. Reisman speaks of "pathological congestion", "homeopathic medicine" and "birth defects" of international law, while using "cost-benefit analysis" and the need to "assess redundancies" when confronting dilemmas about taking policy decisions for the future:

> "For, ultimately, this is a cost-benefit question: courts are nice, of course, and allow more lawyers to become judges, but because public resources are finite, each prospective new institution will preclude the financing and performance of some other urgent community task. So each new institution must justify itself competently. Dispute resolution mechanisms are indispensable, yet like homeopathic medicine which is supposed to heal in the smallest doses but harm in large draughts, is it appropriate to ask whether the increase in adjudicatory bodies in many sectors of international law has become too much of a good thing? Is there 'proliferation'? Will it endlessly increase transaction costs with few corresponding gains for human rights or whatever other social values are at stake? Will the many new and diverse voices of authority prove to be inconsistent on critical issues and ultimately undermine the essentially clarifying and educations function of legal decision? Will the proliferation of institutions transform the lingua franca of international law into a regionalized Babel? Will the financial burden be too heavy?"[608]

## 4.4    (UN)STABLE VOCABULARIES

We have seen how progress associated with the phenomenon of proliferation is closely intertwined with the two vocabularies just described. The two vocabularies, despite their many differences, display uncanny similarities in various components. Let us look at these similarities in turn.

### 4.4.1    Necessity

*First*, both vocabularies laud the arrival of tribunals as the materialization of their respective historical necessities about progress in international law. For the lawyer-as-architect, tribunals are the missing piece in the puzzle of

---

[608] M. Reisman, 'Adapting and Designing Dispute Resolution Mechanisms for the International Protection of Human Rights', in L. Boisson des Chazournes, ed., *Implications of the Proliferation of International Adjudicatory Bodies for Dispute Resolution: Proceedings of a Forum Co-Sponsored by the ASIL* (1995) 8-14, at 8.

international hierarchy of norms and judicial institutions. For the lawyers-as-social-engineer, tribunals confirm the relevance of the comparative advantage and division of labor paradigms, as applied to international law and institutions. For both, international law evolves in a linear fashion and the advent of tribunals is welcomed as an element of progress in this process of evolution.

The jurist assists by creating coherence (fitting the pieces in the puzzle, in the politically agnostic variant) or by intervening to remove failures and pathologies (in the liberal version). Both vocabularies borrow their language and metaphors from biology or economics to accentuate the causal nature of the evolutionary process. The moment conditions are ripe ('maturity' within the discipline for the evolutionists/ liberal democracy as a system of governance for the liberals) the emergence of tribunals follows as the natural consequence of progress in social development, similar to the way in which law has always been the natural product of human socializing. The more pieces of the puzzle in place, the faster the filling up of the blank space in the middle. The less intervention (the less totalitarianism and the more democracy), the quicker the system will find its way to self-fulfillment. The setbacks encountered in the history of international law (too much politics; not enough democracy) explain the originally fragmented nature of the developments, which are eventually now taking shape in the form of a system. Tribunals emerge and disappear on the basis of natural selection, like the flora and fauna of an ecosystem, or like other social-political institutions in liberal societies.

The invocation of historical necessity has a crucial role in the feeling of progress that is generated by the new tribunalism. Tribunals are thereby presented as 'speaking themselves', as a natural development and, consequently, not part of a political-ideological agenda of reform. The accounts accept a formal idea of progress that is catalytic for the production of meaning in the rest of the argument. The historical account immediately situates the reader and the field of study within the context of a historical evolution of internationalism: a story about how things were before, how things are today, and what is the distance traveled; or, to put it differently, a story with well-marked beginning, middle, and end-phases. In Guillaume's or Romano's etiology of the advent of proliferation,[609] to name an example, the

---

[609] Guillaume (Future), *supra* note 506; Romano (Pieces of a Puzzle), *supra* note 474.

emergence of tribunals is a 'natural' development. With this simple move the reader is 'summoned from afar' and placed within a concrete and clearly defined context: a historical continuum (humanity's development) and a concrete social group (a universal community of human beings). Both vocabularies locate the process leading to proliferation to factors exogenous to the agency of the international lawyer. In this account of progress, the "I" of the author is absent. The author adopts the posture of a dispassionate, neutral, objective chronicler that merely transcribes events as they unfold before his sight, from a seemingly external point of view. The movement takes place more in the observable world 'out there' and less within the professional community of international lawyers. In this image, the international jurist is not author but mere witness to the process. She is summoned to report, document, make sense of, ameliorate, and intervene. Either way, to perform legal, system-building, international law work, and not to partake in any kind of ideological-professional project.

In spite of their claim to historical necessity, such accounts are easy to de-center. One only needs to ask whether the transformation occurred *really* or *only* along the lines described, or whether there is such an automatic relationship between the expansion of international law and the turn to adjudication, and so on. Such questions are very important: if the reasons behind the emergence of proliferation are more complex than the ones recounted, then our certainty about what is historically necessary should be different – and different lessons will have to be learned. As it has been demonstrated in Chapter 1, the capacity to envision a set of events as belonging to the same order of meaning requires some principle by which to translate different into similarity. In other words, it requires a "subject" common to all of the referents of the various sentences that register events as having occurred.

In recent years, several authors have challenged the historical necessity of the new tribunalism. Regardless of the extent to which one would agree with each of those critiques, they are sufficient to disrupt the claim of historical necessity. These critiques have been particularly vocal in the area of international criminal justice, where tribunals are often seen not as the apogee of a natural historical process of evolution but as a savvy move of political redemption, as a "fig leaf" effort, and expression of the inability or unwillingness of the international community to prevent or end conflict in the first place.[610] Far from spontaneous social reactions triggered by exogenous factors, tribunals are seen by many as part of a political project of some members of the international community to assuage their guilt for failing to intervene to stop the 1994 genocide by pouring money into the ICTR without making any real commitment to rebuilding Rwanda.[611] It is argued that both ICTY and ICTR were created rather "by the mobilization of shame by non-governmental organizations and especially the grisly pictures beamed to the world by the television camera"[612] and manifest an ex-post facto effort to redeem the international community for its inability to prevent the catastrophe. Even more, it is suggested that tribunals present themselves as an opportunity for the powerful nations to convert a catastrophe into a positive, humanist project for themselves, appropriating for that end the suffering of the victims. In a similar vein, one could turn to the agents of the new tribunalism, namely international lawyers themselves. In opposition to the professional claim of jurists being mere witnesses and reporters of the phenomenon of proliferation, an argument could be made that international jurists could be found to have professional interest in adopting an optimistic view about the importance of international judicial institution building. Given the lucrative terms of employment and the creation of thousands new posts for international lawyers in and around international tribunals, international lawyers have a lot to gain by pursuing a rhetoric which re-situates international law and its professionals in the driving seat of international post-conflict resolution efforts.[613]

## 4.4.2    Unity

*Second*, despite the great diversity of institutional formats, both sets of explanations discern the emergence of a system of international justice, a glo-

---

[610] Murphy (Progress), *supra* note 9, at 95; R. Goldstone, 'Assessing the Work of the United Nations War Crimes Tribunals', 31 *Stanford Journal of International Law* (1997) 1, at 5; see also Mégret (Three Dangers), *supra* note 551, at 232 et seq.

[611] P. Gourevitch, 'Justice in Exile: Hutu Genocide of Tutsi People in Rwanda Can Never Be Fully Brought to Justice', *The New York Times* (24 June 1996) at A15.

[612] M. Mutua, 'Never Again: Questioning the Yugoslav and Rwanda Tribunals', 11 *Temple International and Comparative Law Journal* (1997) 167, at 174.

[613] This argument is made for the world of commercial arbitration by Y. Dezalay and B.G. Garthes, *Dealing in Virtue: International Commercial Arbitration and the Construction of a Transnational Legal Order* (1996).

bal community of courts. Both sides acknowledge the creation of a new profession as well, the international judiciary, and concur with the claim that proliferation brings both systemic benefits and hazards for international law. Similar to the account of history described above, a lot could be said about system-building claims of the sort. For one thing, the methodological tool-kit of the comparative study can easily be problematized. One could argue that considering the ICTY, ITLOS, the Special Court for Sierra Leone and the Ethiopia-Eritrea Claims Commission, as part of the same "puzzle", "system" or "project", is an intellectual leap that may be stretching one's imagination and deny the plethora of political, historical, and other contexts in which these institutions operate.

The 'discovery' of similitude and homologies between different entities is a statement that goes beyond the (self-proclaimed) task of the lawyer/ observer of the transformation of systemic factors or variables. One could instead contend that the actual process of categorization and enumeration is the one that preeminently constructs a system instead of merely recording or discovering its existence. Projects of classification could be seen as conscious and active efforts to bring disparate things under the same symbolic site. It is a process of agency that chooses to emphasize points of convergence and, equally, underplay divergence. Describing all tribunals as a system creates a stable relation between them, the idea for example that a pronouncement before one court has consequences over the functioning of the next one and therefore their relation needs to be studied, and so on. The common site where the system is placed remains symbolic, no matter how intuitive it may appear to be, or regardless of efforts made to vest it with a physical location (e.g. The Hague as the legal capital of the world). This symbolic site is created, as Michel Foucault would say, on the basis of a "grid of identities, similitude, analogies".[614]

> "[T]here is nothing more tentative, nothing more empirical (superficially, at least) than the process of establishing an order among things; nothing demands a sharper eye or a surer, better articulated language; nothing that more insistently requires that one allow oneself to be carried along by the proliferation of qualities and forms. And yet an eye not consciously prepared might well group together certain familiar similar figures and distinguish between

---

[614] Foucault (Order of Things), *supra* note 89, at xxi.

others on the basis of such and such a difference: in fact, there is no similitude or distinction, even for the wholly untrained perception, that is not the result of a precise operation and of the application of a preliminary criterion. [...] Order is, at one and the same time, that which is given in things as their inner law, the hidden network that determines the way they confront one another, and also that which has no existence except in the grid created by a glance, an examination, a language; and it is only in the blank spaces of the grid that order manifests itself in depth as though already there, waiting in silence for the moment of its expression."[615]

If that is indeed the case, one should not wonder what is wrong with the methodological tool kit but, rather, what is the added benefit by calling something a system?

### 4.4.3   Progress

*Third*, the conviction that proliferation is 'in itself' an element of progress in international law. The lawyer-as-architect and the lawyer-as-engineer both adopt a similar sensibility of cautious optimism in their engagement. On the one hand, they share the view that tribunals have a nearly-automatic claim to be regarded as a positive development – by virtue of their alleged systemic effects; on the other, they prescribe caution and the need to study the systemic hazards that may be provoked. The rhetorical strategy that peregrinates between these two positions consolidates the feeling of progress that permeates the debate. The feeling of progress is possible only as long as the link between tribunals and the unity of the system remains presumed. All authors agree that much empirical work still needs to be done to elucidate the precise systemic consequences. Until that work is done "the complacent and the critical alike will be at a disadvantage".[616] Should the empirical base be refuted or proven elusive, what would be left in the project is faith: in international institutions and in the ability of an international community of scholars to establish a well functioning system of checks and balances. The need for empirical research is both the promise and the defeat of the new tribunalism. The nature of comparative and empirical work is a never-ending task: it is an endless accumulation of similitude and com-

---

[615] Ibid.
[616] Miller (An International Jurisprudence), *supra* note 562, at 526.

parisons, infinite as knowledge itself. As international law remains fearful of both idealism and formalism, its support of tribunals needs to remain pinned on the sociologically and empirically basis advocated by both the architect and the social engineer.

But this type of work will *never* come to an end. The end point, proving the deterrent effect of international criminal tribunals, to name only one example, may not even be quantifiable or measurable with empirical analysis.[617] As long as the link between courts and their social effects remains unclear, presumed, or under review, the new tribunalism will continue to reside safely and modestly on the side of progress, on account of the legitimating assumptions that construct it. Not as a panacea but as a token of hope, tribunals seem like a safe extra to an ever-growing repertoire of the professional strategies. Cautious optimism is indeed an irresistible pitch when the alternative is despair.

The question remains however as to whether there is a price to be paid for this sensibility. Tribunalism entrusts the success of the project, once more, to the invisible college of international lawyers: a sophisticated interpretative community trained to establish a tight system of hierarchies or checks-and-balances, norms or standards, and so on. This time, the task in hand is described as one of observation and accumulation of know-how. Operating under the assumption that the creation of international courts and tribunals is generally benign, the role of the international lawyer is to make sure that the development is systemically sustainable. What is needed is technical/ empirical/ statistical work of all sorts, which will create a sufficient information basis to assess each development. The project of mapping and comparing has already begun but much work will have to be done continuously. The role is limited to observations or small-scale engineering, a locus par excellence for the techniques of international law.

Similarly to the claim of historical necessity, the claim of progress that is associated with tribunals is easy to de-center. The reported positive effects of tribunals in resolving disputes could be seen as exaggerated (at best) or

---

[617] See the excellent analysis of Mégret (Three Danfers), *supra* note 551, and in contradistinction to an entire genre of writings in international criminal law which embraces 'pragmatic idealism' and cultivates optimism about the capacity of tribunals to achieve deterrence but without reference to a background theory of how to measure or assess their impact. For an example of this type of writing see P. Akhavan, 'Beyond Impunity: Can International Justice Prevent Future Atrocities?', 95 *American Journal of International Law* (2001) 7.

fictional (at worse). Take the paucity of empirical or statistical analysis to support any of the claims to progress. Or take, as one among many, the critique that tribunals do not take sufficiently into account the interests of the parties to the disputes and/or the victim societies.[618] The argument here is that international courts leave out important parts of the political context, resulting to a formally correct decision which may be only partly relevant to the initial dispute. The handling of the *Hostages* case[619] by the ICJ, was criticized for presenting a very narrow view of the long and complex Iran-United States relationship prior to the Hostages crisis.[620] Reasons can be found, for example, in the definition and use of the concept of "dispute"[621] in international law, whose oppositional structure of claims necessarily reduces the wide scope of interests and conflicts into legal propositions that are accepted or rejected by the tribunal. Tribunals can be seen as giving more emphasis on abstract principles of international law rather than the specific requirements for social reconstruction.[622] When looking at tribunals-related work, one reads more about the systemic effects of their pronouncements (was the quality of the judgment good? Was it in conformity with previous judgments?) rather than about the perception of the involved parties about whether the 'books are closed', to use Jon Elster's expression.[623] In this latter sense, tribunals do not necessarily close or resolve disputes. A narrative of progress that privileges judicial resolution while denigrating alternative strategies would therefore be far from progressive if tested against the very social goals (e.g., justice, peace, etc.) postulated by the new tribunalism itself. As long as the empirical basis for such critiques is missing, however, the vocabulary of progress remains unchallenged.

Such critiques are particularly vocal in the cases of the ICTY and the ICTR, where local scholars claim that the tribunals did not tell the story of how the dispute arose and what were its causes. Indeed in international

---

[618] For criminal justice and the claim of 'neutrality' of international criminal tribunals, see Mégret (Three Dangers), 551 note 541, at 210 et seq.

[619] See text corresponding to note 466, *supra*.

[620] Falk, *supra* note 469.

[621] Jennings states the orthodoxy about the nature of the legal dispute in his oft-cited article: R. Jennings, 'Reflections on the Term "Dispute"', in R.St.J. Macdonald, ed., *Essays in Honor of Wang Tieya* (1993) 401-405 .

[622] See, e.g., the argument in M. Minow, *Between Vengeance and Forgiveness: Facing History after Genocide and Mass Violence* (1998) at 22-51.

[623] J. Elster, *Closing the Books: Transitional Justice in Historical Perspective* (2004).

criminal law, one could argue that lawyers are actively and successfully developing mechanisms of international criminal justice without first developing (at least without debating) a criminology of mass violence, a penology for the perpetrators of this violence, and a victimology for those who are affected by the violence.[624] As a consequence, within the process of international criminal justice, the notion that guilt and wrongdoing can be individualized and placed on the shoulders of a handful of individuals that are brought forward to be prosecuted and punished while it may not be an accurate reflection of the conditions precedent that exist on the ground in order for mass atrocity to be perpetrated on a massive level. Local populations don't always agree with this presumption[625] and may disagree about whether the books were in fact closed or not. Victims are regularly believed to be marginalized in the process, their interests not sufficiently being taken into account. The argument here is that tribunals do not meet their targets of bringing a feeling of justice to the local communities, "closing the books", national reconciliation, and so on. By clearly identifying the guilty individuals and penalizing them for their crimes, an international war crimes tribunal may hope to facilitate a de-escalation of tensions and animosities between the ethnic collectives, and encourage a rapprochement between the formerly warring entities. From the political and social point of view, this was the objective of both the ICTY and ICTR. Many commentators agree that international criminal tribunals have fallen short of such objectives. Both in the cases of the Former Yugoslavia[626] and Rwanda,[627] the

---

[624] M. Drumble, 'Remarks', in S. Ratner and J. Bischoff, 'International War Crimes Trials: Making a Difference?', *Proceedings of an International Conference Held at the University of Texas School of Law*, November 6-7, 2003 (2003) 30; see also M. Drumble, 'Collective Violence and Individual Punishment: The Criminality of Mass Atrocity', 99 *Northwestern University Law Review* (2005) 539.

[625] "For the majority of Rwandans, the ICTR is a useless institution, an expedient mechanism for the international community to absolve itself of its responsibilities for the genocide and its tolerance of the crimes of the RPF"; K. Marks (International Crisis Group), 'Criminal Tribunal for Rwanda: Justice Delayed', <www.globalpolicy.org/tribunals/2001/0607icg.htm> (last visited 17 February 2004), as cited in T. Longman, 'The Domestic Impact of the International Criminal Tribunal for Rwanda', in Ratner and Bischoff (International War Crimes Trials), *supra* note 624, at 33-41.

[626] E.g., A. Fatic, *Reconciliation via the War Crimes Tribunal?* (1999); E. Stover, *The Witness – War Crimes and the Promise of Justice in the Hague* (2003) at 144-145.

[627] Longman (Domestic Impact), *supra* note 624.

argument is made that international criminal proceedings have not helped reconciliation.

## 4.5    CONCLUSION

The case study on international tribunals aimed at exposing the discursive structures by which the new tribunalism rhetoric generates a feeling of progress in international law. The starting point was the intuition that, although the notion of progress may be invoked in order to lend legitimacy for one's argument, progress is a notion that acquires its meaning by being placed in the context of a narrative. In our case study the two vocabularies (lawyer-as-architect and lawyer-as-social-engineer) tell two parallel – if different – historical narratives of progress. Despite many lateral differences, both narratives shake hands in their historical determinism. Both narratives laud the arrival of tribunals as the materialization of their respective historical necessities about progress in international law (rule-oriented approach as progress in law). Both narratives discern the emergence of a system of international justice and a global community of courts (proliferation of courts as a system of international justice). Finally, they share the conviction that proliferation is 'in itself' an element of progress in international law (tribunals has benevolent effects on the international community).

These vocabularies tell a persuasive story of evolution in international law in which a transition to a rule-oriented system supported by an organized international judiciary is tautologically identified with progress, with no room for contestation. The phenomenon of proliferation announces the arrival of this new institutional moment. The persuasiveness of the story is reinforced by the fact that both narratives draw from the credos of two main traditions about international law thinking on both sides of the Atlantic (constitutional formalism and policy pragmatism). In order for the narrative of progress to work, the benefits of the rule oriented approach, the possibility of a system, the social effects of judicialization; all need to be presented as unequivocally true, as 'speaking themselves'.

The chapter demonstrated how the literature sidesteps the empirical proof dimension of all the main assumptions as stated and takes them for granted. The literature relies on the fact that these assumptions are not contested rather than by demonstrating their validity. This way the narratives reverse (and increase) the level of proof needed for the critic, since one would have to adduce empirical evidence contradicting what is believed to be common professional knowledge and experience, even if any such empirical evidence did not originally support the original claim. The creation of a system of international justice in which all institutions performed similar effects is only possible by ignoring their morphological differences, social-political functions, aims and mandate. These narratives once more mystify a before/after historical account that tautologically becomes the interpretative device to explain and understand social reality.

Like the two previous case studies, this chapter took a step further to demonstrate that the structures that produced meaning about progress were unstable and indeterminate. The advantages of the rule-oriented approach, the existence of a system of international justice, the social benefits of judicialization, were shown to be taken for granted instead of having been proven. They key for the persuasiveness of the vocabulary was not its determinacy but its rhetorical capacity to set aside (or disempower) any internal or external critique that would give concrete meaning to these terms. Challenging the empirical basis of the assumptions is enough to immediately position one at the margins of the discipline, where one would have to assume the entire burden of proof. The vocabulary of progress of the new tribunalism, far from based on stable or determinate assumptions, can now be seen as a set of discursive structures that legitimize social and institutional action, allocate resources, and decide the limits of contemporary humanitarianism.

# Chapter 5
# IN CLOSING

## 5.1    FINDINGS

The objective of this book was to test the validity of a set of intellectual propositions relating to the discursive function of the notion of progress in international legal argument. The purpose was neither to define the notion of progress nor to devise a scientific tool that enables one to determine whether a specific international law event (statement, development, doctrine, institution, etc.) constitutes or not progress in public international law. The intention was rather to call to attention the ways in which meaning about progress may be produced in international law texts. The analysis was triggered by the intuition that narratives of progress perform a much more complex role than the one usually ascribed to them. Far from being a neutral discursive form, a mode of representing the objective reality of a world 'out there', progress narratives are suspected to be the product and the expression of non-objective (political, ideological, other) assumptions, while denying that character. Borrowing from the insights of structural linguistics, structuralism, post-structuralism, and related Critical thought movements in law and the social sciences, this enquiry expressed skepticism about the mainstream assumption that progress can ever be a notion that 'speaks itself'. To transpose such intuitions into legal enquiry, three intellectual propositions were put forward, questioning the role of the notion of progress in international law discourse.

i.   *Progress as the product of narratives*: Although progress is a convenient rubric to describe international law events (arguments, developments, actions, and so on), it is a notion that is ultimately devoid of meaning unless placed in the context of a progress narrative.
ii.  *Progress narratives as politics*: Progress narratives are by definition non-objective. As such, they compete with (or exclude) other progress narratives, based on different assumptions. International law discourse tends to deny or mask the non-objective character of its progress narratives.

iii.  *Discourse analysis as action*: Although progress narratives may be a
      useful discursive form, the de-mystification of such narratives may be
      an equally productive and meaningful form of international law argu-
      ment in itself, but one that gives access to a different horizon of action
      and intellectual possibility.

The enquiry was not meant to take place *in abstracto*. It originated in concrete personal-professional experiences with international law situations
and it aspired to engage concrete international law debates in order to demonstrate one's everyday encounter with the use of progress narratives. Not
as an exceptional rhetorical strategy, but as a normalized, mainstreamed,
generally accepted style of legal argument. The propositions were therefore
tested against three case studies, drawn from the everyday practice of public international law. Each case study involved a different use of the notion
of progress, i.e., international law *as* progress, progress *within* international
law, and a combination of the two. Each case study also pointed to different
planes of international law discourse. The first study (Seferiades) told the
story of the lifework of a single scholar. It exemplified how a personal-
ideological project of reform (on the national and international levels) may
gain legitimacy by means of a universalist vocabulary about international
law as progress. The second study (sources) told the story of an international law doctrine. It offered an example of how the notion of progress
may become part of debates about renewalism in the doctrinal structure and
methods of the discipline. The third study (tribunals) told the story of an
institutional development (the proliferation of judicial institutions). It looked
at the ways in which the notion of progress may form part of debates about
resource allocation and decisions about the institutional architecture of the
international system.
    The three case studies were approached by means of the technique of
discourse analysis. The approach, method, and objectives were circumscribed narrowly. The conclusions drawn by the three case studies are limited to the studies in question, although they participate in, and stand in
dialogue with, a wider social constructionist project of international legal
critique. It is now time to turn to some of the findings that this enquiry
resulted in.

## 5.2    PROGRESS AS THE PRODUCT OF NARRATIVES

This first proposition that was put forward seeks to demonstrate that progress in international law, aside from being a convenient label to caption international law events (arguments, developments, actions, and so on), is ultimately a notion devoid of meaning unless placed in the context of a narrative. This is the "structuralist" moment of the analysis, which seeks to identify structures in the text that produce meaning about progress: argumentative structures, a "vocabulary" of progress, which enables determinations of what is acceptable and non acceptable argument within the discourse and gives meaning to the terms used. The analysis of the three case studies confirms this proposition.

All case studies begin by identifying the horizon of the discourse that constitutes the field of their analysis. The first study (Seferiades) turns to the lifework of a single scholar (his writings and actions) as the horizon of the discourse. The second study (sources) turns to interwar (1918-1939) literature on the sources of international law. The third study (tribunals) applies itself to post-1989 literature devoted to the topic of proliferation or multiplication of international judicial institutions.

In addition to specifying the horizon that limits their respective fields of analysis, all case studies propose/identify the specific 'vocabularies of progress' of each discourse. In other words, they point to the presence of discursive structures that, it is argued, produce meaning within that discourse about what is progressive. In the first study (Seferiades), the opposition of the notions of absolutism and democracy is proposed as the vocabulary of progress; in the second study (sources) the narrative moves of standardization and formalization perform the same role; whereas in the third study (tribunals), the vocabularies of the lawyer-as-architect and the lawyer-as-social engineer are fore-grounded as generative of meaning about progress.

How do the vocabularies produce meaning about progress? This operation, it is suggested, involves the deployment of different narrativization techniques, primary among which is the form of historical narrative. The vocabularies just identified form the basis of grand historical narratives of evolution, which are presented as 'speaking themselves' (as true, objective, natural, neutral, diachronic, transcendental, etc.). This hides terrible interpretative pitfalls: the narratives take for granted what still needs to be proven.

Such narratives postulate a specific vision of the future, and a specific account of the past and the present, as inescapable truths, thrusting alternative views beyond the four corners of permissible argument. Progress is thus tautologically identified with itself, with what is projected as the desired future of international law. This is a self-fulfilling prophecy. This way the structure (the vocabulary of progress) becomes a legitimizing structure. It becomes the standard against which options are assessed, the interpretative device by means of which reality is perceived, the mechanism that determines the range of permissible statements.

The narrative production of meaning about progress is not a 'bad thing' in itself. In other words, the purpose of the first proposition is not to suggest a 'regression', error, or fault in legal argument each time meaning is produced via a progress narrative. The purpose is to point to the operations that produce meaning textually and to flag the difference of this approach against the mainstream use of the notion of progress as one that 'speaks itself'.

Thus, in the first study (Seferiades), the opposition of absolutism and democracy was proven to form the backbone of a historical narrative of progress. Seferiades tells a linear story according to which democracy/internationalism has been, for centuries, the catalyst for progress in social organization. In the antipodes, absolutism/sovereignism has been the source of social regression and misery. For a historical account of this sort to be convincing, it needs to be presented as objectively true, as 'speaking itself'. As demonstrated in Chapter 2, Seferiades does exactly that and recounts a story that is complete, universal, diachronic. In his writings, the opposition of democracy and absolutism is 'naturalized' and 'formalized', as the case study explains. The notions of democracy and absolutism acquire fixed and stable meaning and they are defined in opposition to each other. Absolutism *is* the Other of Democracy. This is a totalizing teleology. The history of the world can be recounted through this polarizing prism, where there is no room for alternative explanations. The historical narrative spans the entire course of history, from ancient times till our day, and is applicable to different parts of the world, creating a complete reality which allows no room for doubt: democracy/internationalism appears to be the only path to progress. The notion of progress acquires its meaning through this historical narrative, which determines the range of permissible statements within the discourse. Thus the binary opposition becomes the interpretative device to understand almost any social or political decision.

In the second study (sources), a similar phenomenon occurs. The rhetoric about the reconstruction of international law, which dominated international law debates in the wake of the Great War; and the narrative moves of 'standardization' and 'formalization' in sources literature, which followed the adoption of the Statute of the Permanent Court of International Justice, weave a persuasive historical narrative. This narrative presents pre-1920 doctrine of the sources as unable to fulfill its role as a tool for separating law from non-law. The reason given is that the doctrine was indeterminate: it was too open-ended (nobody knew the exact number and nature of the sources) and too dependent on arbitrary theoretical/political opinion (pinned on partial philosophical theories). On the antipodes, the post-1920 doctrine of the sources (under Art. 38 Statute PCIJ) is presented as hugely superior on account of it being determinate. The problem of open-endedness was resolved with the move to standardization (a new 'closed' and 'universal' list of sources). The problem of dependence on arbitrary political or philosophical opinion was resolved with the move to formalization (the creation of a set of secondary rules belonging to a different register than 'high theory' or politics). The transition from fragmentation to standardization, from philosophy/politics to technique, from academic formalism to pragmatism, is the totalizing narrative that 'speaks itself' and produces meaning about progress in sources discourse. The narrative moves of standardization and formalization capitalize on a background story that privileges determinacy, scientific technique, and pragmatism, to leave no choice as to the meaning of progressiveness in doctrinal debates. Like Seferiades, however, the only way for this story to perform its discursive effect is to buttress its claim to objective truth. The terms themselves (determinacy, pragmatism, technique) need also to be assumed as having stable and determinate meaning. Again, the mystified opposition between a primitive past and an advanced present/future becomes the interpretative device to understand doctrinal progress.

In the third study (tribunals), the two vocabularies (lawyer-as-architect and lawyer-as-social-engineer) tell two parallel – if different – historical narratives of progress. Despite many lateral differences, both narratives shake hands in their historical determinism. Both narratives laud the arrival of tribunals as the materialization of their respective historical necessities about progress in international law (rule-oriented approach as progress in law). Both narratives discern the emergence of a system of international justice and a global community of courts (proliferation of courts as a system of international justice). Finally, they share the conviction that proliferation is 'in itself' an element of progress in international law (tribunals have benevolent effects on the international community). These vocabularies tell a persuasive story of evolution in international law in which a transition to a rule-oriented system supported by an organized international judiciary is tautologically identified with progress, with no room for contestation. The phenomenon of proliferation announces the arrival of this new institutional moment. The persuasiveness of the story is reinforced by the fact that both narratives draw from the credos of two main traditions about international law thinking on both sides of the Atlantic (constitutional formalism and policy pragmatism). In order for the narrative of progress to work, the benefits of the rule oriented approach, the possibility of a system, the social effects of judicialization, all need to be presented as unequivocally true, as 'speaking themselves'. Chapter 4 demonstrated how the literature sidesteps the empirical proof dimension of all the main assumptions as stated and takes them for granted. The literature relies on the fact that these assumptions are not contested rather than by demonstrating their validity. This way the narratives reverse (and increase) the level of proof needed for the critic, since one would have to adduce empirical evidence contradicting what is believed to be common professional knowledge and experience, even if the original claim was not originally supported by any such empirical evidence. The creation of a system of international justice in which all institutions performed similar effects is only possible by ignoring their morphological differences, social-political functions, aims and mandate. These narratives once more mystify a before/after historical account that tautologically becomes the interpretative device to explain and understand social reality.

## 5.3    Progress Narratives as Politics

The second proposition that was put forward takes the argument one step further. It seeks to demonstrate that progress narratives, such as the ones above, are not only responsible for the production of meaning about progress. They are also, and by definition non-objective, despite their claims to objectivity. Being non-objective, progress narratives in fact compete with (often exclude) other narratives, based on different partial vocabularies. As explained in Chapter 1, this proposition finds its origins in post-structuralism, deconstruction, and post-modern work. It aims to demonstrate that, although vocabularies may be the structures that produce meaning about progress in each discourse, the vocabularies themselves are not "true" or "stable". Rather the opposite holds true: the vocabularies acquire different meanings in different contexts, even in ways in which their own authors cannot control or predict. In fact, it is claimed that the instability/indeterminacy of the vocabulary is crucial for the production of meaning.

Along these lines, although a certain vocabulary may be based on the opposition of, say, democracy and absolutism, the proposition here is that neither democracy not absolutism have fixed or stable meaning, although their opposition remains crucial for the production of meaning. A certain notion, such as democracy, acquires its meaning in relation to the notion of absolutism (e.g. in opposition), but both the meaning of democracy and the meaning of absolutism may change in the various contexts in which they are being used. They may in fact collapse into each other. Thus vocabularies, despite their claim to 'speak themselves', are nothing more than ephemeral and unstable structures of the production of meaning which may, nevertheless, constitute powerful mechanisms of (de)legitimation within the context of specific discourses. This would depend on one's capacity to claim decisive use of the vocabulary. The perception of progress is produced by the instability and iterations rather than by the stability of the opposition.

The analysis of the three case studies does not (mean to) lead to the conclusion that these narratives were badly crafted or of poor quality, in the sense of having failed to be determinate enough. This would assume some original state of determinacy that could have been achieved if only they had done 'better' legal work. Rather, the point is that determinacy is no longer the appropriate frame of reference for charting the relation between legal language and the practices it ostensibly seeks to describe. The value of the vocabulary rests in its capacity to legitimize certain events as progressive, *regardless* of whether it is determinate or stable. This way, the presumed authors of each vocabulary (Seferiades, interwar social jurisprudes, the new tribunalists) are not authors of a determinate/rational set of assumptions, but the aspiring controllers of a set of discursive structures that legitimize social outcomes, participating in an intellectual struggle with fellow participants in the discourse for decisive control.

This point was addressed in all three case studies. Take for example the first study (Seferiades). We saw earlier that the opposition of democracy and absolutism became the backbone of a historical narrative, confounding democracy with progress, and absolutism with regression. The case study went however a step further to demonstrate that neither democracy nor absolutism had a stable meaning in the (same) texts of Seferiades. The two notions were de-historicized and de-politicized: they were made appear as forces of nature that somehow simply existed in an absolute form, as traits of humanity. Seferiades presented the dichotomy of the two as a stable one, or at least relatively stable, to the extent that one could ask what is the role of the one versus the other in history. The essentialization of the terms performed a very crucial role in the production of meaning. Not only did it remove from view the problem of linguistic indeterminacy but it also occluded the character and significance of heterogeneity, namely the complexity of social processes in which such concepts have thrived and constituted the banners of ideological opposition. Absolutism thus became a concrete, coherent mode of governance, despite the substantial differences that may have distinguished different types of monarchies from each other; and democracy is presented as a coherent global standard without internal ruptures or discontinuities.

Such use of the narrative was crucial for the persuasive effect of the writings of Seferiades. The deployment of the opposition of absolutism v democracy was a narrative technique that placed Seferiades safely and at all times on the side of progress, even when his argument would fail even its own self-proclaimed standards of what is progressive. The opposition, far from having a stable content, was rather a trope or style of argument that helped vest with legitimacy his liberal ideological-personal project and jump over the ruptures and discontinuities of the experience of reality. The perception of progress was produced by the instability and iterations of the vocabulary rather than its stability. These iterations allowed all claims of Seferiades to be placed on the side of progress (e.g. democracy), even when the claims were in logical contradiction with his own definition of progress at a different point in the text. Despite this incoherence, the vocabulary was nevertheless able to discredit his opponents as regressive (e.g., absolutist).

Ultimately, however, Seferiades was not in control of his own vocabulary. His work, instead of the pursuit of a political-ideological agenda, became devoted to the defense of the opposition of absolutism and democracy.

This strategy prevented Seferiades himself from realizing the contradictions of the bourgeois modernization project and the reasons for its failure. Failure was attributed to an external enemy (regression, absolutism) and not to the instability of the opposition itself.

Likewise, in the second study (sources), the narrative moves of standardization and formalization become the basis of a vocabulary and a historical narrative of progress. According to the story recounted by interwar international layers, the post-1920 version of the doctrine of the sources constituted progress for international law on account of its determinacy (closure, universality, technical nature), and in opposition to the indeterminacy of the pre-1920 doctrine (fragmentation, politics). Like in the case of Seferiades, the case study of Chapter 3 went a step further to demonstrate that the projected virtue of determinacy of the new doctrine was based on notions that were themselves neither stable nor determinate. Closure and universality were subverted each time they were put to application. The 'new' doctrine of the sources (based on Art. 38 PCIJ Statute), despite the claim of limiting the range of sources that could be invoked, allowed two opposing patterns of argument ('hard' and 'soft') to operate simultaneously within each of the sources of the list of Article 38 PCIJ. Instead of bringing closure, the possibility of both 'soft' and 'hard' patterns of argument would enable the debate to continue interminably. The only way to bring closure is the invocation of yet another and new decisive discourse, this time external to Article 38.

The same holds for the narrative move of formalization. Formalization aspired to disconnect the 'registers' of high theory and practical application in order to allow a technical (non-political, non-theoretical) application of the doctrine. It was however demonstrated that the two registers collapsed into each other each time one would seek their autonomous application. Like with the vocabulary of absolutism and democracy, the vocabulary of standardization and formalization, far from having a stable content, was rather a trope or style of argument that helped vest with legitimacy a project for the reconstruction of public international law. 'Talking sources' was not 'more' determinate than 'talking theory'. At the same time, the language of the sources was able to capture anew the fantasy of the international lawyer as a discourse that was able to jump over the ruptures of everyday experience. Legitimacy in sources discourse was produced not because pragmatism or Article 38 PCIJ Statute had the capacity to decisively tell whether a certain norm was one of public international law. Legitimacy was produced by means of the *invocation* of the vocabulary of pragmatism and Article 38. In that sense, progress in sources did not have an essence: it was the product of a narrative whose essence was floating, allowing a multiplicity of meanings according to the occasion. Like with Seferiades, one could argue that the iteration of meanings is what enabled the success of the language of the sources doctrine. As explained in the digression to the contemporary literature, literature on the sources has found peace in bracketing (setting aside) all the hard questions that would bring out the indeterminacy of the doctrine. The feeling of certainty in the literature is forged by standard references to classical cases and materials. In such references the iteration of the vocabulary is either silenced or under-played. The success of the vocabulary of the sources rests in its capacity to legitimize certain events as progressive, regardless of whether it is determinate or stable. The authors of the new doctrine were not the authors of determinate/rational set of technical tools, but the controllers of a set of discursive structures that legitimized social outcomes.

The same holds for the third study (tribunals). As explained earlier, meaning about progress in tribunals discourse is produced by two parallel, if different, vocabularies of progress. The lawyer-as-architect and the lawyer-as-social-engineer differed in many ways but both shook hands in their historical determinism that welcomed the judicialization of international law as synonymous with progress. Like the two previous case studies, however, Chapter 4 went a step further to demonstrate that the structures that produced meaning about progress were unstable and indeterminate. The advantages of the rule-oriented approach, the existence of a system of international justice, the social benefits of judicialization, were taken for granted instead of being proven. They key for the persuasiveness of the vocabulary was not its determinacy but its rhetorical capacity to set aside (or disempower) any internal or external critique that would give concrete meaning to these terms. Challenging the empirical basis of the assumptions is enough to immediately position one at the margins of the discipline, where one would have to assume the entire burden of proof. The vocabulary of progress of the new tribunalism, far from based on stable or determinate assumptions, can now be seen as a set of discursive structures that legitimize social and institutional action, allocate resources, and decide the limits of contemporary humanitarianism.

## 5.4    DISCOURSE ANALYSIS AS ACTION

This leads to the last proposition that was put forward in Chapter 1 concerning the purpose and value of the current enquiry. It is indeed habitual in scholarly writing to conclude one's analysis by providing answers to questions about the academic, social or other significance of the enquiry. What is then the solution, as it emerges from your analysis? What do you propose? What is your alternative? Failure to be re-constructive or normative in answering such questions, failure to provide with an alternative solution, a future perspective or direction, is often taken to betray cynicism, agnosticism, nihilism, or just bad taste. The alleged failure to re-construct has been the primary critique against Critical thought and the various Critical movements in public international law. The tenor of such critiques is that this type of analysis is ultimately unhelpful: despite its occasional intellectual novelty, Critical analysis uses its zeal in order to de-construct and criticize rather than to offer concrete solutions that are badly needed in the everyday practice of the law. In such critiques, the duty to reconstruct is conceived as central to professional identity of the scholar whose task remains incomplete unless she provides the necessary tools to repair the structures that have been found faulty or wanting improvement.

I have no contest with the desire to find solutions to problems. It is claimed here, however, that the 'what is next?' question performs a slightly more complex ideological role than it cares to admit. The question, to begin with, is structured in a way that reproduces precisely the kind of assumption that the present project has set out to disrupt, namely the idea that there *is* something to be done in a better, decisive, foundational, or other progressive meta-way. The 'what is next?' question is posed on the presumption that the author is a rational, coherent, autonomous, subject able to stand outside the problem itself and assume action the moment the 'right' solution is found. The problem is that the adjective 'right' already sets the frame that determines the kind of argument that may come forward. It also assumes the possibility of a decisive meta-narrative that will help one distinguish between different 'right' solutions. The 'what is next?' question therefore embodies and reproduces the idea that there *is* such a thing as a progress narrative that can travel the distance from relativism to a solution that 'speaks itself'. For one to answer the 'what is next?' question in a satisfactory way, one would have to create a decisive meta-narrative. The circularity of this proposition is obvious. It assumes that the creation of 'better' or 'more correct' meta-narratives is the prescribed role of the scholar, as opposed to 'merely' demonstrating that the creation of meta-narratives cannot stand the test of internal criticism. The 'what is next?' question de-legitimizes *ab initio* the conclusions of this enquiry, which aims to demonstrate that there is, ultimately, something problematic in a discourse that endorses progress talk as the only legitimate way of speaking about international law.

In response, and to pay tribute to the customary 'what is next?' question, I close by explaining my own understanding of the motives underlying the present enquiry. These motives may be considered progressive or regressive but hopefully only in context, and in a non-decisive way. While hoping to evade a permanent categorization of the sort, I submit that there is an intrinsic value in this type of analysis as action.

Most of us would agree with Roland Barthes or Hayden White that telling before/after stories about law, history, humanity, specific legal problems, is an intuitive and effective rhetorical technique. Progress narratives help us summon our reader from afar and situate her in a context, they help give a clear account of the author's worldview, and help explain the merit of specific legal or other solutions that emerge as a consequence. A 'progress kick', the zeal generated by feeling part of a moment of disciplinary progress, yields tremendous energy and can be a compelling source of institutional, doctrinal, or social transformation. Associating oneself with a global progressive movement can justify one's renewed commitment to international law and give legitimacy to one's views. It can improve the traction of the discipline as a whole in relation to competing sciences of governance; and can provide the type of cautious optimism that is considered an essential attitude for those on the 'international plane'.

The problem identified here is not the use of narratives of progress or of the notion of progress as such. The present enquiry merely seeks to underline the inevitable exclusions of progress narratives. These exclusions are often times accompanied by a belief, overt or covert, that there 'is' such a thing as progress and that we, as legal professionals, have the capacity to speak it by means of our own legal language. This is not a marginal consideration if it turns out that some of the basic assumptions of the discipline are grounded in grand narratives of progress, such as the ones examined in the three case studies of this book. While most of us subscribe to certain events because we deem them progressive or desirable in context, nothing prevents us from becoming aware of the function of progress narratives in the construction of our own perception of what is progressive. It is hoped that the present study helps illuminate the discursive function of such narratives. This is not a call to abandon progress narratives or the use of the notion of progress. It is a call to assert the limits and potentials of this technique of writing and talking about international law.

While there 'is' nothing in particular to be done in response to the 'what is next?' question, there is plenty to be done in pursuit of goals, strategies, reform projects, re-imagining international law, putting to action deeply felt beliefs. Like Seferiades, our international law work may be inevitably intertwined with personal-ideological projects that shape our agendas, priorities, choices, or preferences. There is nothing incompatible between a commitment to a social, legal, or disciplinary goal and the realization that progress narratives construct our 'progressiveness'. Ultimately, there is nothing inherently progressive or regressive about international law work, even though in many instances most of us will agree that a specific solution is better than others. There may well be no other way of practicing international law but to take a stance in such situations and declare one's preference or commitment to a concrete solution. Narratives of progress always empower some and disempower others, and there may be no way around it.

Revealing the exclusions of progress narratives and contesting their exclusive right to speak the world 'as it is', however, 'is' action. It opens up the field for alternative accounts and histories of progress. It participates in a struggle to redefine the filter of right solutions. In that sense, and unlike Seferiades, there is a lot to be done in terms of re-evaluating our relationship to some of the field's foundational narratives and in terms of exposing what is left out by the type of solutions that they privilege. There may be a lot to be done also in terms of re-writing and teaching international law's orthodoxies, re-evaluating them as we go. There may also be a lot to do in terms of lawyering that takes note of the field's exclusions and uses its ruptures to empower and emancipate. Following this, progress narratives are no longer to be accepted without question – at least not if one wants to know what is occluded, excluded, or included in their claim to progress. Our evaluation of them, in this sense, can remain pending. They can be neither approved nor rejected in a decisive way but the untroubled facility and ease with which they are accepted, incorporated, replicated, cited in the literature must be unsettled and questioned.

Some of international law's founding narratives are primary candidates for such a re-evaluation. This is not an argument to reject them for being wrong, untrue, or political. Every narrative contains a certain degree of truth and falsity. Each may be 'progressive' or 'regressive' in context. Our determination can remain pending, at least while we continuously become aware of its ever-changing social, disciplinary and other outcomes, who gains and who loses each time. Like all texts, the profession's narratives subvert themselves and change over time, acquiring and losing power through use. According to the argument so far, and this is a central claim of this book, the international lawyer is part of this struggle to determine what is progressive and what is not. Our narratives of progress in international law are part of this struggle. So, what must we do?

> "What we must do, in fact, is to tear away from their virtual self-evidence [of narratives], and to free the problems that they pose. To recognize that they are not the tranquil locus on the basis of which other questions (concerning their structure, coherence, systematicity, transformation) may be posed but that they themselves pose a whole cluster of questions (what are they? How can they be defined or limited? What laws do they obey? Which specific phenomena do they give rise to in their field of discourse?). We must recognize that they may not, in the last resort, be what they seem at first sight. In short, they require a theory, and that this theory cannot be constructed unless the field of the facts of discourse on the basis of which those facts are built up appears in its non-synthetic unity. Once this is done an entire field is set free."[628]

In closing, to those who declare the end of history, or any decisive historical narrative of progress, this book merely counter-proposes that history, and the writing of histories of progress, never ends.

---

[628] Foucault (Archaeology of Knowledge), *supra* note 83.

# BIBLIOGRAPHY

Books/Articles

**-A-**

Georges Abi-Saab, 'La "communauté internationale" saisie par le droit. Essai radioscopie juridique', in *Boutros Boutros-Ghali Amicorum Discipulorumque Liber: paix, développement, démocratie* (Bruxelles: Bruylant, 1998) 81-108.

William J. Aceves, 'Liberalism and International Legal Scholarship: The Pinochet Case and the Move towards a Universal System of Transnational Law Litigation', 41 *Harvard International Law Journal* (2000) 129-184.

William J. Aceves, 'Symposium Introduction: Scholarship as Evidence of International Law', 26 *Loyola of Los Angeles International & Comparative Law Review* (2003) 1-5.

Payam Akhavan, 'Beyond Impunity: Can International Justice Prevent Future Atrocities?', 95 *American Journal of International Law* (2001) 7-31.

Roger P. Alford, 'The Proliferation of International Courts and Tribunals: International Adjudication in Ascendance', 94 *American Society of International Law Proceedings of the Annual Meeting* (2000) 160-165.

Nikolaos Alivizatos, *Οι Πολιτικοί Θεσμοί σε Κρίση 1922-1974: Όψεις της Ελληνικής Εμπειρίας* [Political Institutions in Crisis 1922-1974: Aspects of the Greek Experience] (in Greek, Athens, 1982).

Jean Allain, 'The Continued Evolution of International Adjudication', in Johanne Levasseur, ed., *Looking Ahead: International Law in the 21st Century* (Ottawa: Canadian Council on International Law, 2002) 50-71.

Andrew Altman, *Critical Legal Studies: A Liberal Critique* (Princeton, NJ: Princeton University Press, 1993).

Alejandro Álvarez, *Le Droit International Américain: son fondement, sa nature, d'après l'histoire diplomatique des états du Nouveau Monde et leur vie politique et économique* (Paris: A. Pedone, 1910).

Alejandro Álvarez, 'New Conception and New Bases of Legal Philosophy', 13 *University of Illinois Law Review* (1918-1919) 167-182.

Alejandro Álvarez, *The Monroe Doctrine. Its Importance in the International Life of the States of the New World* (New York: Oxford University Press, 1924).

Alejandro Álvarez, 'The Necessity for the Reconstruction of International Law – Its Aim', *Proceedings of the 4th Conference of Teachers of International Law and Related Subjects* (Washington, DC: 1930) 11-16.

Alejandro Álvarez, 'The New International Law', 15 *Transactions of the Grotius Society* (1930) 35-51.

Chittaranjan Felix Amerasinghe, 'History and Sources of the Law of War', 16 *Sri Lanka Journal of International Law* (2004) 263-287.

Sheldon Amos, *Lectures on International Law* (London: Stevens and Sons, 1874).

Leigh Anderson and Janet W. Looney, eds., *Making Progress: Essays in Progress and Public Policy* (Lanham, MD: Lexington Books, 2002).

Nisuke Ando et al., eds., *Liber Amicorum Judge Shigeru Oda* (The Hague: Kluwer Law International, 2002).

Antony Anghie, *Imperialism, Sovereignty and the Making of International Law* (Cambridge: Cambridge University Press, 2005).

Anonymous, 'The League of Nations and the Laws of War', 1 *British Yearbook of International Law* (1920-21) 109-124.

Louise Arbour, 'Progress and Challenges in International Criminal Justice', 21 *Fordham International Law Journal* (1997) 531-540.

Samuel J. Astorino, 'The Impact of Sociological Jurisprudence on International Law in the Inter-war Period', 34 *Duquesne Law Review* (1996) 277-298.

Antony Aust, *Handbook of International Law* (Cambridge: Cambridge University Press, 2005).

Antony Aust, *Modern Treaty Law and Practice* (2nd edn.; Cambridge: Cambridge University Press, 2007).

John Austin, *The Province of Jurisprudence Determined*, new edn. (Cambridge: Cambridge University Press, 1995).

**-B-**

Hans W. Baade, 'The Legal Effects of Codes of Conduct for Multinational Enterprises', in Norbert Horn, ed., *Legal Problems of Codes of Conduct for Multinational Enterprises* (Deventer: Kluwer, 1980) 3-38.

John Baillie, *The Belief in Progress* (Oxford: Oxford University Press, 1950).

Ilias Bantekas, 'Reflections on Some Sources and Methods of International Criminal and Humanitarian Law', 6 *International Criminal Law Review* (2006) 121-136.

Harry Elmer Barnes, *World Politics in Modern Civilization: The Contributions of Nationalism, Capitalism, Imperialism and Militarism to Human Culture and International Anarchy* (New York: Knopf, 1930).

L.A.N.M. Barnhoorn and K.C. Wellens, eds., *Diversity in Secondary Rules and the Unity of International Law* (The Hague: Nijhoff, 1995).

Roland Barthes, 'Introduction to the Structural Analysis of Narratives', in Roland Barthes, *Image, Music, Text* (Translated by Steven Heath; London: Fontana Press, 1977).

Jules Basdevant, *Peace through International Adjudication?* (Translated from the French by Arthur W.A. Cowan, Le judiciaire dans l'organisation international actuelle, Brochure, Peace Palace Library, 1949).

M. Cherif Bassiouni, 'From Versailles to Rwanda in Seventy-Five Years: The Need to Establish a Permanent International Criminal Court', 10 *Harvard Human Rights Law Journal* (1997) 11-62.

M. Cherif Bassiouni, 'The Normative Framework of International Humanitarian Law: Overlaps, Gaps, and Ambiguities', 8 *Transnational Law & Contemporary Problems* (1998) 199-275.

M. Cherif Bassiouni, 'The Sources and Content of International Criminal Law: A Theoretical Framework', in Kalliopi Koufa, ed., *The New International Criminal Law: 2001 International Law Sassion* (Athens: Sakkoulas, 2003) 19-207.

Richard R. Baxter, 'Two Cheers for International Adjudication', 65 *American Bar Association Journal* (1979) 1185-1189.

Peri Bearman, Rudolph Peters and Frank E. Vogel, eds., *The Islamic School of Law: Evolution, Devolution, and Progress* (Harvard: Harvard Law School Islamic Legal Studies Program, 2005).

Roderick Beaton, Γιώργος Σεφέρης – Περιμένοντας τον Αγγελο [George Seferis – Waiting for an Angel. A Biography] (Athens, 2004).

Max Beloff, *The Age of Absolutism 1660-1815* (London: Hutchinson, 1954).

Harold J. Berman, 'The Law of International Commercial Transactions (Lex Mercatoria)', 2 *Emory Journal of International Dispute Resolution* (1988) 235.

Marshall Berman, *All That Is Solid Melts into Air: The Experience of Modernity* (London: Verso, 1982).

Nathaniel Berman, 'A Perilous Ambivalence: Nationalist Desire, Legal Autonomy, and the Limits of the Interwar Framework', 33 *Harvard International Law Journal* (1992) 353-379.

Nathaniel Berman, '"But the Alternative is Despair": European Nationalism and the Modernist Renewal of International Law', 106 *Harvard Law Review* (1992-1993) 1792-1903.

Nathaniel Berman, 'In the Wake of Empire', 14 *The American University International Law Review* (1999) 1521-1554.

Ralph Beddard and Dilys M. Hill, eds., *Economic, Social and Cultural Rights: Progress and Achievement* (Houndmills: MacMillan, 1992).

Yves Beigbeder, *International Justice against Impunity: Progress and New Challenges* (Boston: Nijhoff, 2005).

Isaiah Berlin, 'History and Theory: The Concept of Scientific History', 1 *History and Theory* (1960-1961) 1-31 .

Fritz K. Bieligk, *Progress to World Peace: A Study of the Development of International Law and the Social and Economic Conditions of Peace* (Translated by E. Fitzgerald, London: Hutchinson & Co., 1945).

Patricia Birnie and Alan Boyle, *International Law and the Environment* (2nd edn.; Oxford: Oxford University Press, 2002).

Willem Roosegaarde Bisschop, 'Sovereignty', 2 *British Yearbook of International Law* (1921-1922) 122-132.

Meriel Bloor and Thomas Bloor, *The Practice of Critical Discourse Analysis: An Introduction* (London: Hodder Arnold, 2007).

Florence Brewer Boeckel, *Progress of the Centuries toward World Organization* (Washington, DC: National Council for the Prevention of War, 1927).

Laurence Boisson de Chazournes, 'Les résolutions des organes des Nations Unies, et en particulier celles du Conseil de sécurité, en tant que source de droit international humanitaire', in Luigi Condorelli, Anne-Marie La Rosa and Sylvie Scherrer, *Les Nations Unies et le droit international humanitaire: actes du Colloque international à l'occasion du cinquantième anniversaire de l'ONU* (1996) 149-173.

Laurence Boisson de Chazournes, 'Multiplication des instances de règlement des différends: vers la promotion de la règle de droit', (Zero Issue) *Forum* (1998) 14-15.

John R. Bolton, 'Is There Really "Law" in International Affairs?', 10 *Transnational Law and Contemporary Problems* (2000) 1-48.

Alan E. Boyle, 'Dispute Settlement and the Law of the Sea Convention: Problems of Fragmentation and Jurisdiction', 46 *The International and Comparative Law Quarterly* (1997) 37-54.

Alan E. Boyle and Christine M. Chinkin, *The Making of International Law* (Oxford: Oxford University Press, 2007).

James Boyle, *Critical Legal Studies* (New York: New York University Press, 1994).

Benjamin Braude and Bernard Lewis, eds., *Christians and Jews in the Ottoman Empire: The Functioning of a Plural Society* (New York: Holmes & Meier Publishers, 1982).

James Leslie Brierly, 'Le fondement du caractère obligatoire du droit international', 23 *Recueil des Cours* (III-1928) 463-552.

James Leslie Brierly, 'The Future of Codification', 12 *British Yearbook of International Law* (1931) 2.

James Leslie Brierly, *The Law of Nations – An Introduction to the International Law of Peace* (2nd edn.; Oxford: Clarendon Press, 1936).

James Leslie Brierly, 'The Shortcomings of International Law', in Hersch Lauterpacht and Claude Humphrey Meredith Waldock, eds., *The Basis of Obligation in International Law and Other Papers by the Late J.L. Brierly* (Oxford: Clarendon Press, 1958) 68.

James Leslie Brierly, 'The Lotus Case', in Hersch Lauterpacht and Claude Humphrey Meredith Waldock, eds., *The Basis of Obligation in International Law and Other Papers by the Late J.L. Brierly* (Oxford: Clarendon Press, 1958) 68.

Chester Brown, 'The Proliferation of International Courts and Tribunals: Finding Your Way through the Maze', 3 *Melbourne Journal of International Law* (2002) 453-475.

Chester Brown, *A Common Law of International Adjudication* (Oxford: Oxford University Press, 2007).

Edith Brown Weiss, 'The Rise or the Fall of International Law?', 69 *Fordham Law Review* (2000) 345-372.

Gillian Brown and George Yule, eds., *Discourse Analysis* (Cambridge: Cambridge University Press, 1983).

Ian Brownlie, 'Legal Effects of Codes of Conduct for Multi-National Enterprises: Commentary', in Norbert Horn, ed., *Legal Problems of Codes of Conduct for Multinational Enterprises* (Deventer: Kluwer, 1980) 39-43.

Ian Brownlie, 'Problems Concerning the Unity of International Law', in (no editor) *International Law at the Time of its Codification: Essays in Honor of Roberto Ago* (Milano: Giuffrè, 1987) 153-162.

Ian Brownlie, *Principles of International Law* (6th expanded and revised edn.; Oxford: Oxford University Press, 2003).

Jutta Brunée, 'Coping with Consent: Law-Making under Multilateral Environmental Agreements', 15 *Leiden Journal of International Law* (2002) 1-52.

Mary Buckley and Robert Singh, eds., *The Bush Doctrine and the War on Terrorism: Global Responses, Global Consequences* (London: Routledge, 2006).

Thomas Buergenthal, 'The American Convention on Human Rights: An Illusion of Progress', in *Miscellanea W.J. Ganshof van der Meersch: studia ab discipulis amicisque in honorem egregii professoris edita* (Mélanges publiés sous l'begide et avec l'appui du Centre Interuniversitaire de Droit Public et de l'Université Libre de Bruxelles, Vol. 1, Brussels, Bruylant, 1972).

Thomas Buergenthal, 'Proliferation of International Courts and Tribunals: Is It Good or Is It Bad?', 14 *Leiden Journal of International Law* (2001) 267-275.

John Bagnell Bury, *The Idea of Progress: An Inquiry into Its Origins and Growth*, new edn. (orig. London: Macmillan, 1920; new edition, New York: Dover Publications, 1987).

Nicholas Murray Butler, *The International Mind: An Argument for the Judicial Settlement of International Disputes* (New York, 1912).

Antoine C. Buyse, *Post-Conflict Housing Restitution: The European Human Rights Perspective, with a Case Study on Bosnia and Herzegovina* (Ph.D. Thesis, Utrecht: Intersentia: 2007).

Gionata Piero Buzzini, 'La théorie des sources face au droit international général: réflexions sur l'émergence du droit objectif dans l'ordre juridique international', 106 *Revue Générale de Droit International Public droit des gens histoire diplomatique, droit penal, droit fiscal, droit administrative* (2002) 581-617.

Michael Byers, Custom, *Power and the Power of Rules: International Relations and Customary International Law* (Cambridge: Cambridge University Press, 1999).

**-C-**

Lucius C. Caflisch, The Law of International Waterways and Its Sources', in Ronald St. J. Macdonald, ed., *Essays in Honour of Wang Tieya* (Dordrecht: Nijhoff, 1994) 115-129.

Charles Calvo, *Le droit international théorique et pratique précédé d'un exposé historique des progrès de la science du droit des gens*, 5e éd. rev. et compl. par un supplément (Paris: Durand et Pedone-Lauriel, 1896).

Robert H. Canary and Henry Kozicki, eds., *The Writing of History: Literary Form and Historical Understanding* (Madison/London: University of Wisconsin Press, 1978).

Thomas E. Carbonneau, ed., *Lex Mercatoria and Arbitration – A Discussion of the New Law Merchant* (Dobbs Ferry, NY: Transnational Juris Publications, 1990).

David D. Caron, 'The ILC Articles on State Responsibility: The Paradoxical Relationship Between Form and Authority', 96 *American Journal of International Law* (2002) 857-873.

Anthony Carty, ed., *Post-Modern Law: Enlightenment, Revolution, and the Death of Man* (Edinburgh: Edinburgh University Press, 1990).

Anthony Carty, 'Critical International Law: Recent Trends in the Theory of International Law', 2 *European Journal of International Law* (1991) 66-96.

Anthony Carty, 'A Renewed Place for Doctrine as a Source of International Law in a Time of Fragmentation', in Rosario Huesa Vinaixa and Karel Wellens, eds., *L'influence des sources sur l'unité et la fragmentation du droit international* (Bruxelles: Bruylant, 2006) 239-261.

Deborah Z. Cass, 'Navigating the Newstream: Recent Critical Scholarship in International Law', 65 *Nordic Journal of International Law* (1996) 341-383.

Antonio Cassese, *International Law* (2nd edn.; Oxford/New York: Oxford University Press USA, 2005).

Antonio Cassese, 'The Proper Limits of Individual responsibility under the Doctrine of Joint Criminal Enterprise', 5 *Journal of International Criminal Justice* (2007) 109-133.

Louis Cavaré, 'L'arrêt du "Lotus" et le positivisme juridique', 10 *Travaux juridiques et economiques de l'Université de Rennes* (1930) 144.

Jean-Paul Chapdelaine, 'À la recherche d'une éthique en droit international économique', 22 *Revúe Générale de Droit* (1991) 471-475.

Hilary Charlesworth, Christine Chinkin and Shelley Wright, 'Feminist Approaches to International Law', 85 *American Journal of International Law* (1991) 613-645.

Jonathan I. Charney, 'International Lawmaking: Article 38 of the Statute Reconsidered', in Joost Delbrück, ed., *New Trends in International Lawmaking, International "Legislation" in the Public Interest* (Berlin: Duncker & Humblot, 1997) 171-230.

Jonathan I. Charney, 'The Impact on the International Legal System of the Growth of International Courts and Tribunals', 31 *New York University Journal of International Law and Politics* (1999) 697-708.

Jonathan I. Charney, 'Is International Law Threatened by Multiple International Tribunals?', 271 *Recueil des Cours* (1998) 101-382.

Jonathan I. Charney, 'Progress in International Criminal Law?', 93 *American Journal of International Law* (1999) 452-464.

Abram Chayes and Antonia Handler, *The New Sovereignty: Compliance With International Regulatory Agreements* (Cambridge, MA: Harvard University Press, 1995).

Bhupinder S. Chimni, 'Third World Approaches to International Law: A Manifesto', 8 *International Community Law Review* (2006) 3-27.

Christine Chinkin, 'A Mirage in the Sand? Distinguishing Binding and Non-Binding Relations between States', 10 *Leiden Journal of International Law* (1997) 223-247.

Christine Chinkin and Hilary Charlesworth, *The Boundaries of International Law: A Feminist Analysis* (Manchester: Manchester University Press, 2000).

Nikita Sergeevic Crushchev, 'Peace and Progress Must Triumph in Our Time' (report of N.S. Khrushchov on his visit to the United States to a meeting of Moscow people at the Sports Palace of the Lenin Stadium September 28, 1959, translated from Russian, London, 1959).

Inis L. Claude Jr., *Swords into Plowshares: The Problems and Progress of International Organization* (4th edn.; New York: Random House, 1988).

Richard Clogg, *A Concise History of Greece* (2nd edn.; Cambridge: Cambridge University Press, 2002).

Bernard Colas, 'Acteurs, sources formelles, et hiérarchie des normes en droit international économique', 22 *Revue générale du droit* (1991) 385-395.

Sanford D. Cole, 'Codification of International Law', 12 *Grotius Society Transactions* (1927) 49-61.

Luigi Condorelli, 'Les progrès du droit international humanitaire et la circulaire du secrétaire général des Nations Unies du 6 août 1999', in Laurence Boisson de Chazournes, Vera Gowlland-Debbas and Georges Michel Abi-Saab, eds., *The international Legal System in Quest of Equity and Universality: Liber Amicorum Georges Abi Saab* (The Hague: Martinus Nijhoff, 2001) 495-505.

Percy Corbett, 'The Consent of States and the Sources of the Law of Nations', 6 *British Yearbook of International Law* (1925) 20-30.

Matthew Craven and Malgosia Fitzmaurice, eds., *Interrogating the Treaty: Essays in the Contemporary Law of Treaties* (Nijmegen: Wolf Legal Publishers, 2005).

Matthew Craven, 'Unity, Diversity, and the Fragmentation of International Law', 14 *Finnish Yearbook of International Law* (2003) 3-34.

James Crawford, ed., *The International Law Commission's Articles on State Responsibility: Introduction, Text, and Commentaries* (Cambridge: Cambridge University Press, 2002).

Jonathan D. Culler, *Structuralist Poetics: Structuralism, Linguistics, and the Study of Literature* (Ithaca: Cornell University Press, 1975).

Jonathan D. Culler, ed., *On Deconstruction: Theory and Criticism after Structuralism* (London: Routledge, 1983).

Henri Culot, 'Soft Law et droit de l'OMC', 19 *Revue internationale de droit économique* (2005) 251-289.

**-D-**

Patrick Daillier and Alain Pellet, *Droit International Public* (6th edn.; Paris: LGDJ, 1999).

Douglas Dakin, *The Unification of Greece*, 1770-1923 (London: Benn, 1972).

Antony Alfred D'Amato, *International Law Sources* (Leiden: Nijhoff, 2004).

Dan Danielsen and Karen Engle, eds., *After Identity: A Reader in Law and Culture* (London: Routledge, 1995).

Gennady Danilenko, *Law Making in the International Community* (Dordrecht: Nijhoff, 1993).

George B. Davis, *The Elements of International Law, with an Account of Its Origin Sources and Historical Development* (3rd revised edn., including the results of the Second Peace Conference at The Hague in 1907 and other new material; New York, 1908).

Emmanuel Decaux, 'La Forme et la Force Obligatoire des Codes de Bonne Conduite', 29 *Annuaire Francais de Droit International* (1983) 81-97.

Vladimir-Djuro Degan, *Sources of International Law* (The Hague: Nijhoff, 1997).

Vladimir-Djuro Degan, 'On the Sources of International Criminal Law', 4 *Chinese Journal of International Law* (2005) 45-83.

Ige F. Dekker and Harry H.G. Post, eds., *On the Foundations and Sources of International Law* (The Hague: T.M.C. Asser Press, 2003).

Barbara Delcourt, 'The Doctrine of the "Responsibility to Protect" and the EU Stance: Critical Appraisal', 59 *Studia Diplomatica* (2006) 69-93.

Mireille Delmas-Marty, 'Present-day China and the Rule of Law: Progress and Resistance', 2 *Chinese Journal of International Law* (2003) 11-28.

Mireille Delmas-Marty et al., eds., *Les sources du droit international pénal: l'expérience des tribunaux pénaux internationaux et le statut de la Cour Pénale Internationale* (sous la dir. de Mireille Delmas-Marty, Emanuela Fronza, Elisabeth Lambert-Abdelgawad, Paris: Société de Législation Comparée, 2004).

Jacques Derrida, *Of Grammatology* (Translated by Gayatri Chakravorty Spivak, Baltimore/London: The John Hopkins University Press, 1997).

Edouard-Eugène-François Descamps, 'Le droit international nouveau: L'influence de la condamnation de la guerre sur l'évolution juridique international', 31 *Recueil des Cours* (1930) 393-559.

Yves Dezalay and Bryan G. Garth, *Dealing in Virtue: International Commercial Arbitration and the Construction of a Transnational Legal Order* (Chicago, MI: The University of Chicago Press, 1996).

Pieter van Dijk, 'Nature and Function of Equity in International Economic Law', 7 *Grotiana* (1986) 4-48.

Odysseas Dimitrakopoulos and Thanos Veremis, eds., *Μελετήματα Γύρω απο τον Βενιζέλο και τιν Εποχή του* [Studies on Venizelos and his Era, in Greek] (Athens, 1980).

Marco Divač Öberg, 'The Legal Effects of Resolutions of the UN Security Council and General Assembly in the Jurisprudence of the ICJ', 16 *European Journal of International Law* (2005) 879-906.

Martin Dixon, *Textbook on International Law* (5th edn.; Oxford: Oxford University Press, 2005).

Costas Douzinas, Peter Goodrich and Yifat Hachamovitch, eds., *Politics, Postmodernity and Critical Legal Studies: The Legality of the Contingent* (London: Routledge, 1994).

Mark Drumble, 'Remarks', in Steven R. Ratner and James L. Bischoff, eds., 'International War Crimes Trials: Making a Difference?', *Proceedings of an International Conference Held at the University of Texas at Austin School of Law, November 6-7, 2003* (University of Texas at Austin School of Law, 2003).

Mark Drumble, 'Collective Violence and Individual Punishment: The Criminality of Mass Atrocity', 99 *Northwestern University Law Review* (2005) 539-611.

Oswald Ducrot and Tzvetan Todorov, *Encyclopedic Dictionary of the Sciences of Language* (Baltimore/London: The Johns Hopkins University Press, 1979).

John Dugard, ed., *The South West Africa/Namibia Dispute: Documents and Scholarly Writings on the Controversy between South Africa and the United Nations* (Berkeley, CA: University of California Press, 1973).

John Dugard, *International Law: A South African Perspective* (3rd edn., revised and expanded; Lansdowne: Juta, 2005).

Pierre-Marie Dupuy, 'Soft Law and the International Law of the Environment', 12 *Michigan Journal of International Law* (1991) 420-435.

Pierre-Marie Dupuy, *Droit International Public* (2nd edn.; Paris: Dalloz, 1993).

Pierre-Marie Dupuy, 'The Danger of Fragmentation or Unification of the International Legal System and the International Court of Justice', 31 *New York University Journal of International Law and Politics* (1999) 791-808.

Pierre-Marie Dupuy, 'L'unité de l'ordre juridique international, Cours général de droit international public', 297 *Recueil des Cours* (2002) 15-489.

**-E-**

Terry Eagleton, *Ideology: An Introduction* (London: Verso, 1991).

Ludwig Edelstein, *The Idea of Progress in Classical Antiquity* (ed. by Harold Cherniss, Baltimore: The John Hopkins University Press, 1967).

Sterling E. Edmunds, *The Lawless Law of Nations: An Exposition of the Prevailing Arbitrary International Legal System in Relation to Its Influence upon Civil Liberty, Disclosing It as the Last Bulwark of Absolutism against the Political Emancipation of Man* (Washington, DC: Byrne and Company, 1925).

Dwight D. Eisenhower, *The Atom for Progress and Peace* (Washington, DC: Office of Public Affairs, 1953).

Olufemi Elias, 'The Nature of the Subjective Element in Customary International Law', 44 *The International and Comparative Law Quarterly* (1995) 501-520.

Olufemi Elias and Chin Lim, 'General Principles of Law, "Soft Law", and the Identification of International Law', 28 *Netherlands Yearbook of International Law* (1997) 3-49.

Olufemi Elias and Chin Lim, 'The Role of Treaties in the International Legal Order', 66 *Nordic Journal of International Law* (1997) 1-21.

Olufemi Elias and Chin Lim, *The Paradox of Consensualism in International Law* (The Hague: Kluwer Law International, 1998).

Taslim Olawale Elias, 'Does the International Court of Justice, as It Is Presently Shaped, Correspond to the Requirements Which Follow from Its Functions as the Central Judicial Body of the International Community?', in Max Planck Institut für Ausländisches Öffentliches Recht und Völkerrecht, Herman Mosler and Rudolf Bernhardt, eds., *Judicial Settlement of International Disputes: International Court of Justice, Others Courts and Tribunals, Arbitration and Conciliation: An International Symposium* (Berlin: Springer, 1974) 19-31.

Robert C. Ellickson, *Order without Law: How Neighbors Settle Disputes* (Cambridge, MA: Harvard University Press, 1991).

Jon Elster, *The Cement of Society: A Study of Social Order* (Cambridge: Cambridge University Press, 1989).

Jon Elster, *Closing the Books: Transitional Justice in Historical Perspective* (Cambridge: Cambridge University Press, 2004).

Arthur Eyffinger, *The 1899 Peace Conference: 'The Parliament of Man, The Federation of the World'* (The Hague: Kluwer Law International, 1999).

**-F-**

Norman Fairclough, *Critical Discourse Analysis: The Critical Study of Language* (London: Longman, 1995).

Richard A. Falk, 'On the Quasi-Legislative Competence of the General Assembly', 60 *American Journal of International Law* (1966) 782-791.

Richard A. Falk, 'The South West Africa Cases: An Appraisal', XXI *International Organization* (1967) 1-23.

Richard A. Falk, 'Realistic Horizons for International Adjudication', 11 *Virginia Journal of International Law* (1971) 314-326.

Richard A. Falk, 'The Iran Hostage Crisis: Easy Answers and Hard Questions', 74 *American Journal of International Law* (1980) 411-417.

Richard A. Falk, *Reviving the World Court* (Charlottesvile, VA: University Press of Virginia, 1986).

Richard A. Falk, 'On the Quasi-Legislative Competence of the General Assembly', in J.A.M. Klabbers, ed., *International Organizations* (Aldershot: Ashgate, 2005) 297-306.

Aleksandar Fatic, *Reconciliation via the War Crimes Tribunal?* (Aldershot: Ashgate, 2000).

Charles G. Fenwick, 'The Progress of International Law during the Past Forty Years', 79 *Recueil des Cours* (1951).

George A. Finch, *The Sources of Modern International Law* (Publications of the Carnegie Endowment for International Peace, Division of international law, 1937).

George A. Finch et al., *The International Law of the Future: Postulates, Principles and Proposals* (Publications of the Carnegie Endowment for International Peace, Division of international law, 1944).

William W. Fisher III, Morton J. Horwitz and Thomas A. Reed, eds., *American Legal Realism* (Oxford: Oxford University Press, 1993).

Andreas Fischer-Lescano and Gunther Teubner, 'Regime-Collisions: The Vain Search for Legal Unity in the Fragmentation of Global Law', 25 *Michigan Journal of International Law* (2004) 999-1046.

Gerald G. Fitzmaurice, 'Some Problems Regarding the Formal Sources of International Law', in Frederik Mari van Asbeck et al., eds., *Symbolae Verzijl: présentées au professeur J.H.W. Verzijl à l'occasion de son LXX-ième anniversaire* (La Haye: Nijhoff, 1958) 153-176.

Malgosia Fitzmaurice and Olufemi Elias, *Contemporary Issues in the Law of Treaties* (Utrecht: Eleven International Publishing, 2005).

Michel Foucault, *The Archaeology of Knowledge* (Translated by A.M. Sheridan Smith, London: Tavistock, 1972).

Michel Foucault, *Discipline and Punish: The Birth of the Prison* (Translated by Alan Sheridan, New York: Random House, 1977).

Michel Foucault, 'Truth and Power', in Colin Gordon. ed., *Power/Knowledge – Selected Interviews and Other Writings 1972-1977* (New York: Pantheon Books/Random House, 1980).

Michel Foucault, *The Order of Things: An Archaeology of the Human Sciences* (orig. 1966, Routledge, 2002).

Roland R. Foulke, *A Treatise on International Law: With an Introductory Essay on the Definition and Nature of the Laws of Human Conduct* (Philadelphia, J.C. Winston,1920).

Gregory H. Fox and Brad R. Roth, eds., *Democratic Governance and International Law* (Cambridge: Cambridge University Press, 2000).

Thomas M. Franck, 'Legitimacy in the International System', 82 *American Journal of International Law* (1988) 705-759.

Thomas M. Franck, *The Power of Legitimacy among Nations* (Oxford: Oxford University Press, 1990).

Elena Frangakis-Syrett, *The Commerce of Smyrna in the Eighteenth Century (1700-1820)* (Athens: Centre for Asia Minor Studies, 1992) .

David Freestone, Richard Barnes and David M. Ong, *The Law of the Sea: Progress and Prospects* (Oxford: Oxford University Press, 2006).

Wolfgang Friedmann, 'The Jurisprudential Implications of the South West Africa Case', 6 *Columbia Journal of Transnational Law* (1967) 1-16.

Francis Fukuyama, *The End of History and the Last Man* (New York: Avon Books, 1992).

**-G-**

Ralph Gaebler and Maria Smolka-Day, eds., *Sources of State Practice in International Law* (Ardsley, NY: Transnational Publishers, 2002).

Giorgio Gaja, 'Les obligations et les droits erga omnes en droit international', 71 *Annuaire de l'Institut de Droit International* (2006) 81-136.

Bryan A. Garner, ed., *Black's Law Dictionary* (8th edn.; Thomson West, 2004).

James Paul Gee, *An Introduction to Discourse Analysis: Theory and Method* (2nd revised edn.; London: Routledge, 2005).

Martin van Gelderen and Quentin Skinner, eds., *Republicanism: A Shared European Heritage* (Cambridge: Cambridge University Press, 2002).

Gérard Genette, 'Boundaries of Narrative', 8 *New Literary History* (1976) 1-13.

Helen Ghebrewebet, *Identifying Units of Statehood and Determining International Boundaries: A Revised Look at the Doctrine of 'Uti Possidetis' and the Principle of Self-Determination* (Frankfurt am Main: Lang, 2006).

Torsten Gihl, *International Legislation: An Essay on Changes in International Law and in International Legal Situations* (Translated from the Swedish by Sydney J. Charleston, London: Oxford University Press, 1937).

Torsten Gihl, 'The Legal Character and Sources of International Law', 1 *Scandinavian Studies in Law* (1957) 51-92.

Alexander Gillespie, *The Illusion of Progress: Unsustainable Development in International Law and Policy* (London: Earthscan, 2001).

Marlies Ellen Glasius and Mary Kaldor, eds., *A Human Security Doctrine for Europe: Project, Principles, Practicalities* (London: Routledge, 2006).

Jack L. Goldsmith and Eric A. Posner, *The Limits of International Law* (New York: Oxford University Press, 2005).

Richard J. Goldstone, 'Justice as a Tool for Peace-Making: Truth Commissions and International Criminal Tribunals', 28 *New York University Journal of International Law and Politics* (1996) 485-503.

Richard J. Goldstone, 'Assessing the Work of the United Nations War Crimes Tribunals', 33 *Stanford Journal of International Law* (1997) 1-8.

Richard J. Goldstone and Erin P. Kelly, 'Progress and Problems in the Multilateral Human Rights Regime', in Edward Newman, Ramesh Thakur and John Tirman, eds., *Multilateralism under Challenge? Power, International Order, and Structural Change* (Tokyo: United Nations University Press, 2006) 259-288.

Edward Gordon, 'Old Orthodoxies amid New Experiences: The South West Africa (Namibia) Litigation and the Uncertain Jurisprudence of the International Court of Justice', 1 *Denver Journal of International Law and Policy* (1971) 65-92.

Philip Gourevitch, 'Justice in Exile: Hutu Genocide of Tutsi People in Rwanda Can Never Be Fully Brought to Justice', *The New York Times* (June 24, 1996).

Philip Babcock Gove, ed., *Merriam-Webster's Third New International Dictionary of the English Language Unabridged* (Merriam-Webster, 2002).

Antonio Gramsci, *Gli Intellettuali e L'Organizzazione della Cultura* [Intellectuals and the Organization of Culture] (Torino: Einaudi, 1949) .

Donald W. Greig, 'Sources of International Law', in Sam Blay, Ryszard Piotrowicz and
    Martin Tsamenyi, eds., *Public International Law: An Australian Perspective* (Melbourne:
    Oxford University Press, 2005) 52-84.
Gilbert Guillaume, 'The Future of International Judicial Institutions', 44 *The International
    and Comparative Law Quarterly* (1995) 848-862.
Gilbert Guillaume, 'The Proliferation of International Judicial Bodies: The Outlook for the
    International Legal Order', 27 October 2000, Speech to the Sixth Committee of the
    General Assembly of the United Nations, <www.icj-cij.org/court/index.php?pr=85&pt=3
    &p1=1&p2=3&p3=1> (visited 15 September 2009).
Isabelle R. Gunning, 'Modernizing Customary International Law: The Challenge of Human
    Rights', 31 *Virginia Journal of International Law* (1991) 211-247.

**-H-.**
Gerhard Hafner, 'Should One Fear the Proliferation of Mechanisms for the Peaceful Settle-
    ment of Disputes?', in Lucius Caflisch, *Règlement Pacifique des différends entre états:
    perspectives universelle et européenne* (The Hague: Kluwer law International, 1998)
    25-41.
Gerhard Hafner, 'Pros and Cons Ensuing from Fragmentation of International Law', 25
    *Michigan Journal of International Law* (2003-2004) 849-863.
William Edward Hall, *A Treatise on International Law* (6th edn.; edited by J.B. Atlay, Ox-
    ford: Clarendon Press, 1909).
Henry Wagner Halleck, *International Law or Rules Regulating the Intercourse of States in
    Peace and War* (Vol. 1) (3rd edn., thoroughly revised and in many parts rewritten by
    Sherston Baker; London: Kegan Paul, Trench, Trübner & Co., 1893).
Herbert Lionel Adolphus Hart, *The Concept of Law* (Oxford: Clarendon Press, 1961).
Wybo P. Heere, ed., *International Law and Its Sources: Liber Amicorum Maarten Bos*
    (Deventer: Kluwer Law and Taxation Publishers, 1989).
Paul Heilborn, 'Les sources du droit international', 11 *Recueil des Cours* (1926) 1-63.
Veijo Heiskanen, 'The Doctrine of Indirect Expropriation in Light of the Practice of the
    Iran-United States Claims Tribunal', 8 *Journal of World Investment & Trade* (2007)
    215-231.
Laurence R. Helfer and Anne-Marie Slaughter, 'Toward a Theory of Effective Suprana-
    tional Adjudication', 107 *Yale Law Journal* (1997) 273-392.
Laurence R. Helfer and Anne-Marie Slaughter, 'Why States Create International Tribunals:
    A Response to Professors Posner and Yoo', 93 *California Law Review* (2005) 899-956.
Jean-Marie Henckaerts et al., eds., *Customary International Humanitarian Law* (Vols. I-III)
    (Cambridge: Cambridge University Press, 2005).
Louis Henkin, *How Nations Behave: Law and Foreign Policy* (2nd edn.; New York: Colum-
    bia University Press, 1979).
Nicholas Henshall, *The Myth of Absolutism: Change and Continuity in Early Modern Euro-
    pean Monarchy* (London: Longman, 1992).
Alexander Pearce Higgins, 'The Law of Peace', 4 *British Yearbook of International Law*
    (1923-1924) 153-159.
Rosalyn Higgins, *Problems and Process: International Law and How We Use It* (Oxford:
    Clarendon Press, 1994).
Rosalyn Higgins, 'The ICJ, the ECJ and the Integrity of International Law', 52 *The Interna-
    tional and Comparative Law Quarterly* (2003) 1-20.
Jens Hinricher, 'The Law-Making of the International Telecommunication Union (ITU):
    Providing a New Source of International Law?', 64 *Zeitschrift für ausländisches
    öffentliches Recht und Völkerrecht* (2004) 489-501.

Eric Hobsbawm, *Nations and Nationalism since 1780: Program, Myth, Reality* (2nd edn.; Cambridge: Cambridge University Press, 1992).

Michael Hoey, *Textual Interaction: An Introduction to Written Discourse Analysis* (London: Routledge, 2001).

Godefridus Josephus Henricus van Hoof, *Rethinking the Sources of International Law* (Deventer: Kluwer Law International, 1983).

Morton J. Horwitz, *The Transformation of American Law (1870-1960): The Crisis of Legal Orthodoxy* (New York: Oxford University Press, 1992).

Marjorie Housepian Dobkin, *Smyrna 1922: The Destruction of a City* (London: Faber & Faber, 1972).

Manley Ottmer Hudson, 'The Outlook for the Development of International Law' (An Address before the American Branch of the International Law Association: New York, January 1925) (Pamphlet, 1925).

Manley Ottmer Hudson, 'The Prospect for International Law in the Twentieth Century', 10 *The Cornell Law Quarterly* (1925) 419-459.

Manley Ottmer Hudson, *Progress in International Organization* (Stanford University Press, 1932).

Rosario Huesa Vinaixa et Karel Wellens, eds., *L'influence des sources sur l'unité et la fragmentation du droit international* (Brussels: Bruylant, 2006).

Cecil J.B. Hurst, 'The Effect of War on Treaties', 2 *British Yearbook of International Law* (1921-1922) 37-47.

Graham Hutton, *The War as a Factor in Human Progress* (Pamphlet no. 36; Chicago, IL: 1942).

**-J-**

John H. Jackson, *The World Trading System: Law and Policy of International Economic Relations* (2nd edn.; Cambridge, MA: MIT Press, 1997).

Fredric Jameson, *Marxism and Form: Twentieth Century Dialectical Theories of Literature* (Princeton University Press, 1972).

Fredric Jameson, *The Prison-House of Language: A Critical Account of Structuralism and Russian Formalism* (Princeton University Press, 1975).

Fredric Jameson, *Postmodernism or, the Cultural Logic of Late Capitalism* (Duke University Press, 1991).

Sir Robert Y. Jennings, 'What Is International Law and How Do We Tell It When We See It', 37 *Annuaire Suisse de Droit International* (1981) 59-91.

Sir Robert Y. Jennings, 'The Identification of International Law', in Bin Cheng, ed., *International Law: Teaching and Practice* (London: Stevens and Sons, 1982) 9.

Sir Robert Y. Jennings, 'The Proliferation of Adjudicatory Bodies: Dangers and Possible Answers', in Laurence Boisson des Chazournes, ed., *Implications of the Proliferation of International Adjudicatory Bodies for Dispute Resolution: Proceedings of a Forum Co-Sponsored by the ASIL and the HEI* 2-5 (Washington, DC: American Society of International Law, 1995).

Sir Robert Y. Jennings, 'Reflections on the Term "Dispute"', in Ronald St. J. Macdonald, ed., *Essays in Honor of Wang Tieya* (Dordrecht: Martinus Nijhoff Publishers, 1994) 401-405.

Sir Robert Y. Jennings, 'The Judiciary, International and National, and the Development of International Law', 45 *The International and Comparative Law Quarterly* (1996).

Sir Robert Y. Jennings, 'Reflections on the Subsidiary Means for the Determination of Rules of Law', in Gaetano Arangio-Ruiz, *Studi di diritto internazionale in onore di Gaetano Arangio-Ruiz* (Napoli: Ed. Scientifica, 2003) 319-338.

Sir Robert Y. Jennings and Sir Arthur Watts, eds., *Oppenheim's International Law* (9th edn.; London: Longman, 1996).

Philip C. Jessup, 'Do New Problems Need New Courts?', 65 *Proceedings of the American Society of International Law* (1971) 261-268.

Fleur Johns, Thomas Skouteris and Wouter Werner, eds., *The Law and Periphery Series: Alejandro Álvarez*, 19 *Leiden Journal of International Law* (2006) 875-1040.

George Alexander Johnston, *International Social Progress: The Work of the International Labour Organization of the League of Nations* (London: Allen & Unwin, 1924).

Emmanuelle Jouannet, 'Regards sur un siècle de doctrine française du droit international', 46 *Annuaire Français de Droit International* (2001) 1-57.

Emmanuelle Jouannet, 'La critique de la pensée classique durant l'entre-deux guerres: Vattel et van Vollenhoven: Quelques réflexions sur le modèle classique du droit international)', in Péter Kovacs, ed., *History in International Law: Historia ante Portas* (Bíbor Kiadó, 2005) 61-83.

**-K-**

Stratos Kalogeropoulos et al., eds., *Mélanges Séfériadès* (Athens, 1961) .

Frits Kalshoven and Liesbeth Zegveld, *Constraints on the Waging of War: An Introduction to international Humanitarian Law* (3rd edn.; International Committee of the Red Cross, 2001).

Jörg Kammerhofer, 'Uncertainty in the Formal Sources of International Law: Customary International Law and Some of its Problems', 15 *European Journal of International Law* (2004) 523-553.

Immanuel Kant, 'Perpetual Peace: A Philosophical Sketch', in H.S. Reiss, ed., *Immanuel Kant, Political Writings* (2nd edn.; Cambridge: Cambridge University Press, 1991).

Giorgos Katiforis, *Η Νομοθεσία των Βαρβάρων* [The Legislation of the Barbarians] (in Greek, Athens, 1975).

Milton Katz, *The Relevance of International Adjudication* (Cambridge, MA: Harvard University Press, 1968).

Mark Kelman, *A Guide to Critical Legal Studies* (Cambridge, MA: Harvard University Press, 1990).

David Kennedy, 'The Turn to Interpretation', 58 *Southern California Law Review* (1985) 1.

David Kennedy, 'Critical Theory, Structuralism, and Legal Scholarship', 21 *New England Law Review* (1985-1986) 209-290.

David Kennedy, 'The Move to Institutions', 8 *Cardozo Law Review* (1986-1987) 841-988.

David Kennedy, *International Legal Structures* (Baden Baden: Nomos, 1987).

David Kennedy, 'The Sources of International Law', 2 *American University Journal of International Law & Policy* (1987) 1-96.

David Kennedy, 'A New Stream of International Law Scholarship', 7 *Wisconsin International Law Journal* (1988-1989) 1-49.

David Kennedy, 'International Law in the Nineteenth Century: History of an Illusion', 65 *Nordic Journal of International Law* (1996) 385-420.

David Kennedy, 'When Renewal Repeats: Thinking Against the Box', 32 *New York Journal of International Law and Politics* (2000) 335-500.

David Kennedy, *The Dark Sides of Virtue: Reassessing International Humanitarianism* (Princeton University Press, 2004).

David Kennedy, *Of War and Law* (Princeton University Press, 2006).

David Kennedy and William W. Fischer III, eds., *The Canon of American Legal Thought* (Princeton University Press, 2006).

Duncan Kennedy, *A Critique of Adjudication [fin de siècle]* (Cambridge, MA: Harvard University Press, 1997).

John F. Kennedy, *Alliance for Progress* (Washington, DC: U.S. Government Printing Office, 1961).

Benedict Kingsbury, 'Is the Proliferation of International Courts and Tribunals a Systematic Problem?', 31 *New York University Journal of International Law and Politics* (1999) 679-696.

Henry Kissinger, *Does America Need a Foreign Policy? Toward a Diplomacy for the 21ˢᵗ Century* (New York: Simon & Schuster, 2001).

Jan Klabbers, *The Concept of Treaty in International Law* (The Hague: Kluwer Law International, 1996).

Jan Klabbers, 'The Scope of International Law: Erga Omnes Obligations and the Turn to Morality', in Matti Tupamäki et al., eds., *Liber Amicorum Bengt Broms: Celebrating His 70th Birthday, 16 October 1999* (Helsinki: Finnish Branch of the International Law Association, 1999) 149-179.

Jan Klabbers, 'Compliance Procedures', in Daniel Bodansky, Jutta Brunnée, and Ellen Hey, eds., *The Oxford Handbook of International Environmental Law* (Oxford: Oxford University Press, 2007) 995-1009.

Karen Knop, 'Reflections on Thomas Franck, *Race and Nationalism* (1960): "General Principles of Law" and Situated Generality', 35 *New York University Journal of International Law and Politics* (2003) 437-469.

Karen Knop, *Diversity and Self-Determination in International Law* (Cambridge: Cambridge University Press, 2002).

Karen Knop, '"General Principles of Law" and Situated Generality', 35 *New York Journal of International Law and Politics* (2003) 437-469.

Marcelo G. Kohen, *La pratique et la théorie des sources du droit international, in Société Française pour le Droit international, La pratique et le droit international: Colloque de Genève* (Paris: Pedone, 2004) 81-111.

Robert Kolb, 'Théorie du Ius Cogens International', 36 *Revue Belge de droit International* (2003) 5-55.

Robert Kolb, 'Principles as Sources of International Law (with Special Reference to Good Faith)', 53 *Netherlands International Law Review* (2006) 1-36.

Outi Korhonen, 'New International Law: Silence Defence or Deliverance', 7 *European Journal of International Law* (1996) 1-28.

Outi Korhonen, *International Law Situated: An Analysis of the Lawyer's Stance Towards Culture, History and Community* (The Hague: Kluwer Law International, 2000).

Martti Koskenniemi, *From Apology to Utopia: The Structure of International Legal Argument* (Helsinki: Finnish Lawyer's Publishing Company, 1989).

Martti Koskenniemi, 'The Normative Force of Habit: International Custom and Social Theory', 1 *Finnish Yearbook of International Law* (1990) 77-153.

Martti Koskenniemi, ed., *Sources of International Law* (Ashgate: Aldershot, 2000).

Martti Koskenniemi, *The Gentle Civilizer of Nations: The Rise and Fall of International Law 1870-1960* (Cambridge: Cambridge University Press, 2002).

Susanne Kratzsch, *Rechtsquellen des Völkerrechts außerhalb von Artikel 38 Absatz 1 IGH-Statut* (Doctoral Thesis, Tübingen: Köhler-Druck, 2000).

Peter J. van Krieken and David McKay, eds., *The Hague: Legal Capital of the World* (The Hague: T.M.C. Asser Press, 2005).

Julia Kristeva, *Desire in Language: A Semiotic Approach to Literature and Art* (Collected Essays, New York: Columbia University Press, 1980).

Julia Kristeva, *Revolution in Poetic Language* (New York: Columbia University Press, 1984).

Martin Kuijer, *The Blindfold of Lady Justice: Judicial Independence and Impartiality in Light of the Requirement of Art. 6 ECHR* (Nijmegen: Wolf Legal Publishers, 2004).

Thomas S. Kuhn, *The Structure of Scientific Revolutions* (Chicago, MI: University of Chicago Press, 1962).

Josef L. Kunz, 'On the Theoretical Basis of the Law of Nations', 10 *Grotius Society Transactions* (1925) 115-143.

Josef L. Kunz, 'The Swing of the Pendulum: From Over-estimation to Under-estimation of International Law', 44 *American Journal of International Law* (1950) 135-140.

**-L-**

Ernesto Laclau, 'Discourse', in Robert E. Goodin and Philip Pettit, eds., *A Companion to Contemporary Political Philosophy* (Oxford: Blackwell Publishing, 1993).

Ernesto Laclau and Chantal Mouffe, *Hegemony and Socialist Strategy: Towards a Radical Democratic Politics* (London: Verso, 1985).

Ernesto Laclau and Chantal Mouffe, 'Post-Marxism without Apologies', in Ernesto Laclau, *New Reflections on the Revolutions of Our Time* (London: Verso, 1997).

Jacob M. Landau, ed., *Atatürk and the Modernization of Turkey* (Boulder, CO: Westview Press, 1984).

Carl Landauer, 'J.L. Brierly and the Modernization of International Law', 25 *Vanderbilt Journal of Transnational Law* (1992-1993) 881-917.

Carl Landauer, 'The Gentle Civilizer: Declension Narratives in International Law', Presented in the 3rd Birkbeck Workshop on Critical Approaches to International Law (Manuscript, on file with Thomas Skouteris, London, May 16, 2006).

Walter Consuelo Langsam, *The World Since 1914* (New York: MacMillan, 1933).

Paul de La Pradelle, *Progrès ou déclin du droit international, in Mélanges offerts à Charles Rousseau: la communauté internationale* (Paris: Pedone, 1974) 139-152.

Larry Laudan, *Progress and Its Problems: Towards a Theory of Scientific Growth* (University of California Press, 1978).

Hersch Lauterpacht, *Private Law Sources and Analogies of International Law (With Special Reference to International Arbitration)* (London: Longmans, Green and Co., 1927).

Hersch Lauterpacht, *The Function of Law in the International Community* (Oxford: The Clarendon Press, 1933).

Hersch Lauterpacht, 'Brierly's Contribution to International Law', 32 *British Yearbook of International Law* (1955-1956) 1-14.

Hersch Lauterpacht, *The Development of International Law by the International Court*, revised edn. (London: Longmans, 1958).

Hersch Lauterpacht, *The Development of International Law by the International Court* (Cambridge: Grotius Publications Ltd., 1982).

Nikolaos Lavranos, 'Concurrence of Jurisdictions between the ECJ and Other International Courts and Tribunals', 14 *European Environmental Law Review* (2005) 213-225.

Thomas Joseph Lawrence, *The Principles of International Law* (4th edn., revised and rewritten; London, 1911).

Claude Lévi-Strauss, *The Savage Mind* (Chicago, MI: University Of Chicago Press, 1966).

Cecil C. Lingard and R.G. Trotter, *Peace with Progress* (Toronto: Canadian Institute of International Affairs, 1945).

Alejandro Lorite Escorihuela, 'Cultural Relativism the American Way: The Nationalist School of International Law in the United States', 5 *Global Jurist Frontiers* (2005), <www.be press.com/gj/frontiers/vol5/iss1/art2> (visited 25 May 2008).

John Losee, *Theories of Scientific Progress: An Introduction* (Routledge, 2004).

Vaughan Lowe, 'Overlapping Jurisdiction of International Tribunals', 20 *Australian Yearbook of International Law* (1999) 191-204.

Edward C. Luck, 'Reforming the United Nations: Lessons from a History of Progress', in Paul F. Diehl, ed., *The Politics of Global Governance: International Organizations in an Interdependent World* (Boulder, CO: Lynne Rienner, 2005) 445-482.

Georg Lukács, 'Narrate or Describe', in G. Lukács, ed., *Writer and Critic and Other Essays* (edited and translated by Arthur D. Khan, New York: Grosset and Dunlap, 2005).

Philip de Ly, *International Business Law and Lex Mercatoria* (Amsterdam: North-Holland, 1992).

Jean-François Lyotard, *The Postmodern Condition: A Report on Knowledge* (translated from French by Geoff Bennington and Brian Massumi, Minneapolis: University of Minnesota Press, 1984).

**-M-**

William McGrew, *Land and Revolution in Modern Greece, 1800-1881: The Transition in the Tenure and Exploitation of Land from Ottoman Rule to Independence* (Kent, Ohio: Kent State University Press, 1985).

Ruth Mackenzie and Philippe Sands, 'International Courts and Tribunals and the Independence of the International Judge', 44 *Harvard International Law Journal* (2003) 271-286.

Henry Sumner Maine, *International Law* (The Whewell Lectures, 2nd edn.) (London: Murray, 1894).

Peter Malanczuk, *Akehurst's Modern Introduction to International Law* (7th revised edn.; London: Routledge, 1997).

Andrew Mango, *Atatürk* (London: John Murray, 1991).

Andrew Mango, *The Turks Today: After Atatürk* (London: John Murray, 2004).

William Oke Manning, *Commentaries on the Law of Nations*, revised edn. (London, 1875).

David W. Marcell, *Progress and Pragmatism: James, Dewey, Beard and the American Idea of Progress* (Greenwood Press, 1974).

Susan Marks, *The Riddle of All Constitutions: International Law, Democracy and the Critique of Ideology* (Cambridge: Cambridge University Press, 2000).

Susan Marks, 'International Law, Democracy, and the End of History', in Gregory H. Fox and Brad R. Roth, eds., *Democratic Governance and International Law* (Oxford: Oxford University Press, 2000) 220-251.

Giorgos Mavrogordatos, *Stillborn Republic: Social Coalitions and Party Strategies in Greece, 1922-1936* (Berkeley, CA: University of California Press, 1983).

Giorgos Mavrogordatos and Constantinos Hatziiosif, eds., *Βενιζελισμός και Αστικός Εκσυγχρονισμός* [Venizelism and Bourgeois Modernization, in Greek] (Athens, 1988).

Sir Arnold D. McNair, 'The Present Position of the Codification of International Law', 13 *Grotius Society Transactions* (1928) 129-141.

Sir Arnold D. McNair, 'The Function and Differing Legal Character of Treaties', 11 *British Yearbook of International Law* (1930) 99-118.

Frédéric Mégret, 'Three Dangers for the International Criminal Court: A Critical Look at a Consensual Project', 12 *Finnish Yearbook of International Law* (2001) 192-247.

Maurice Mendelson, 'The International Court of Justice and the Sources of International Law', in Alexander Samuel Muller, David Raić and Johanna Thuránszky, eds., *The International Court of Justice: its Future Role After Fifty Years* (The Hague: Nijhoff, 1996) 63-89.

Nathan Miller, 'An International Jurisprudence? The Operation of "Precedent" Across International Tribunals', 15 *Leiden Journal of International Law* (2003) 483-526.

Russell Miller and Rebecca Bratspies, eds., *Progress in International Law* (Leiden: Brill, 2008).

Gary Minda, *Post-Modern Legal Movements: Law and Jurisprudence at Century's End* (New York: NYU Press, 1995).

Panu Minkkinen, *Thinking without Desire: A First Philosophy of Law* (Oxford: Hart Publishing, 1999).

Martha Minow, *Between Vengeance and Forgiveness: Facing History after Genocide and Mass Violence* (Boston, MA: Beacon Press, 1998).

Loukas Mistelis, 'Is Harmonization a Necessary Evil? The Future of Harmonization and New Sources of International Trade Law', in Ian Fletcher, Loukas Mistelis and Marise Cremona, eds., *Foundations and Perspectives of International Trade Law* (Sweet & Maxwell, 2001) 3-27.

David Mitrany, *The Progress of International Government* (New Haven, 1933).

Frank Moorhouse, *Grand Days* (Picador, 1994).

Hermann Mosler and Rudolf Bernhardt, eds., *Judicial Settlement of International Disputes: International Court of Justice, Others Courts and Tribunals, Arbitration and Conciliation: An International Conference* (Berlin: Springer, 1974).

Thorburn Muirhead, *Amber Light: A Formula for Peaceful Progress* (London: Cranton Press, 1945).

Benjamin Mulamba Mbuyi, *Introduction à l'étude des sources modernes du droit international public* (Laval: Les Presses de l'Université Laval, 1999).

Sean D. Murphy, 'Progress and Jurisprudence of the International Criminal Tribunal for the Former Yugoslavia', 93 *American Journal of International Law* (1999) 57-97.

Makau Wa Mutua, 'Never Again: Questioning the Yugoslav and Rwanda Tribunals', 11 *Temple International and Comparative Law Journal* (1997) 167-187.

Makau Wa Mutua, 'What is TWAIL?', 94 *Proceedings of the American Society of International Law Annual Meeting* (2000) 31-40.

**-N-**

Jacob Nieuwenhuis and Carel Stolker, eds., *Vooruit met het recht: wat geldt in de rechtenwetenschap als vooruitgang?* (The Hague: Boom, 2006).

Otfried Nippold, *The Development of International Law after the World War* (Oxford: Clarendon Press, 1923).

Robert A. Nisbet, *Social Change and History: Aspects of the Western History of Development* (New York: Oxford University Press, 1969).

Robert A. Nisbet, *History of the Idea of Progress* (New York: Basic Books, 1980).

Philip Noel Baker, 'The Codification of International Law', 5 *British Yearbook of International Law* (1924) 38-65.

**-O-**

Shigeru Oda, 'The International Court of Justice Viewed from the Bench', 244 *Recueil des Cours* (1993) 9-190.

Shigeru Oda, 'Dispute Settlement Prospects in the Law of the Sea', 44 *The International and Comparative Law Quarterly* (1995) 863-872.

Obiora Okafor, *Re-defining Legitimate Statehood: International Law and State Fragmentation in Africa* (The Hague: Kluwer Law International, 2000).

Obiora Okafor, 'Viewing International Legal Fragmentation from a Third World Plane: A TWAIL Perspective', in *Fragmentation: Diversification and Expansion of International Law: Proceedings of the 34th Annual Conference of the Canadian Council of International Law* (Ottawa: Canadian Council of International Law, 2006) 115-132.

Yasuaki Onuma, 'The ICJ: An Emperor without Clothes? International Conflict Resolution, Article 38 of the ICJ Statute and the Sources of International Law', in Nisuke Ando et al., eds., *Liber Amicorum Judge Shigeru Oda* (The Hague: Kluwer Law International, 2002) 191-212.

Lassa Oppenheim, *International Law: A Treatise* (Vol. I) (2nd edn.; London: Longmans, 1912).

Lassa Oppenheim, *The Future of International Law* (Oxford: Clarendon Press, 1921).

Alexander Orakhelashvili, *Peremptory Norms in International Law* (Oxford: Oxford University Press, 2006).

Anne Orford, *Reading Humanitarian Intervention: Human Rights and the Use of Force in International Law* (Cambridge: Cambridge University Press, 2003).

Anne Orford, ed., *International Law and its Others* (Cambridge: Cambridge University Press, 2006).

Francisco Orrego-Vicuña, 'Law-Making in a Global Community: Does Consent still Matter?', in Juergen Bröhmer et al., eds., *Internationale Gemeinschaft und Menschenrechte: Festschrift für Georg Ress zum 70. Geburtstag am 21. Januar 2005* (Carl Heymanns Verlag, 2005) 191-206.

**-P-**

Alexander A. Pallis, *Greece's Anatolian Venture – and After: A Survey of the Diplomatic and Political Aspects of the Greek Expedition to Asia Minor* (1915-1922) (London: Methuen, 1937).

David Palmeter and Petros C. Mavroidis, 'The WTO Legal System: System of Law', 92 *American Journal of International Law* (1998) 398-413.

Brian Paltridge, *Discourse Analysis: An Introduction* (Continuum, 2007).

Clive Parry, *The Sources and Evidences of International Law* (Manchester: Manchester University Press, 1965).

Joost Pauwelyn, *Conflict of Norms in Public International Law: How WTO Law Relates to Other Rules of International Law* (Cambridge: Cambridge University Press, 2003).

Joost Pauwelyn, 'Bridging Fragmentation and Unity: International Law as a Universe of Inter-Connected Islands', 25 *Michigan Journal of International Law* (2004) 903-916.

Alain Pellet, 'Article 38', in Andreas Zimmermann, Christian Tomuschat and Karin Oellers-Frahm, eds., *The Statute of the International Court of Justice: A Commentary* (Oxford: Oxford University Press, 2006).

Anne Peters, 'International Dispute Settlement: A Network of Cooperational Duties', 14 *European Journal of International Law* (2003) 1-34.

Ernst-Ulrich Petersmann, 'Constitutionalism and International Adjudication: How to Constitutionalize the U.N. Dispute Settlement System?', 31 *New York University Journal of International Law and Politics* (1999) 753-790.

Louise Phillips and Mariane Jørgensen, *Discourse Analysis as Theory and Method* (London: Sage, 2002).

Robert Phillimore and Reginald James Mure, *Commentaries upon International Law* (3rd edn.; London: Buttersworth, 1879).

Navanethem Pillay, 'International Criminal Tribunals as a Deterrent to Displacement', in Anne Bayefsky and Joan Fitzpatrick, eds., *Human Rights and Forced Displacement* (The Hague: Martinus Nijhoff Publishers, 2000) 262-266.

Navanatheem Pillay, 'Protection of the Health of Women through International Criminal Law: How Can International Criminal Law Contribute to Efforts to Improve Criminal Justice', 22 *Emory International Law Review* (2008) 15-27.

M.C.W. Pinto, 'Pre-eminence of the International Court of Justice', in Connie Peck and Roy Lee, eds., *Increasing the Effectiveness of the International Court of Justice* (The Hague, Martinus Nijhoff Publishers, 1997).

Fausto Pocar, 'The Proliferation of International Criminal Courts and Tribunals: A Necessity in the Current International Community', 2 *Journal of International Criminal Justice* (2004) 304-308.

Leon Poinsard, *Comment se prépare l'unité sociale du monde: le droit international au XXe siècle, ses progrès et ses tendances* (Paris, 1907).

Nicolas Politis, 'Le problème des limitations de la souveraineté et de la théorie de l'abus des droits dans les rapports internationaux', 6 *Recueil des Cours* (1925) 1-121.

Nicolas Politis, *The New Aspects of International Law: A Series of Lectures Delivered at Columbia University in July 1926* (Washington, DC: Carnegie Endowment for International Peace, 1928).

Karl Raimund Popper, *The Logic of Scientific Discovery* (New York: Basic Books, 1959).

Karl Raimund Popper, *The Open Society and Its Enemies. Vol. 1, The Spell of Plato* (4th revised edn.; New York: Harper and Row, 1963).

Karl Raimund Popper, 'The Rationality of Scientific Revolutions', in Ian Hacking, ed., *Scientific Revolution* (Oxford: Oxford University Press, 1981) 80-106.

Eric A. Posner, 'International Law and the Disaggregated State', 32 *Florida State University Law Review* (2005) 797-842.

Eric A. Posner, 'The Decline of the International Court of Justice', in Stefan Voigt, Max Albert and Dieter Schmidtchen, eds., *International Conflict Resolution* (Tübingen: Mohr-Siebeck, 2006).

Eric A. Posner and John Choon Yoo, *A Theory of International Adjudication*, John M. Olin Law and Economics Working Paper No. 206, <www.law.uchicago.edu/node/652/publications> (visited 19 September 2009).

Eric A. Posner and John Choon Yoo, 'Judicial Interdependence in International Tribunals', 93 *California Law Review* (2005) 1-74.

Harry H.G. Post, 'Some Curiosities in the Sources of the Law of Armed Conflict Conceived in as General International Legal Perspective', in Bert Barnhoorn and Karel C. Wellens, eds., *Diversity in Secondary Rules and the Unity of International Law* (The Hague: Martinus Nijhoff, 1995) 83-117.

Paul Louis Ernest Pradier-Fodéré, *Traité de droit international public européen et américain suivant les progrès de la science et de la pratique contemporaine* (Paris: G. Pedone-Lauriel, 1885-1906).

Dietmar Praeger, 'The Proliferation of International Judicial Organs: The Role of the International Court of Justice', in Niels Blokker and Henry G. Schermers, eds., *Proliferation of International Organizations: Legal issues* (The Hague: Kluwer Law International, 2001) 279-295.

Nigel Purvis, 'Critical Legal Studies in Public International Law', 32 *Harvard International Law Journal* 7 (1991) 81-12.

**-Q-**

Juan José Quintana, 'The International Court of Justice and the Formulation of General International Law: The Law of Maritime Delimitation as an Example', in Alexander Samuel Muller, David Raić and Johanna Thuránszky, eds., *The International Court of Justice: Its Future Role after Fifty Years* (The Hague: Nijhoff, 1996) 367-381.

**-R-**

Maurizio Ragazzi, *The Concept of International Obligations 'Erga Omnes'* (Oxford: Clarendon Press, 1997).

Balakrishnan Rajagopal, *International Law from Below: Development, Social Movement, and Third World Resistance* (Cambridge: Cambridge University Press, 2003).

Nayukulu Gogigeni Ranga, *The Colonial and Colored Peoples: A Programme for their Freedom and Progress* (Bombay: Hing Kitabs, 1946).

Raymond Ranjeva, 'Quelques observations sur l'intérêt à avoir une juridiction internationale unique', *International Law Forum* (1998) 10.

Pemmaraju Sreenivasa Rao, 'Multiple International Judicial Forums: A Reflection of the Growing Strength of International Law or Its Fragmentation?', 25 *Michigan Journal of International Law* (2004) 929-961.

Ignacio de la Rasilla del Moral, 'All Roads Lead to Rome or the Liberal Cosmopolitan Agenda as a Blueprint for a Neoconservative Legal Order', 7 *Global Jurist* (2007) 1-15.

Catherine Redgwell, 'International Soft Law and Globalization', in Barry Barton et al., eds., *Regulating Energy and Natural Resources* (New York, NY: Oxford University Press, 2006) 89-107.

Lucy Reed, 'Great Expectations: Where Does the Proliferation of International Dispute Resolution Tribunals Leave International Law?', 96 *American Society of International Law Proceedings* (2002) 219-231.

Michael Reisman, 'International Law after the Cold War', 84 *American Journal of International Law* (1990) 859-866.

Michael Reisman, 'Creating, Adapting and Designing Dispute Resolution Mechanisms for the International Protection of Human Rights', in Laurence Boisson des Chazournes, ed., *Implications of the Proliferation of International Adjudicatory Bodies for Dispute Resolution: Proceedings of a Forum Co-Sponsored by the ASIL* 8-14 (Washington, DC: American Society of International Law, 1995).

Michael Reisman, 'Judge Shigeru Oda: A Tribute to an International Treasure', 16 *Leiden Journal of International Law* (2003) 57-65.

Michael Reisman, 'Islamic Fundamentalism and Its Impact on International Law and Politics', in Mark Janis and Carolyn Evans, eds., *Religion in International Law* (Kluwer Law International, 2004) 357-384.

Louis Renault, *Les progrès récents du droit des gens* (Groningen: Wolters, 1912).

Paul Ricoeur, 'Narrative Time', 7 *Critical Inquiry* (1980) 169-190.

Annelise Riles, 'The View from the International Plane: Perspective and Scale in the Architecture of Colonial International Law', 6 *Law and Critique* (1995) 39-54.

Roberto Rivello, 'Les principes généraux de droit et le droit international pénal', in Mario Chiavario, ed., *La justice pénale internationale entre passé et avenir* (Milano: Giuffrè, 2003) 89-111.

Anthea Roberts, 'Traditional and Modern Approaches to Customary International Law: A Reconciliation', 95 *American Journal of International Law* (2001) 757-791.

William Francis Roemer, *The Ethical Basis of International Law* (Chicago, MI: Loyola University Press, 1929).

Cesare Romano, 'The Proliferation of International Judicial Bodies: The Pieces of the Puzzle', 31 *New York University Journal of International Law and Politics* (1999) 709-751.

Cesare Romano, 'The Shift from the Consensual to the Compulsory Paradigm in International Adjudication: Elements for a Theory of Consent', 39 *New York University Journal of International Law and Politics* (2007) 791-872.

Elihu Root, 'The Codification of International Law', 19 *American Journal of International Law* (1925) 671-684.

Shabtai Rosenne, *The World Court: What It Is and How It Works* (Leiden: Sijthoff, 1962).

Shabtai Rosenne, ed., *Conference for the Codification of International Law of 1930* (Dobbs Ferry, NY: Oceana, 1975).

Shabtai Rosenne, *The Law and Practice of the International Court 1920-1996* 529 (Leiden: Sythoff, 1997).

Shabtai Rosenne, ed., *The Hague Peace Conferences of 1899 and 190 and International Arbitration – Reports and Documents* (The Hague: T.M.C. Asser Press, 2001).

Shabtai Rosenne, *The Perplexities of Modern International Law* (The Hague: Kluwer Law International, 2004).

Alf Niels Christian Ross, *On Law and Justice* (London: Stevens & Sons, 1958).

Alf Niels Christian Ross, *The United Nations: Peace and Progress* (Totowa, NJ: The Bedminster Press, 1966).

Charles Rousseau, *Scientific Progress and the Evolution of International Law* (Paris: UNESCO, 1954).

Charles Rousseau, *Droit International Public*, Vol. I (Paris: Sirey, 1970).

Bruce Russett, *Grasping the Democratic Peace: Principles for a Post-Cold War World* (Princeton: Princeton University Press, 1994).

**-S-**

William Samore, 'The New International Law of Alejandro Álvarez', 52 *American Journal of International Law* (1958) 41-54.

Antonio Sanchez de Bustamante, *The World Court* (New York: MacMillan, 1925).

Philippe Sands, *Manual on International Courts and Tribunals* (London: Butterworths, 1999).

Philippe Sands, 'Turtles and Torturers: The Transformation of International Law', 33 *New York Journal of International Law and Politics* (2001) 527-559.

Paul C. Szasz, 'The Proliferation of Administrative Tribunals', in Niels Blokker and Henry Schermers, eds., *Proliferation of International Organizations* (The Hague: Kluwer Law International, 2001) 241-249.

William A. Schabas, *The UN International Criminal Tribunals: The Former Yugoslavia, Rwanda and Sierra Leone* (Cambridge: Cambridge University Press, 2006).

Frederick Schauer, *Playing by the Rules: A Philosophical Examination of Rule-Based Decision-Making in Law and Life* (Oxford: Clarendon Press, 1991).

Deborah Schiffrin, Deborah Tannen and Heidi E. Hamiton, eds., *The Handbook of Discourse Analysis* (Blackwell Publishing, 2005).

Dietrich Schindler, 'Contribution à l'étude des facteurs sociologiques et psychologiques du droit international', 46 *Recueil des Cours* (1933) 229-326.

Pierre Schlag, 'Normative and Nowhere to Go', 43 *Stanford Law Review* (1990-1991) 167-192.

Bernadotte E. Schmitt and Harold C. Vedeler, *The World in the Crucible 1914-1919* (New York: Harper & Row, 1984).

Georg Schwarzenberger, *International Law and Totalitarian Lawlessness* (London: Cape, 1943).

Steven Schwebel, Address by the President of the International Court of Justice to the General Assembly of the United Nations, 28 October 1998, <www.icj-cij.org/presscom/index.php> (visited 25 May 2008).

Iain Scobbie, 'Towards the Elimination of International Law: Some Radical Skepticism about Skeptical Radicalism', 61 *British Yearbook of International Law* (1990) 339-362.

David Scott, *Conscripts of Modernity: The Tragedy of Colonial Enlightenment* (Dyrham & London: Duke University Press (2004).

James Brown Scott, 'The Gradual and Progressive Codification of International Law', 21 *American Journal of International Law* (1927) 417-450.

James Brown Scott, *Le progrès du droit des gens* (Paris: Les Editions Internationales, 1930).

James Brown Scott, 'The Progress of International Law During the Last 25 Years', 25 *Proceedings of the American Society of International Law* (1931) 2-34.

George Scott, *The Rise and Fall of the League of Nations* (London: Hutchinson, 1973).

Stelios Seferiades, *Etude Critique sur la théorie de la cause* (Paris: Ouvrage couronne par la Faculté de droit de Paris, 1897).

Stelios Seferiades, *Les Jeux de Bourse en droit international privé* (Paris, 1902).

Stelios Seferiades, *Réflexions sur le Boycottage en droit international* (Paris, 1912).

Stelios Seferiades, *Le Régime immobilier en Turquie au point de vue du droit international* (Paris, 1913).

Stelios Seferiades, 'Les Tribunaux de Prises en Grèce – Leur Constitution, Leur Fonctionnement et Leur Jurisprudence', 23 *Revue Générale de Droit International Public* (1916) 31-81.

Stelios Seferiades, 'Chronique sur l'arrestation des consuls d'Allemagne, d'Autriche-Hongrie etc. a Salonique', 23 *Revue Générale de Droit International Public* (1916) 84-88.

Stelios Seferiades, *Το Μέλλον του Διεθνούς Δημοσίου Δικαίου* [The Future of International Public Law] (Pamphlet, in Greek, Athens, 1919).

Stelios Seferiades, 'L'échange des populations', 24 *Recueil des Cours* (1928) 307-439.

Stelios Seferiades, *Μαθήματα Διεθνούς Δημοσίου Δικαίου* [Courses on International Public Law] (Vol. I, Athens, 1920; Vol. II, Athens, 1928-1929).

Stelios Seferiades, *Le problème de l'accès de particuliers a des juridictions internationales* (Paris, 1929).

Stelios Seferiades, *Principes généraux du droit international de la paix, 34 Recueil des Cours* (1930) 177-492.

Stelios Seferiades, 'Le problème de l'accès de particuliers a des juridictions internationales', 51 *Recueil des Cours* (1935) 1-120.

Stelios Seferiades, *Ο Ηθικός Οπλισμός* [Moral Armament, in Greek] (Athens, 1935).

Stelios Seferiades, *Contribution a l'Etude du régime international de la mer de Marmara, in Mélanges Mahaim*, Vol. II (1935) 320-331.

Stelios Seferiades, 'Aperçus sur la Coutume Juridique internationale', 43 *Revue Générale de Droit International Public* (1936) 129-196.

Stelios Seferiades, *Απο το συρτάρι μου, Ποιηματα 1895-1912* [From My Drawer, Poems 1895-1912, in Greek] (Athens, 1939).

Vincent Seligman, *The Victory of Venizelos: A Study of Greek Politics 1910-1918* (London: Allen & Unwin, 1920).

Mortimer N.S. Sellers, 'The Doctrine of Precedent in the United States of America', 54 *American Journal of Comparative Law* (2006) 67-88.

Mohammed Shahabuddeen, *Precedent in the World Court* (Cambridge: Cambridge University Press, 1996).

Yuval Shany, *The Competing Jurisdictions of International Courts and Tribunals* (Oxford: Oxford University Press, 2003).

Malcolm N. Shaw, *International Law* (5th edn.; Cambridge: Grotius, 2003).

Dinah Shelton, 'Legal Norms to Promote the Independence and Accountability of International Tribunals', 2 *The Law and Practice of International Courts and Tribunals* (2003) 27-62.

Marcel Sibert, 'Quelques aspects de l'organisation et de la technique des conférences internationales', 48 *Recueil des Cours* (1934) 387-458.

Bruno Simma, 'Self-Contained Regimes', 16 *Netherlands Yearbook of International Law* (1985) 112-136.

Bruno Simma et al., eds., *The Charter of the United Nations: A Commentary* (Oxford: Oxford University Press, 2002).

Bruno Simma and Dirk Pulkowski, 'Of Planets and the Universe: Self-Contained Regimes in International Law', 17 *European Journal of International Law* (2006) 483-529.

Walter Simons, *The Evolution of International Public Law in Europe Since Grotius* (New Haven: Yale University Press, 1931).

Gerry Simpson, *Great Powers and Outlaw States: Unequal Sovereigns in the International Legal Order* (Cambridge: Cambridge University Press, 2004).

Sir Ian Sinclair, *The Vienna Convention on the Law of Treaties* (2nd revised and enlarged edn.; Manchester: Manchester University Press, 1984).

Thomas Skouteris, 'The New Approaches to International Law and Its Impact on Contemporary International Legal Scholarship', 10 *Leiden Journal of International Law* (1997) 415-420.

Thomas Skouteris, 'Bridging the Gap: The 1999 Annual Meeting of the American Society of International Law', 12 *Leiden Journal of International Law* (1999) 505-509.

Thomas Skouteris, 'The Vocabulary of Progress in Interwar International Law: An Intellectual Portrait of Stelios Seferiades', 16 *European Journal of International Law* (2005) 823-856.

Thomas Skouteris and Outi Korhonen, 'Under Rhodes's Eyes: The "Old" and the "New" International Law at Looking Distance', 11 *Leiden Journal of International Law* (1998) 429-440.

Anne-Marie Slaughter, 'International Law in a World of Liberal States', 6 *European Journal of International Law* (1995) 503-538.

Anne-Marie Slaughter, 'A Global Community of Courts', 44 *Harvard International Law Journal* (2003) 191-219.

Anne-Marie Slaughter, *A New World Order* (Princeton, NJ: Princeton University Press, 2004).

Anne-Marie Slaughter and Alec Stone Sweet, 'Assessing the Effectiveness of International Adjudication', 89 *Proceedings of the American Society of International Law* (1995) 91-93.

Anthony D. Smith, *Nationalism and Modernism, A Critical Survey of Recent Theories of Nations and Nationalism* (Routledge, 1998).

Herbert A. Smith, 'International Law Making', 16 *Grotius Society Transactions* (1930) 93.

Louis B. Sohn, 'Enhancing the Role of the General Assembly of the United Nations in crystallizing International Law', in Jerzy Makarczyk, ed., *Theory of International Law at the Threshold of the 21st Century* (The Hague: Kluwer Law International, 1996) 549-561.

Georges Sorel, *The Illusion of Progress* (Translated by John and Charlotte Stanley, Berkeley, CA: University of California Press, 1969).

Max Sørensen, *Les sources du droit international: étude sur la jurisprudence de la Cour Permanente de la Justice International* (Copenhagen: Munsgaard, 1946).

Shane Spelliscy, 'The Proliferation of International Tribunals: A Chink in the Armor', 40 *Columbia Journal of Transnational Law* (2001) 143-175.

Ole Spiermann, *International Legal Argument in the Permanent Court of International Justice: The Rise of the International Judiciary* (Cambridge: Cambridge University Press, 2005).

Ole Spiermann, 'Twentieth Century Internationalism in Law', 18 *European Journal of International Law* (2007) 785-814.

Arthur Steiner, 'Fundamental Conceptions of International Law in the Jurisprudence of the Permanent Court of International Justice', 30 *American Journal of International Law* (1936) 414-438.

Henry Steiner and Philip Alston, eds., *International Human Rights in Context: Law, Politics, Morals* (3rd edn.; New York: Oxford University Press, 2008).

Eric Stover, *The Witnesses: War Crimes and the Promise of Justice in The Hague* (Philadelphia, PA: University of Pennsylvania Press, 2005).

Ellery C. Stowell, *International Law: A Restatement of Principles in Conformity with Actual Practice* (New York: Henry Holt and Company, 1931).
Michael Stubbs, *Discourse Analysis: The Sociolinguistic Analysis of Natural Language* (Chicago, MI: The University of Chicago Press, 1983).
John Sturrock, ed., *Structuralism and Since: From Lévi Strauss to Derrida* (Oxford: Oxford University Press, 1981).
Daniel S. Sullivan, 'Effective International Dispute Settlement Mechanisms and the Necessary Condition of Liberal Democracy', 81 *Georgetown Law Journal* (1992) 2369.

-T-
Immi Tallgren, 'We Did It? The Vertigo of Law and Everyday Life at the Diplomatic Conference on the Establishment of an International Criminal Court', 12 *Leiden Journal of International Law* (1999) 683-707.
Christian J. Tams, *Enforcing Obligations Erga Omnes in International Law* (Cambridge: Cambridge University Press, 2005).
Frederick J. Teggart, ed., *The Idea of Progress: A Collection of Readings* (Berkeley, CA: University of California Press, 1929).
Ruti G. Teitel, *Transitional Justice* (Oxford University Press, 2004).
Giorgos Tenekides, ed., *Stylianos Prodromou Seferiades* (in Greek, Athens, 1961).
Daniel Terris, Cesare P.R. Romano and Leigh Swigart, eds., *The International Judge: An Introduction to the Men and Women Who Decide the World's Cases* (Oxford University Press, 2007).
Fernando R. Tesón, 'The Kantian Theory of International Law', 92 *Columbia Law Review* (1992) 53-102.
Hugh Thirlway, 'The Proliferation of International Judicial Organs and the Formation of International Law', in Wybo Heere, ed., *International Law and the Hague's 750th Anniversary* (The Hague: T.M.C. Asser Press, 1999) 433-441.
Hugh Thirlway, 'The Proliferation of International Judicial Organs: Institutional and Substantive Questions: The International Court of Justice and Other International Courts', in Niels Blokker and Henry Schermers, eds., *Proliferation of International Organizations* (The Hague: Kluwer Law International, 2001) 251-278.
Hugh Thirlway, 'The Sources of International Law', in Malcolm Evans, ed., *International Law* (Oxford: Oxford University Press, 2003) 117-143.
John B. Thomson, *Ideology and Modern Culture: Critical Social Theory in the Era of Mass Communications* (Polity, 1990).
Christian Tomuschat, 'International Courts and Tribunals with Regionally restricted and/or Specialized Jurisdiction', in Herman Mosler and Rudolf Bernhardt, eds., *Judicial Settlement of International Disputes: International Court of Justice, Others Courts and Tribunals, Arbitration and Conciliation: An International Conference* (Berlin: Springer, 1974) 285-416.
Christian Tomuschat and Jean-Marc Thouverin, eds., *The Fundamental Rules of the International Legal Order: Jus Cogens and Obligations Erga Omnes* (Leiden: Nijhoff, 2006).
Joel P. Trachtman, 'The International Economic Law Revolution', 17 *Pennsylvania Journal of International Economic Law* (1996) 33-61.
Tullio Treves, 'Judicial Lawmaking in an Era of "Proliferation" of International Courts and Tribunals: Development or Fragmentation of International Law?', in Rüdiger Wolfrum and Völker Röben, eds., *Development of International Law in Treaty Making* (Berlin: Springer, 2005) 587-620.

Nikolaos Tsagourias, 'The Will of the International Community as a Normative Source of International Law', in Ige Dekker and Wouter Werner, eds., *Governance and International Legal Theory* (Leiden: Nijhoff, 2004) 97-124.
Ioanna Tsatsou, *Ο Αδελφός μου Γιώργος Σεφέρης* [My Brother Giorgos Seferis, in Greek] (Athens, 1974).
Travers Twiss, *The Law of Nations Considered as Independent Political Communities: On the Rights and Duties of Nations in Time of Peace* (Oxford: Clarendon Press, 1884).

-U-
Roberto Mangabeira Unger, *The Critical Legal Studies Movement* (Cambridge: Harvard University Press, 1986).
Francisco José Urrutia, 'La codification du droit international en Amérique', 22 *Recueil des Cours* (1928) 81-236.

-V-
Mark E. Villiger, *Customary International Law and Treaties: A Manual on the Theory and Practice of the Interrelation of Sources* (2nd revised edn.; The Hague: Nijhoff, 1997).
Charles de Visscher, 'La codification du droit international', 6 *Recueil des Cours* (1925) 325-455.
Theo Vogelaar, 'The OECD Guidelines: Their Philosophy, History, Negotiation, Form, Legal Nature, Follow-up Procedures, and Review', in Norbert Horn, ed., *Legal Problems of Codes of Conduct for Multinational Enterprises* (Kluwer Law International, 1980) 127-139.
Tassos Vournas, Ιστορία της Νεώτερης και Σύγχρονης Ελλαδας [History of Later and Modern Greece, in Greek] (Athens: Patakis, 1977).

-W-
Daniel L. Wade, 'A Basic Guide to the Sources of International Criminal Law', in Ellen G. Schaffer and Randall J. Snyder, eds., *Contemporary Practice of Public International Law* (Dobbs Ferry, NY: Oceana, 1997) 189-220.
Thomas Wälde, 'A Requiem for the "New International Economic Order": The Rise and Fall of Paradigms in International Economic Law', in N. Al-Nauimi and Richard Meese, eds., *International Legal Issues Arising Under the United Nations Decade of International Law* (Den Haag: Nijhoff, 1995) 1301-1338.
W. Warren Wagar, ed., *The Idea of Progress Since the Renaissance* (New York/London: John Wiley & Sons, 1969).
Sir C. Humphrey M. Waldock, 'Decline of the Optional Clause', 32 *British Yearbook of International Law* (1955-1956) 244-287.
Francis Paul Walters, *A History of the League of Nations*, Vol. I. (London and New York: Oxford University Press, 1952).
Hans Wehberg, 'La contribution des conférences de la paix de La Haye au progrès du droit international', 37 *Recueil des Cours* (1931).
Prosper Weil, 'Le Droit International Économique: Mythe ou Réalité?', in *Colloque D'Orléans, Aspects du Droit International Économique: Élaboration, Contrôle, Sanction* (Paris: Pedone, 1972).
Prosper Weil, 'Towards Relative Normativity in International Law?', 77 *American Journal of International Law* (1983) 413-442.
Karel C. Wellens, 'Diversity in Secondary Rules and the Unity of International Law: Some Reflections on Current Trends', Bert Barnhoorn and Karel Wellens, eds., *Diversity in Secondary Rules and the Unity of International Law* (The Hague: Martinus Nijhoff, 1995).

Carl Wellman, *The Proliferation of Rights: Moral Progress or Empty Rhetoric?* (Boulder, CO: Westview Press, 1999).

John Westlake, *International Law* (2nd edn.; Cambridge, 1910).

Henry Wheaton, *Histoire des progrès du droit des gens en Europe depuis la paix de Westphalie jusqu'au Congrès de Vienne: avec un précis historique du droit des gens européen avant la paix de Westphalie* (Leipzig: F.A. Brockhaus, 1841).

Henry Wheaton, *Elements of International Law* (8th edn.; Oxford: Clarendon Press, 1936).

Hayden V. White, 'Historicism, History, and the Figurative Imagination', 14 *History and Theory* (1975) 48-67.

Hayden V. White, 'The Value of Narrativity in the Representation of Reality', in Hayden White, *The Content of the Form. Narrative Discourse and Historical Representation* (Baltimore: The John Hopkins University Press, 1987) 1-25.

Henry George Widdowson, *Text, Context, Pretext: Critical Issues in Discourse Analysis* (Blackwell Publishing, 2005).

John Fischer Williams, *International Change and International Peace* (London: Milford, 1932).

John Fischer Williams, *Aspects of Modern International Law – An Essay* (London: Oxford University Press, 1939).

Adrien Katherine Wing, ed., *Global Critical Race Feminism: An International Reader* (New York: NYU Press, 2000).

Karol Wolfke, *Custom in Present International Law* (2nd revised edn.; Nijhoff, 1993).

Theodore Dwight Woolsey, *Introduction to the Study of International Law: Designed as an Aid in Teaching and in Historical Studies* (6th revised and enlarged edn. by Theodore Salisbury Woolsey; 1899).

Jan Wouters, 'Bronnen van het internationaal recht' [Sources of International Law], in Nathalie Horbach, René Lefeber and Olivier Ribbelink, eds., *Handboek internationaal recht* [Handbook of International Law] (The Hague: T.M.C. Asser Press, 2007) 81-122.

Quincy Wright, *Problems of Stability and Progress in International Relations* (Berkeley, CA: University of California Press, 1954).

**-Y-**

Sienho Yee, 'Strategies for Settling the Hierarchy of the Sources of International Law', in Vesna Crnić-Grotić and Miomir Matulović, eds., *International Law and the Use of Force at the Turn of Centuries: Essays in Honor of V.D. Degan* (Rijeka: Faculty of Law, University of Rijeka, 2005) 341-375.

**-Z-**

Stephen Zamora, 'Is There Customary International Economic Law?', 32 *German Yearbook of International Law* (1989) 9-42.

Karl Zemanek, 'New Trends in the Enforcement of Erga Omnes Obligations', 4 *Max Planck Yearbook of United Nations Law* (2000) 1-52.

Alfred Zimmern, *The League of Nations and the Rule of Law 1918-1935* (London: Macmillan, 1936).

Slavoj Žižek, 'Introduction: The Spectre of Ideology', in Slavoj Žižek, ed., *Mapping Ideology* (Verso, 1994).

REPORTS/CASES

Roberto Ago, Fifth Report on State Responsibility, *Yearbook of the International Law Commission* (1976, Vol. II).

*Aegean Sea Continental Shelf* Case (*Greece* v. *Turkey*), Judgment of 19 December 1978, *ICJ Reports* (1978).

Case *Concerning Maritime Delimitation and Territorial Questions between Qatar and Bahrain* (*Qatar* v. *Bahrain*), Jurisdiction and Admissibility, Judgment of 15 February 1995, *ICJ Reports* (1995).

Case *Concerning the Payment of Various Serbian Loans Issued in France*, *PCIJ Series* A – No. 20/21 (July 12th, 1929).

Case *Concerning United States Diplomatic and Consular Staff in Tehran* (*United States of America* v. *Iran*), Judgment, *ICJ Reports* (1980).

Codification du droit International américain (Washington D.C.: Pan-American Union, 1925 & 1926).

Fragmentation of International Law: Difficulties Arising from the Diversification and Expansion of International Law, Report of the Study Group of the International Law Commission, Finalized by Martti Koskenniemi, UN Doc. A/CN.4/L.682 (13 April 2006).

International Labor Office, The ILO in the Service of Social Progress: A Workers' Education Manual (1969).

International Law Association Study Group's 'The Burgh House Principles on the Independence of the International Judiciary' (<www.ila-hq.org/en/committees/study_groups.cfm/cid/1012>).

International Peace Forum, The World Court: A Magazine of International Progress Supporting a Union of Democratic Nations (New York: World's Court League 1916-1919).

Jurisdiction of the European Commission of the Danube between Galatz and Braila, PCIJ Series B, No. 14 (December 8, 1927).

League of Nations Union, The Progress of the League of Nations (1923).

*Lighthouses* Case between France and Greece, Judgment of 17 March 1934, *PCIJ Series* A/B, No. 62 (1934).

*Loizidou* v. *Turkey*, Judgment of 23 March 1995, Judgment No. 40/1993/435/514.

*Lotus* Case (*France* v. *Turkey*), *PCIJ Series* A, No. 10 (1927).

*The Mavrommatis Jerusalem Concessions* Case, *Greece* v. *United* Kingdom, *PCIJ Series* A, No. 5 (March 26th 1925).

Nottebohm case (*Lichtenstein* v. *Guatemala*), Judgment of 6 April 1955, *ICJ Reports* (1955).

Procès-verbaux of the Proceedings of the Committee, June 16th – July 24th 1920.

Security Council Resolution 827, U.N. Doc. S/INF/49 (1993).

Societé Française pour le Droit International, La Juridictionnalisation du droit international: Colloque de Lille (Paris: Pedone, 2003).

*South West Africa Cases* (*Ethiopia* v. *South Africa*; *Liberia* v. *South Africa*), Judgment of 21 December 1962, *ICJ Reports* (1962).

*South West Africa Cases* (Second phase), (*Ethiopia* v. *South Africa*; *Liberia* v. *South Africa*), *ICJ Reports* (1966).

Supplement to the *American Journal of International Law* (Special Number, 1926) 1-387.

Eleftherios Venizelos, 'The Internal Situation in Greece and the Amnesty of Political Officers', Speech of E. Venizelos in the Greek Chamber, April 23, 1920 (pamphlet, Library of Leiden University).

# INDEX